'Michael Fordham was a towering figure w[...] viewpoint and child analysis into Jungian thin[...] mutually enriching collaboration with those of other theoretical persuasions. Elizabeth Urban's book builds on this endeavour. She is widely known as a sensitive and creative clinician, and here the reader has the opportunity to follow her interrogation of her clinical and observational practice in the light of formulations by Fordham, Jung, Freud, Klein, Bion and Winnicott as well as infant researchers such as Trevarthen and Stern. Urban often addresses topics that are little explored or difficult to conceptualise – primary identification and Fordham's "working from the self", for example – and what she has to say is illuminating and original. This book will be of interest to practising clinicians as well as trainees, and to all those concerned with Jungian and psychoanalytic thought, with theory building, and with the foundations of the self.'

Maria Rhode, *Emeritus Professor of Child Psychology, Tavistock & Portman NHS Foundation Trust*

'This is a helpful book firstly because there has not been very much written about Michael Fordham's theoretical and clinical model as well as his significant innovations in Analytical Psychology, and secondly because Elizabeth had a close professional relationship with Fordham that spanned over a long period of time. I met Elizabeth in the 1970's during my own analytical training with Fordham, and she has always impressed me as a very devoted and conscientious follower of Fordham and his ideas. She both has an excellent understanding of his model as well as a clear way of communicating and expanding upon it with the integration of infant observation work, infant research, and psychoanalytical theory especially of Freud, Klein, Bion and Winnicott. Fordham believed very strongly in the integration of psychoanalytic theory into analytical psychology but he had less knowledge and experience in the area of infant research and he himself did not conduct his own infant observation but relied on the work of his students in the seminars that he taught over many years with Gianna Williams at the SAP (Society of Analytical Psychology).'

Brian Feldman, PhD, *Senior Training Analyst for Inter-Regional Society of Jungian Analysts*

'Elizabeth Urban, an experienced clinician and teacher, is a knowledgeable student of the work of Michael Fordham, having studied with him, over many years. She brings to her understanding of Fordham's original contributions to Jungian child development her integration of the research and clinical studies of other psychologists, and neuro scientists. This work is a significant addition not only to Fordham's work but to our understanding of infant and child development. This approach illuminates how we come to realize our individuality. Her work evidences the surges of development that occur in infancy, its impact on consciousness, a sense of self, language and social awareness. Like Fordham she has conceptualised her clinical discoveries into a Jungian metapsychological model of how the infant's mind emerges. If Fordham left an outline of a model, it has been Elizabeth Urban's task to fill this in with detailed clinical and observational material. Her work has implications for assessment, treatment, and the appropriateness of different kinds of intervention when development is delayed. Elizabeth Urban's capacity to present clearly complicated ideas makes her work an invaluable addition to the literature of child development, and the realization of the self from a Jungian perspective.'

James Astor, *Emeritus Training Analyst of Society of Analytical Psychology*

'When I first heard about Fordham's work, I was studying in Zurich in 1959 when Jung was still alive. I heard that Fordham approach to Jung's ideas was creating a new ground that would open up to analytic work with children. Nobody was in the least interested in analytic work with children at the Jung Institute in Zurich. My experience of work at the SAP in London, with students influenced by Fordham's work and with Fordham himself gave me the experience that one could exchange ideas about early development and object relations and discover that they could be integrated with Jung's theory. This is the core of Fordham's creative work and it is the core of Elizabeth Urban's beautiful book. Jung was explicitly focussing on the second half of life. Fordham opened up Jungian theory to the first and even the very early half of life. Elizabeth Urban's book captures the originality of Fordham's developments as an extremely creative Post Jungian.'

Gianna Williams, *Child Psychotherapist and Psychoanalyst, Tavistock Clinic*

'I could try to puff this book by praising Elizabeth's unusually penetrating thinking about Fordham's contribution to Jung's archetypal theory as it pertains to infancy and the self. I could point out her gifts of symbolic understanding and interpretation and their effects on the healing of her patients. But I'd rather say that I wish I had had this text when I was training and working as a child psychotherapist. And I'd like to recall the help that she gave me with a 14-year old girl who left me feeling rebuffed and fixed in a state where it was impossible to reach her. In a phone discussion Elizabeth loosened my thinking which had got stuck, as though fixed in the girl's dream image that Elizabeth understood as depicting a self object. I was able to write up the ensuing material and pass on Elizabeth's insights at a Berlin-London conference and in a published paper. To me her book is invaluable.'

Miranda Davies, *retired Professional Member of the Society of Analytical Psychology*

'This remarkable book shares deep insights into infancy and the mother-baby relationship. The author has worked with Michael Fordham during his last ten years of life, discussing observations of her clinical work with mothers and babies as well as her work with adult and child patients. Based on forty-five years of clinical experience, Urban makes a unique contribution through demonstrating typical, universal (archetypal) patterns of behaviour at significant points of development during the first two years of infants' lives. She significantly augments Fordham's modified theories through her descriptions of clinical work elaborating upon and applying his theories.'

Jeanne Magagna, *Psychotherapy Services,*
Great Ormond Street Hospital

Understanding Infants Psychoanalytically

Focussing on infants and the relationship between child and parent, this book presents a discourse on eminent Jungian child analyst Michael Fordham's model of development that extended Jung's theory to infancy and childhood.

In this book, Elizabeth Urban, a Jungian psychotherapist in weekly conversations with Fordham, proposes five key areas, such as identifying periods of primary self-functioning and the active participation of the infant in development, that contribute to the Fordham model of infant development. Drawing extensively on her observations and experiences working in a London child and adolescent unit, and a mother and baby unit, as well as using real-life observations to support the proposed contributions, the author provides a deeper understanding of infant development in the context of the relationship with the parents.

This book is a unique contribution to the study of child development and is of great interest to paediatricians, psychotherapists and other mental health professionals who work with children and their parents.

Elizabeth Urban trained in child and adult analysis at the Society of Analytic Psychology. During her training she was supervised by Michael Fordham, Jungian analyst, and continued to work with him until his death in 1995. Her work with Fordham deepened her interest in infancy, which resulted in her developing and integrating Fordham's theories into her clinical work with mothers with their babies in a psychiatric in-patient unit, her work with deaf children, her psychotherapeutic work in a London CAMHS unit, her private psychotherapy practice and her teaching internationally.

Understanding Infants Psychoanalytically

A Post-Jungian Perspective on Michael Fordham's Model of Development

Elizabeth Urban

Routledge
Taylor & Francis Group

LONDON AND NEW YORK

Cover image: © OR Images/Getty Images

First published 2022
by Routledge
4 Park Square, Milton Park, Abingdon, Oxon OX14 4RN

and by Routledge
605 Third Avenue, New York, NY 10158

Routledge is an imprint of the Taylor & Francis Group, an informa business

British Library Cataloguing-in-Publication Data
A catalogue record for this book is available from the British Library

Library of Congress Cataloging-in-Publication Data
Names: Urban, Elizabeth (Psychotherapist), author.
Title: Understanding infants psychoanalytically : a post-Jungian
    perspective on Michael Fordham's model of development /
    Elizabeth Urban.
Description: Abingdon, Oxon ; New York, NY : Routledge, 2022. |
    Includes bibliographical references and index.
Identifiers: LCCN 2021044159 | ISBN 9781032105048 (paperback) |
    ISBN 9781032105062 (hardback) | ISBN 9781003215639 (ebook)
Subjects: LCSH: Infant analysis. | Infant psychology. |
    Jungian psychology.
Classification: LCC RJ502.5 .U73 2022 | DDC 155.42/2—dc23
LC record available at https://lccn.loc.gov/2021044159

ISBN: 978-1-032-10506-2 (hbk)
ISBN: 978-1-032-10504-8 (pbk)
ISBN: 978-1-003-21563-9 (ebk)

DOI: 10.4324/9781003215639

Typeset in Times New Roman
by Apex CoVantage, LLC

This book is dedicated to the memory of Michael Fordham, Dorothy Davidson and the Children's Section of the Society of Analytical Psychology (1974–2006). My gratitude is extended to Jane Dwyer, who introduced me to Jung's ideas, and Jeanne Magagna, who encouraged me and enabled me to publish this book.

Contents

Introduction

Elizabeth Urban

The aim of this book is to present a discourse on Michael Fordham's developmental model extending Jung's theory to infancy and childhood. The chapters indicate how infant research, my own clinical and observational work, and ideas from related fields have contributed to my understanding of infant development. Throughout, Fordham's model has provided a useful and enduring framework for my thinking. What I have learned from research and my own experience adds new contributions to the model, based on, as Fordham would have put it, 'sufficient evidence' (Fordham 1993a, p. 5).

Michael Fordham

Michael Fordham is best known as a theoretical innovator and for a range of accomplishments still carrying his imprint. Besides developing a comprehensive Jungian model of development from foetal life to old age, he was on the editorial team of Jung's *Collected Works*, a leader in establishing the Society of Analytical Psychology, and the first editor of the *Journal of Analytical Psychology*; he set up an accredited Child Analytic Training and authored nine books and more than two hundred papers and reviews. These achievements speak to Fordham's intellectual strength, emotional robustness and character. Following Fordham's death, Donald Meltzer paid tribute to him, commenting, 'He was one of three great men I have known' (Meltzer 1996, p. 26). Expanding on this, James Astor wrote: 'Some . . . have compared him with Freud, Klein and Bion, but distinguished him from them in his capacity to combine pioneering clinical work with wearing the mantle of office, of running the Society, fostering the trainees and being neither inflated nor destroyed by the spoilers great men attract' (Fordham 1993b). Fordham's life (1905–1995) covered most of the 20th century and, correspondingly, the first century of psychoanalysis.

He was born in London, the third of three children. His early family life was spent in Edwardian comfort, raised by liberal parents who were involved in social issues and mixed with various writers and artists; John Galsworthy was Fordham's godfather. In his memoir (1993b) Fordham described himself as a naughty child who loved his mother passionately. His accounts give less attention to her

DOI: 10.4324/9781003215639-1

precarious health (he had been born during one of her asthma attacks). Her unexpected death just as he was turning fifteen shattered Michael, leaving him cut off from his emotional life in a way that left him little sense of direction. This remained, despite the distractions of medical studies and his first marriage, until he entered therapy with a London Jungian and soon after met Jung. Fordham had informed Jung before going to Zurich that he required an income if he were to train with Jung. Despite this, Jung crushed Fordham's hopes, saying there were no opportunities for making a living there because of Swiss laws disallowing foreigners to work. He did however invite Fordham to a lecture the following day, and Fordham was impressed with Jung's humanity, directness, vitality and erudition. Back in London Fordham was furious at what he experienced as Jung's lack of sensitivity to his situation and then realised that his rage was the expression of a strong tie that had formed. This was accompanied by a lasting loyalty to Jung, preventing him from making close ties with psychoanalysts; he did not have analysis with a psychoanalyst, but at the end of his life he was engaged in discussions of ideas regarding infancy with the psychoanalysts Donald Meltzer and Gianna Polacco Williams.

In 1934 Fordham was awarded a fellowship at the London Child Guidance Clinic on Tavistock Square. He was the only Jungian amongst psychoanalysts at a time when Jungians were apprehensive, even disapproving, of child analysis, on the basis it would overwhelm the child's nascent ego. This initially handicapped him in his work with children until he discovered from Melanie Klein how to make emotional contact with his child patients through play. I understand that this was in response to the influx of pre-war refugees.

Linking with psychoanalysis and Kleinians

In 1944 London Jungians invited Fordham to set up a training, the first outside Zurich. At the same time Fordham became actively involved with the Medical Section of the British Psychological Society. Members were working analytically with patients with psychotic personality structures, as Jung had done, and the Medical Section provided a forum for analysts to discuss new concepts that applied to their work. Fordham recognised how these related to some of Jung's established ideas and drew attention to this in the introduction to his third volume. 'In recent years considerable changes have occurred in psychoanalysis in Britain. These have made it desirable to relate its new formulations to those of analytical psychology' (Fordham 1958, p. 2).

Although Fordham's thinking is essentially Jungian, his model lacked conceptual clarity without the ideas coming from new developments in psychoanalysis. The most significant influence was Klein herself: 'Winnicott, Bion and Scott . . . all derived their work from her, but she was the real innovator' (1985, p. 216). Fordham referred to her in all eight of his analytic books, beginning with his recognition in the first that unconscious phantasies are conceptually virtually identical to Jung's archetypes (Fordham 1944). Although Jung and Klein drew upon quite different data, both conceptualised innate, instinctual features and processes, the expressions of which develop and become more complex while also continuing to operate on a primitive level throughout life. Both also realised that analytic access to these primitive operations is achieved through transference and countertransference. While Jung 'thought of the analyst as just as much in the analysis as the patient' (Fordham 1985, p. 140), Klein's definition of projective and introjective identification contributed detailed dynamics that indicated how affects in the analyst can be used to further analysis.

Fordham was also a significant influence on Winnicott. Their hospital clinics were not far from each other, and they shared a close and warm relationship, discussing work. Fordham's personal admiration, respect and affection for Winnicott are evident in his tribute given to the British Psycho-Analytical Society in honour of Winnicott. He refers to the reciprocity between them by quoting from Winnicott's review of Jung's memoir, 'If we [psychoanalysts] fail to come to terms with Jung we are self-proclaimed partisans, partisans in a lost cause' (Fordham [1972], quoted in Fordham 1995, p. 196). In sparring with ideas, and contributing to each other's thinking, Fordham had especially high praise for Winnicott's clinical work (Fordham 1972, 1995) and also made use of the concept of transitional objects, although later holding reservations about generalising the idea because Fordham did not observe transitional objects in infancy as Winnicott had described (Fordham 1985). While Fordham acknowledged the importance to him of both Klein and Winnicott, he did not accept their metapsychologies.

The Society of Analytical Psychology had been set up in 1946. By 1955, under Fordham's influence, the Society was absorbing psychoanalytic ideas and technique, thereby creating an ideational split that was eventually resolved in 1976 by a group of predominantly Zurich-trained analysts separating from the SAP. Over the same period clinical discussions for members working with children gradually shaped into the Child Analytic Training. This entailed providing an infant observation seminar and, at Esther Bick's recommendation, Gianna Polacco Williams, an established Kleinian familiar with Jung's ideas, was appointed its leader. Fordham joined the group as a 'guest observer', and he at last acquired data from direct observations of infants. Fordam stated, 'Here, it seemed, was my hypothesis being enacted graphically and often dramatically. . . . The integrative sequences stared me in the face' (Fordham 1987, p. 357). Williams' and Fordham's discussions were so rich that a second monthly seminar including trainees was formed, separating discussions on observations from those on theory. In linking Jungian and Kleinian ideas, Williams drew Fordham's interest to the post-Kleinians, in particular Bion, whose ideas of 'O' and beta elements closely parallel Jung's concepts of the self and psychoids. Fordham focused on Bion in his review of Meltzer's series *The Kleinian Development* (Meltzer 1978), drawing further comparisons (Fordham 1980). Bion's influence appears in Fordham's late writing (post-1980), as did Meltzer's. In 1981 Fordham nearly died from a viral infection that affected his heart. As he convalesced he met weekly with Meltzer, to whom he credited 'my surprisingly good recovery' and from whom he 'developed . . . a rich professional and literary existence' (Fordham 1993b, p. 142).

An understanding of the links Fordham established between Jung and Klein would be incomplete without a comment on the historical context in which they occurred. The post-war period was highly productive for both psychoanalysis and analytical psychology yet fell in the shadow of the breakdown of the Freud-Jung relationship. As James Astor points out, Jung became deeply introverted and drawn into dreams and envisioned phantasies that had hallucinatory elements. Although Jung was internally broken up, he did not experience a psychosis that impaired his sense of reality; he continued to work and maintain family life. In contrast Freud's response was extroverted. Fearing that Jung would try to dominate psychoanalysis with his ideas, Freud contributed to the view that Jung was 'mad' in order to explain his defection. Thereby it became the politics of psychoanalysts to isolate Jung through defamation.

> This was the professional climate in which Fordham began his work: a climate in which psychoanalysts, trained at the Institute of Psycho-Analysis, as a matter of loyalty to Freud did not read Jung – or at least did not admit to doing so.
>
> (Astor 1995, p. 4)

Some of the SAP membership felt a sense of inferiority combined with resentment at what they considered to be psychoanalysts' intentional lack of acknowledgement of Jung's contributions.

> For instance, [Fordham] emphasised Jung's recognition that the total involvement of the analyst in the [analytic] process was relevant to a successful therapeutic encounter – a point of view now widely acknowledged by psychoanalysts but not attributed to Jung.
>
> (Astor 1995, p. 121)

Bion appears to be an example. Bion did know about Jung's ideas; he attended Jung's Tavistock Lectures in the autumn of 1935 with his patient Samuel Beckett, who was particularly taken with a comment Jung made about one of his cases. One of Beckett's biographers, Anthony Cronin, suggested that Bion and Beckett discussed Jung's diagnosis of the little girl's case, and Bion's theory concerning psychological and biological birth (Cronin, 1999). This raises the question as to whether Bion was influenced more by Jung or Beckett. Or, alternatively, as Williams commented, was it that 'these thoughts . . ., to use Bion's phrase, [were] "looking for a thinker" . . .?' (Davies and Urban 1996, pp. 57–58).

Winnicott, and possibly other psychoanalysts, may have been directly influenced by Jung and used Jung's ideas with a patient, or patients, thereby claiming that the experience had become their own and then conceptualising this according to the analyst's theoretical point of view. While perhaps wanting in intellectual diligence, might this have presented a pragmatic and not entirely dishonest solution to a dark dilemma?

In the course of these decades Fordham's assimilation of Kleinian principles into Jungian theory has been passed down to become the hallmark of the SAP. Providing the SAP with an identity of its own did much to resolve the SAP's need for finding it by comparison with the Institute of Psychoanalysis, while facilitating continuing links between SAP analysts and their psychoanalytic colleagues.

The Fordham model

In this section I introduce concepts that are developed in most of the chapters of this book. I regard the concepts from a post-Jungian perspective that draws upon Fordham's links with Kleinian thought. Here it is important to appreciate that the Jung-Freud collaboration broke down in part because they did not agree on the essential nature of psychic energy: for Freud it was sexual and object-related, and for Jung it was neutral and directed overall towards self-realisation in its deepest meaning.

The self

There is little consensus in psychology, sociology or philosophy on what is meant by 'the self'. Jung first identified what became his theory of the self from a series of drawings he made as he recovered from the breakdown of his relationship with Freud. He soon realised that they were mandalas, ancient spiritual and ritual symbols in Hinduism and Buddhism which represent the universe. In Kleinian thought the self is based on Freud's structural theory. Although 'not explicitly defined . . . [it] seems to indicate a concept of wholeness which embraces the ego, super-ego, and id, and is even perhaps something more as well' (Fordham 1957, p. 198); that is, it implies a wholeness that unites the structural parts.

For Jung the self is explicitly the whole of the individual, which is more than the sum of its constituents. This gives it a conceptually superordinate position in relation to the parts, as it operates autonomously as an overall organising principle providing the functional unity of mind and body in a constant flux of states of the organism. As the totality, the self transcends and unites all its parts, and thus opposites; for instance, container and contained, good and evil, beauty and ugliness, instinct and spirit. As this includes the opposites of conscious and unconscious, the self is ultimately beyond experience and unknowable. Here lies the historical reference in Eastern thought: the self is inherently mysterious; it is mystical. Bion captured this in his succinct abstraction of 'O':

> Its existence as indwelling has no significance whether it is supposed to dwell in an individual person or in God or the Devil; it is not good or evil; it cannot be known, loved or hated. It can be represented by such terms as ultimate reality or truth. . . . L, H, K are links and by virtue of that fact are substitutes

for the ultimate relationship with O which is not a relationship or an identification or an atonement or a reunion.

(Bion 1984, pp. 139–140)

The primary self

Jung's work and interests were with the adult mind, and his thinking and concepts
apply accordingly. Initially Fordham accepted that self theory did not pertain to
childhood or his child patients, but by the mid-1940's he had acquired clinical
evidence that put 'back very much earlier than Jung's view had supposed the
capacity of the child to have a "centrum"' (Fordham 1947, p. 271).

Winnicott had theorised that the initial state in infancy is unintegration followed by integration, but Fordham turned this around and postulated a primary
state of integration, a primary self which is the source out of which development
emerges.

Acknowledging Bion, Fordham wrote:

> I take (the primary self) to represent a state in which there is no past and no
> Future, though is present like a point which position but no magnitude. It
> has no desires, no memory, no images, but out of it by transformation all of
> these can deintegrate. There is consciousness and no unconsciousness– -it is
> a permanent absence.
>
> (Fordham 1985, p. 33)

> As a biologist, Fordham postulated what refers to a species-specific life force:
> a primary self expressed in individuality, adaptability and mixing and blur-
> ring categories of discourse, embracing contradictions, and sliding between
> ideas rather than linking them. . . . Yet in scientific writings, such transgres-
> sions lead us to anything and everything we fancy – because, as is readily
> logically demonstrable, from a contradiction any proposition follows.
>
> (O'Shaughnessy 2003, p. 1523)

O'Shaughnessy sees this from the perspective of the reality principle, which has
its own means of validation. What Jung and Bion are referring to is a different
order of reality having its own noumenal epistemology, in contrast to the sensate grasp of the phenomenal and its logical ordering. Thus it can be argued that
non-scientific language is appropriate because it captures the nature of this other
sensed reality, the 'ultimate'.

The ego

Klein posited that the ego is an innate, discrete organising structure, while Jung
held that the ego is a derivative of the self and thus a secondary organiser. In

Fordham's model, the ego is a deintegrate, that is, it emerges out of the self in the course of development.

The individual and individuation

Jung maintained that personal identity derives from innate contents (archetypal objects/unconscious phantasies) while Freud held (for the most part) that ego identity is not intrinsic and is built up through identifications with external figures. As Fordham noted, 'Freud exalts the process [of identification] while Jung demotes it' (Fordham 1995, pp. 63–64). Fordham's model incorporates the principle of individuality in his postulate of a unique mind-body unity from the outset and by drawing attention to the infant's active contribution to relating to externals.

For Jung, the inherent goal of the self is the realisation of one's individuality, termed individuation. Bion expresses the same notion in his definition of O:

> The most, and the least that the individual can do is to be it. . . . The qualities attributed to O, the links with O, are all transformations of O and being O. The human person is himself and by 'is' I mean in both instances a positive act of being for which L, J, K are only substitutes and approximations.
>
> (Bion 1984, p. 140)

Fordham regarded individuation from a developmental perspective, whereby the sense of having an individual self develops in the ego via the resolution of conflicts between opposites in the self; most notably is that between love and hate, leading to the depressive position.

Archetypes

Jung understood archetypes to be inherent structuring functions likened to Bion's idea of preconception:

> Archetypes are the modes of apprehension, and wherever we meet with uniform and regularly recurring modes of apprehension we are dealing with an archetype, no matter whether its mythological character is recognized or not.
>
> (Jung CW 8, para 280)

Both Jung and Klein referred to their respective concepts (archetypes and unconscious phantasies) as images of the instinct. Fordham defines an archetype as follows:

> [The infant] does react in a way that is characteristic and typical and it is at once mental and physical. That's the characteristic of an archetype.
>
> (Fordham 1984)

The dynamics of the primary self: deintegration and reintegration

In Fordham's model, development occurs via the interplay between two-fold complementary actions of the self. Together they account for the overall functioning of a self-organising system and how the essentially individual self relates to and internalises the external world. Fordham reasoned that if the original state is one of integration, there needs to be a way of conceptualising how the organism relates to the environment in order to survive and develop. He looked for a term that referred to an extroverted action arising from within the self that 'opened it up' or 'reached out' to the environment. When assigning a term, he discounted 'disintegration' and 'unintegration' as inapt and came up with 'deintegration'.

The complementary action to deintegration is a process of introversion accounting for how a complex experience, say, a baby's feeding, is absorbed into the self. This he termed 'reintegration'. This term, like its counterpart, is based on logic: if the original state is of integration which becomes disrupted by deintegration, then any subsequent return to an integrated state is a re-integration. What is reintegrated are deintegrates, that is, pre-objects that can become formed into internal objects via further deintegration and reintegration, that is, development. As mental life becomes more complex through these dual processes, representations and symbols emerge.

Significant sources for my work

The principal source and inspiration for my work is Fordham and our discussions arising from our shared interest in early development. Following his death, to get a sense of the progression of Fordham's thinking I read his papers on development chronologically up to the mid-1970's.

A number of researchers have been instrumental to my studies. Foremost has been Colwyn Trevarthen, whose research into the precursors of language identified typical and universal patterns of relating that I recognised as archetypal. Stem's classic, *The Interpersonal World of the Infant* (1985), opened my eyes to early infant amodal and transmodal perception and distinguished it from later perception (see Chapter 2). From various researchers (Trevarthen [1989], Trevarthen and Marwick [1986], Stem [1985], Schore [1994], Panksepp [1998] and Hobson [2002]) I developed an understanding of the sequencing and identifying characteristics of surges of global changes, or massive deintegrations, that mark the development toward having a mind linked to other minds. This knowledge has been invaluable in my work at the mother- baby unit and an important contribution to what I consider I have added to Fordham's model. James Astor's volume *Michael Fordham: Innovations in Analytical Psychology* (1995) is the most comprehensive and authoritative source on Fordham's work. His book has been helpful to my broader understanding of Fordham as well as setting out ideas that I have studied but that he presents from a different vertex. Lastly, my observations of mothers and their infants have been central to the development of my thinking and have made early development vivid and real. To those mothers and babies, who suffered and struggled to discover or recover their affectionate bonds, I owe not only acknowledgement but also indebtedness.

Contributions to Fordham's model

In his late eighties Fordham introduced a paper summarising his model:

> I regard what I shall say as notes for beginning to construct a model. It may be said that I have . . . defined a model using Jung's concepts of the ego, the archetypes and the self. . . . [T]here is not much that I would go back on, but I was then, and continue to be, aware that it needed filling out, and that may now be possible.
>
> (Fordham 1993a, p. 5)

In this section I put forward five areas 'filling out' the model, based on research and my own clinical experience and observations of infants. These are implicitly conveyed in various chapters and are here explicitly stated. They do not significantly change the model but, inasmuch as they are new to it, can be considered to be innovations, and thus original.

I. Identifying periods of massive deintegration

> It was only late in life that Fordham referred to periods of massive deintegratio (Fordham 1993a), specifying birth to be the first.

According to Trevarthen (2000), Schore and other researchers cited in the chapters, surges of development accompanied by global changes are manifestations of the emergence of functional brain systems. These occur at typical periods:

1   at six weeks to three months, when, due to the changes to developments in visual perception, the infant becomes drawn to the mother's (or another's) face and begins to engage in proto-conversations with this partner;
2   at four to six months, when the infant's attention is drawn to physical objects which are manipulated and examined with almost scientific interest, thereby promoting self-agency and prompting gross control and fine motor dexterity; and
3   between ten and twelve months, when the prefrontal cortex 'comes on-line', and person andobject combine with a new anticipation from another mind of what can be done with the object.

This last shift marks a revolution in consciousness and a vast array of related developments, including an emergent sense of self and other, shared play, language development and social affects, such as shame (Chapters 5, 7 and 8).

This identification of universal and typical periods of massive deintegrative surges adds considerable form and detail to Fordham's model. I observed the regularity and consistency with which these archetypal shifts occurred at predictable times during the first year. Therefore I could introduce my court reports with a summary of relevant age-related capacities against which I could assess if a baby was developing according to expectation. Also, I could assess whether a mother was meeting these expectations and, if not, I could turn to experienced nurses, try myself to draw out these behaviours in order to confirm an infant's capacities or, alternatively, identify possible indications of developmental delay or impairments (Chapter 7).

To know what to look for and when to look for it also served useful in parent-infant therapy. For instance, some four- to five-month-old babies became fussy, aversive or passively dulled if the mother continued to engage primarily face-to-face, although this quickly changed into interest and curiosity when the babies were allowed to explore objects. The fourteen-month-old toddler I describe in Chapters 7 and 8 concerned me because his play with his mother was aimless and solitary, and it moved quickly from one thing to another. My shared play with him demonstrated that his capacities were appropriate to his age and that they needed support from his mother and the nurses.

II. Primary self functioning: amodal perception and primary consciousness

Stern (1985) describes research that indicates that infant perception is not distinct sense modes, such as sights, sounds and touches, but rather is amodal, that is, of qualities such as shapes, intensities and rhythms. I realised that amodal properties and their perception also apply to affect, for instance, the soft contour, low intensity and slow rhythm of tenderness. In practice this drew my awareness to how I used my voice and its prosody to attune to babies and help mothers to do the same (Chapter 3).

Also, I observed how babies on the cusp of language acquisition reached into their mothers' mouths as if they perceived spoken language amodally, that is, perceiving language sounds as objects in the mouth that have physical properties which can be grasped with the hands as a prelude to becoming grasped conceptually as representational (Chapter 3). I happened to notice that the few children with whom I worked who had autistic features seemed to perceive amodally when in emotionally aroused states (Chapters 1 and 2). I note these points as observations as opposed to generalising assertions.

The shift at the end of the first year of life marks a development in consciousness. Various related fields, from neurology to philosophy, distinguish between primary and secondary consciousness (Edelman 1989). The former is conceived as 'a form of consciousness that humans share with non-human animals; it is sense experience' (Tallis 2010, p. 26). Primary consciousness exists from birth and remains throughout life, while secondary or higher consciousness (the equivalent of ego consciousness) begins to emerge toward the end of the first year and becomes the conscious awareness of being conscious, as in Descartes' 'Cogito ergo sum'.

Fordham had maintained that the division between consciousness and the unconscious is not helpful when thinking about young infants but is a result of deintegration and reintegration. The distinction between primary and secondary consciousness corroborates this. Although my studies have not gone far into amodal perception and primary and higher consciousness, I consider that I have put forward enough to be able to refer meaningfully to an initial 'period of primary self functioning', which is marked by a preponderance of amodal perception, deintegrates/part objects and archetypal patterns of relating.

III. The infant's active participation in development

Fordham repeatedly pointed out how a very young infant, even before birth, contributes to their own development by taking initiatives via signalling and giving feedback. Fordham's point is that the infant is hardly a passive recipient of parenting.

I also show work in which I describe a film of a fourteen-month-old boy. Examined closely the film reveals how he actively assembled sensate experiences (see Picture 7, Chapter 8) in the process of constructing a dawning concept of inside-outside/container-contained/three-dimensionality.

IV. Developmental components of projective and introjective identification

Klein's concepts of projective and introjective identification are probably the most useful tools in understanding human unconscious communication. In Chapter 6 I refer to neurological studies providing a microanalysis of early neurochemical phenomena that underlie instantaneous communication of affective states between infant and mother, prior to projective and introjective identification, that is, when there are contents to project (Schore 2002). I propound that early phenomena comprise the contents of what becomes projective and introjective identification, thus filling in details of primary self functioning and affective communication. Furthermore, young infants avert their gaze when faced with depressed, psychotically withdrawn, or persistently non-responsive mothers, often turning to bright lights or spaces.

V. Symbol formation and the principle of emergence

Complexity theory has led me to view reintegration according to the principle of emergence. I introduce this in Chapter 6, where I use this principle to describe how concept building develops into thinking, reflection and reflecting on reflection.

This is not inconsistent with Fordham's understanding of how symbol formation occurs as part of the development from whole objects (the mother as the whole world) to part objects (the mother as 'good' and/or 'bad'). Yet what I put forward adds another dimension and shape and incorporates them with an ever-changing emergent whole that is more than the sum of its parts.

Michael Rustin has recognised the contribution of emergence to a new understanding of how sustained developments arise from recurring shifts of state, namely those between the paranoid schizoid and depressive positions. Rustin's work adds to Fordham's model and merits further examination (Rustin 2002).

Toward the end of my Child Analytic Training, Mara Sidoli and Miranda Davies edited a collection of papers by mainly SAP child analysts, titled *Jungian Child Psychotherapy: Individuation in Childhood* (1988). While sharing the same heritage of ideas with my colleagues, my work, like theirs, has been individualised by particular experiences with particular patients in particular settings. Mine have been my experience with profoundly deaf children and the rare position I held as a child psychotherapist in a perinatal inpatient psychiatric unit. As a result of my experiences the chapters in this book convey the further developments in thinking about infancy.

The chapters in this book are divided into three sections. The first, 'Theory', contains theoretical expositions of Fordham's model (Chapters 1 and 2); the second, 'Developments', brings together three chapters in which Fordham's concepts are elucidated by clinical and observational material (Chapters 3, 4 and 5); and the third, 'Extensions', discusses publications that implicitly or explicitly include my innovations to Fordham's model (Chapters 6, 7 and 8).

All chapters refer to Fordham's model, and most include clinical material and infant observation as well as theory. My own clinical material used throughout is from infants and children. Others' observations have come from my observation group with Gianna Polacco Williams and from observers in infant observation groups I have led.

Part I: Theory

These two chapters are aimed at putting forward Fordham's theoretical model and clarifying his ideas and the terms he uses. This is done through the use of metaphor and simile, by drawing parallels with other theoreticians, and by illustrating his concepts with clinical and observational material. Throughout I am aware that theories cannot be proved, only disproved; hence I am not arguing the 'truth' of the model but, rather, fleshing out Fordham's more abstract constructs.

Chapter 1, The Primary Self and Related Concepts in Jung, Klein and Isaacs, sorts out a theoretical muddle described in the introduction. The theoretical section reviews how Jung, Klein and Isaacs conceptualise early psychic contents and processes, followed by an exposition of Fordham's model of a deintegrating and reintegrating primary self.

Chapter 2, Infant Observation, Experimental Infant Research and Psychodynamic Theory Regarding Lack of Self/Other Differentiation, examines different analytic views on early states of what are variously termed identity, identification, projective identification and fusion. Based on my understanding of the early pre-dominance of amodal perception, I suggest that young infants perceive the other as separate, but the difference is irrelevant in early life and until later feature-based perception and attachment processes emerge at the end of the first year.

Part II: Developments

These chapters describe Fordham's model and its essential theoretical elements. Each chapter aims to illustrate the model and to bring its conceptual formulations to life through the use of clinical material and infant research and observation.

Chapter 3, Out of the Mouths of Babes: An Enquiry into the Sources of Language Development, details my work with a profoundly deaf ten-year-old girl who attended the school for the deaf where I worked. The chapter demonstrates how the foundations of language rest on object relations and phantasies about communication. Secondly, it illustrates deintegration by describing how the sources of language follow a 'normal' course of deintegrations that leads from the nipple-in-the-mouth to the word-in-the-mouth and how compensatory deintegra-tions evolve in infants with profound deafness.

Chapter 4, 'With Healing in Her Wings . . .': Integration and Repair in a Self-Destructive Adolescent, refers to Jung's idea that the cure is in the symptom. After a theoretical sketch of Fordham's model I introduce three corollaries elaborating his view that internal development proceeds from whole objects to part objects to the depressive position. I then link this progression with periodic surges of global change during the first year.

Chapter 5, Developmental Aspects of Trauma and Traumatic Aspects of Devel-opment, draws attention to how 'the stuff of trauma' is part of healthy devel-opment and describes how pathological splitting comes about. I illustrate the massive deintegration at the end of the first year relevant to the development of perceived differences between self and other. I assert that at this point the baby has a new awareness of self and other that includes the difference of status in the relationship.

Part III: Extensions

The chapters in this section represent the point at which I began to add my own discoveries and formulations to Fordham's model. While Chapter 8 concerns technique, chapters 6 and 7 are theoretical. All three chapters include my innova-tions to the Fordham model, although some are subsidiary to the aims I had in writing each chapter.

Chapter 6, Fordham, Jung and the Self: A Re-examination of Fordham's Con-tribution to Jung's Conceptualisation, makes an argument for the usefulness of Jung's distinction by regarding the self and the ego from a developmental point of view.

I turn to Fordham's conceptual analysis of Jung's use of 'self', in which he identifies an apparent contradiction between Jung's definition of the self as the psychosomatic whole of the individual, while also referring to it as an archetype (a part of the whole). Fordham resolves this by drawing in a concept, the 'central archetype of order', which he then leaves undeveloped. I make use of Fordham's idea of a central archetype by hypothesising its emergence at the end of the first year along with a new order of reintegrating 'bits' of ego consciousness, and support this with infant and neurobiological studies.

At the end of the chapter I propose that 'primary self can be understood to refer to a period of development which is pre-consciousness (that is, before secondary consciousness) and marked by the predominance of deintegrates (primitive part objects), and which draws to a close around the end of the first year.

Chapter 7, The 'Self' in Analytical Psychology: The Function of the 'Central Archetype' Within Fordham's Model, is essentially an extension of Chapter 6 and further argues the usefulness of the concept of a central archetype. I summarise Fordham's statements about the term in order to define it before applying it to the changes that occur during the massive surge of deintegration at the end of the first year. I detail a session with a young toddler to demonstrate the developmental shift from face-to-face to mind-to-mind. In the last part of the chapter I introduce the use of 'emergence' from mathematics and complexity theory in order to make the case that deintegration and reintegration function as emergent processes, which lead from sentience to mentalisation and the increasing complexity of the mind over the course of life.

Chapter 8, Reflections on Research and Learning from the Patient: The Art and Science of What We Do, asserts that interpretive analytic work rests on the patient's capacity for three-dimensionality. Here I describe the treatment and slow development of a grossly deprived six-year-old boy over two years of therapy. I contribute to Fordham's description by adding further considerations of the intrapersonal and interpersonal components that comprise 'working out of the self'.

Further reflections

These chapters link infant research to the periods of massive deintegration in the first year. The description of Baby Toby's development from the nipple-in-the-mouth to a word-in-the-mouth (Chapter 3) connects to the toddler's purposeful use of his body to construct a concept of inside-outside/container-contained/three-dimensionality (Chapter 7), and both of these link to the six-year-old boy's construction (as opposed to expression) of a three-dimensional space in which he could hold his loving feelings (Chapter 8).

Upon reflection, I consider that my most substantial and well-substantiated contribution to Fordham's model has been the identification and dating of surges of massive deintegration in the first year of life. My most exciting discovery has been how active a young toddler was in constructing – and then discovering – a new mental concept arising from shared activity with another mind.

In his obituary of Jung, Fordham wrote, 'The best monument that can be raised to Jung is to make use of and develop his work rather than let it be passively accepted and sterilized' (Fordham 1961, p. 168). My chapters were written to clarify my thinking and link it to what I was learning from research and my clinical experience. Yet, looking back, I realise that what I have done has been in similar spirit to Fordham's monument to Jung: honouring Fordham and expressing my admiration, loyalty and affection to him.

References

Astor, J. (1995). *Michael Fordham: Innovations in Analytical Psychology*. London: Routledge.

Bion, W. (1984). *Transformations*. London: Maresfield. Reprint of 1963 first edition.

Cronin, A. (1999). *Samuel Beckett: The Last Modernist*. London: Flamingo.

Davies, M. and Urban, E. (1996). 'Fordham and the society of analytical psychology infant observations: An interview with Gianna Williams'. *Journal of Child Psychotherapy*, 22: 49–63.

Edelman, G. (1989). *The Remembered Present*. New York: Basic Books.

Fordham, M. (1944). *The Life of Childhood*. London: Kegan Paul, Trench. Trubner & Co.

———. (1947). 'Integration and disintegration and early ego development'. *The Nervous Child*, 6(3).

———. (1957). 'Critical notice of M. Klein, P. Heinmann, R. Money-Kyrle (eds.), New directions in psycho-analysis', *Journal of Analytical Psychology*, 2: 195–200.

———. (1958). *The Objective Psyche*. London: Routledge and Kegan Paul.

———. (1961). 'Obituary: C. G. Jung'. *British Journal of Medical Psychology*, 4(3/4).

———. (1972). 'A tribute to D. W. Winnicott'. *The Scientific Bulletin of the British Psychoanalytical Society and Institute of Psycho-Analysis*, No. 57.

———. (1980). 'Critical notice of D. Meltzer, The Kleinian Development'. *Journal of Analytical Psychology*, 25: 201–204.

———. (1984). Portrait of an Analyst: Michael Fordham in Conversation with Roger Hobdell, filmed interview. London: Society of Analytical Psychology.

———. (1985). *Explorations into the Self*, Library of Analytical Psychology, Vol. 7. London: Academic Press.

———. (1987). 'Actions of the self'. Chapter 16 in P. Young-Eisendrath and J. Hall (eds), *The Book of the Self*. New York: New York University Press

———. (1993a). 'Notes on the formation of a model'. *Journal of Analytical Psychology*, 38: 5–12.

———. (1993b). *The Making of an Analyst: A Memoir*. London: Free Associations.

———. (1995). 'Identification'. Chapter 2 in R. Hobdell (ed.), *Freud, Jung, Klein – The Fenceless Field: Essays on Psychoanalysis and Analytical Psychology.* London: Routledge.

Fordham, M. and Gordon, R. (1958). 'Critical notice of M. Klein, Envy and Gratitude: A study of unconscious sources'. *Journal of Analytical Psychology*, 3: 172–175.

Hobson, P. (2002). *The Cradle of Thought; Exploring the Origins of Thinking*. London: Macmillan.

Meltzer, D. (1978). *The Kleinian Development, Parts 1–111*. Perthshire: Clunie Press.

———. (1996). 'A personal response to the making of an analyst'. *Journal of Child Psychotherapy*, 22: 26–27.

Panksepp, J. (1998). *The Foundations of Human and Animal Emotions*. Oxford: Oxford University Press.

Rustin, M. (2002). 'Looking in the right place: Complexity Theory, psychoanalysis and infant observation. *The International Journal of Infant Observation*, 5: 122144. Reprinted in Andrew Briggs (ed.). *Surviving Space: Papers on Infant Observation.* Karnac/Tavistock Clinic Book Series (2002).

Schore, A. (1994). *Affect Regulation and the Origin of the Self: The Neurobiology of Emotional Development.* Hove, UK: Lawrence Erlbaum Associates.

———. (2002). 'Clinical implications of a psychoneurobiological model of projective identification'. Chapter 1 in S. Alhanati (ed.), *Primitive Mental States*, Vol. 2: *Psychobiological and Psychoanalytic Perspectives on Early Trauma and Personality Development.* London: Karnac.

Sidoli, M. and Davies, M. (1988). *Jungian Child Psychotherapy: Individuation in Childhood.* London: Karnac.

Stern, D. (1985). *The Interpersonal World of the Infant.* London: Basic Books.

Stewart, I. (1998). *Life's Other Secret: The New Mathematics of the Living World.* London: Allen Lane.

Tallis, R. (2010). *Michelangelo's Finger: An Exploration of Everyday Transcendence.* London: Atlantic Books.

Trevarthen, C. (1989). 'Development of early social interactions and the affective regulation of brain growth'. in C. von Euler, H. Forssberg, and H. Lagercrantz (eds.), *Neurobiology of Early Infant Behaviour.* Basingstoke, UK: Macmillan.

Trevarthen, C. and Marwick, H. (1986). 'Signs of motivation for speech in infants, and the nature of a mother's support for development of language'. In B. Lindblom and R. Zetterstrom (eds.), *Precursors of Early Speech.* Basingstoke, Hants: Macmillan.

Urban, E. (1996). ' "With healing in her wings . . .": Integration and repair in a self-destructive adolescent'. *Journal of Child Psychotherapy*, 22: 64–81.

———. (2003a). 'Developmental aspects of trauma and traumatic aspects of development'. *Journal of Analytical Psychology*, 48: 171–190.

———. (2003b). 'Review of Primitive Mental States, Vol. 2: *Psychological and Psychoanalytic Perspectives on Early Trauma and Personality Development*, S. Alhanati (ed.)'. *The International Journal of Infant Observation and its Applications*, 6: 117–123.

———. (2005). 'Fordham, Jung and the self: A re-examination of Fordham's contribution to Jung's conceptualisation'. *Journal of Analytical Psychology*, 50: 571–594.

———. (2008). 'The "self" in analytical psychology: The function of the "central archetype" within Fordham's model'. *Journal of Analytical Psychology*, 53: 329350.

———. (2009). 'Conjugating the self'. *Journal of Analytical Psychology*, 54: 399–403.

———. (2013). 'Reflections on research and learning from the patient: The art and science of what we do'. *Journal of Analytical Psychology*, 58: 510–529.

Part I

Theory

Chapter 1

The primary self and related concepts in Jung, Klein and Isaacs

Introduction

This chapter has its source in some comments made by Dr Fordham in one of my supervision sessions. The patient under discussion was a boy with autistic features, who had been seeing me in analysis for three years. When Dr Fordham said, almost as an aside, that it is not possible to analyse someone who has autism, I was considerably taken aback, because that was what I thought I had been trying to do. When I asked what he meant, he answered that analysis is of internal objects, and autistic children have no internal objects. What do they have inside? I wondered, and Dr Fordham answered that the primary self is lacking in contents. This made me realise that I had confusions and misconceptions about the primitive mind and its contents. This chapter represents my attempt to address these questions. It is a study of early psychic contents and processes, beginning with a consideration of the differences between Jung, Klein and Isaacs, on the one hand, and Fordham, on the other. I then examine Fordham's theory of a primary self and its actions, I and attempt to describe how contents are built up in the psyche. Some of the primary processes described are illustrated by an infant observation. At the end of the chapter I give clinical material through which I hope to show how the same psychic processes that contribute co psychic growth can also result in the failure of psychic development.

A, if not the, major difference between Freud and Jung lay in their views about the inner world. Freud's main emphasis was on the way contents of the mind are derived from personal experience, whereas Jung's studies viewed the mind as innately endowed with priori configurations that encompass far more than personal contents.

Klein too departed from Freud on this point, and the Controversial Discussions of the British Psycho-Analytic Society revolved around this issue (Hinshelwood 1989). Both Jung and Klein thought that the primary contents of the mind are inextricably bound up with the instincts, that in fact they are the mental representations of the instincts.

DOI: 10.4324/9781003215639-3

According to Jung, the primary content of the psyche is the archetype. In contrast to instincts the ' "archetypes" are inborn forms of "intuition" ' (Jung 1919, p. 133).

> Analogous to instinct, with the difference that whereas the impulse to carry out some highly complicated purposive apprehension of a highly compli-cated action, intuition is the unconscious purposive apprehension of a highly complicated situation.
>
> (ibid., p. 133)

Jung also noted the similarities between archetypes and instincts. The archetypes make up the collective unconscious, which is universal and impersonal; that is, it is the same for all individuals. Instincts, according to Jung, are also impersonal and universal, and are, also like the archetypes, hereditary factors of a dynamic or motivating character. Thus, instincts form very close analogues to the archetypes, so close, in fact, that there is good reason for supposing that the archetypes are the unconscious phantasies. Klein writes, 'I believe that phantasies operate from the outset, as do the instincts, and are the mental expression of the activity of both the life and death instincts' (Klein 1952, p. 58). Isaacs presents a fuller exposi-tion of the relationship between phantasies and instincts than does Klein. Isaacs states that 'phantasies are the primary content of unconscious mental processes' (Isaacs 1952, p. 82). 'The mental expression of instinct is unconscious phantasy. Phantasy is (in the first instance) the mental corollary, the psychic representative, of instinct' (ibid., p. 83).

Although for the most part Klein and Isaacs describe phantasies in terms of stories, for example, 'I want to eat her all up', these stories are based upon images:

> What, then, does the infant hallucinate? We may assume, since it is the oral impulse which is at work, first, the nipple, then the breast, and later his mother as a whole person; and he hallucinates the nipple or the breast in order to enjoy it. As we can see from his behaviour (sucking movements, sucking his own lip or a little later his fingers, and so on), hallucination does not stop at the mere picture, but carries him on to what he is, it in detail, going to do with the desired object which he imagines (phantasies) he has obtained.
>
> (Ibid., p. 86)

The 'picture' of the breast that is an image of the instinct make Isaacs's descrip-tion of unconscious phantasies virtually identical to Jung's description of the archetype as the 'self-portrait of the instinct'. When Isaacs wrote, 'such knowl-edge (of the breast) is in the *aim* of instinct' (ibid., p. 94), she can be understood to be talking about the same thing that Jung described when he stated that the yucca moth has an image of the yucca flower and its structure, so that, when present externally, the flower sets off instinctual behaviour (Jung 1919). Both Jung and Isaacs stated that there is an image of the aim of the instinct – the object that fulfils the instinctual urge that exists within the psyche, enabling the instinct to know that for which it is looking.

Important differences do, however, exist between Jung and Klein. Klein was a psychoanalyst who extended Freud's concepts of libidinal and destructive instincts to pre-Oedipal development, focusing on how infancy lies at the core of the personality. On the other hand, although Jung drew attention to the inherent richness of the mind before Klein began writing, his interest in childhood and infancy was limited. Although he referred to the individuality of the infant (Jung 1911, 1921), for the most part he thought that the infant is in primary identity with the mother (Jung 1927). The issue of primary identity raises a number of questions which have since been addressed by Fordham.

The self, the primary self and 'the ultimate': Jung and Fordham

My misconception was that I had pictured an innate, internal realm of images and phantasies that from birth were projected onto the external world. Sorting this out required that I 'empty out' the contents of the infant mind and differentiate between the self described by Jung and the primary self described by Fordham. Jung concluded from his studies 'that a class of images, expressing totality, symbolises the self, defined as the total personality, conscious and unconscious' (Fordham 1976, p. 11). Jung's awareness of the self arose from the period following his break with Freud. At this time he discovered the meaning of the mandala symbols that preoccupied him. In *Memories, Dreams and Reflections*, Jung wrote, 'Only gradually did I discover what the mandala really is: "Formation, Transformation, Eternal Mind's eternal recreation". . . . Mandalas were cryptograms concerning the state of the self which were presented to me anew each day. In them I saw the self – that is my whole being actively at work' Jung 1963a, p. 221). Later he added, 'I knew that in finding the mandala as the expression of the self I had attained what was for me the ultimate' (ibid., p. 222).

The 'ultimate' to which he referred is the individuating self, which, according to Jung, emerges out of an initial primary identity with the mother (Jung 1927). Fordham applied Jung's ideas about the self and individuation to early childhood and introduced clinical material from his work in support of the idea that children show signs of individuation at a very early age (Fordham 1969). He revised Jung's ideas and postulated that the child's individuation emerges not out of a primary identity with the mother, but out of an original, or primary self, which is a pre-individuating self (Fordham 1976). Drawing from Jung's definition of the self as 'the totality unconscious' (Jung 1955, p. 389) of the psyche altogether, i.e. 'conscious and unconscious' (Jung 1955, p. 389), and also on the claim that 'the self embraces the bodily sphere as well as the psyche' (Jung 1963b, p. 503), Fordham defined the primary self as 'a psychosomatic integrate – a blueprint for psychic maturation – from which the behaviour of infants may be derived as they gradually develop and differentiate into children, adolescents and adults'

(Fordham 1976, p. 11). Thus 'the ultimate' for Jung is the individuating self, and for Fordham it is the primary self.

Together these two concepts describe the self as alpha and omega. To understand this more fully, I have found it important to consider how the 'empty' primary self (Fordham's 'ultimate', the ultimate source), which has the potential for providing the space for inner objects, acquires the characteristics of inside and outside and develops into a container for psychic contents to which the ego might then relate Jung's 'ultimate', the ultimate goal. For me this has meant going back to 'the very beginning', to the point at which the primary self is in its most primary state, before it has any characteristics and when it is 'pure' potential. This – Fordham's 'ultimate' in its ultimate form – would be at the instant when the foetal organism acquires a psychic constituent (thereby becoming psychosomatic) but prior to deintegration and reintegration, that is to any further relating to the environment. This state exists only as a theoretical construct. But, for my purposes here, it is important to describe it.

The fertilised egg at the instant of union more aptly illustrates the primary self at 'the very beginning' than does the infant at birth. This is because deintegration and reintegration occur in utero. These processes are accelerated at birth and lead eventually to the internalisation of objects and, later, to symbolisation. But, at birth, the primary self has developed beyond its original state. Originally the primary self exists as nothing but potential. As Fordham described it, it is a 'pregnant void':

> I conclude with a reflection on the 'ultimate'. I take it to represent a state in which there is no past and no future, though it is present like a point which has position but no magnitude. It has no desires, no memory, no thoughts, no images but out of it by transformation all of these can deintegrate. There is no consciousness and so no unconscious – it is a pregnant absence.
>
> (Fordham 1985, p. 33)

The primary self at birth has developed from the 'ultimate' but is still mainly without contents; that is, it is primarily void-but-predisposed-to-receive objects from without that can be internalised. Furnishing the internal world really gets under way only after increased deintegrative and reintegrative processes have taken place after birth. However, the primary self has undergone transformations from 'the very beginning' up until birth and to the point at which there are the primary contents described by Jung, Klein and Isaacs. That is, the images considered by them to be innate are not; what is innate is the potential and predisposition to have images.

Fordham drew upon Freud's analogy of the protozoa amoeba to the ego to describe his postulate of the primary, pre-individuating self, and I would like to extend the analogy to describe Fordham's 'ultimate'. In Fordham's analogy, the amoeba, like the primary self, is a living organism. It is a nucleated mass of protoplasm, most dense at the outside, which forms a boundary with the outside world. Finger-like extensions called pseudopodia protrude from the amoeba and engulf food, which is then incorporated into the organism. In this analogy, the nucleated endoplasm of the amoeba corresponds to the centralising and ordering functions of the primary self. The pseudopodia correspond to deintegrates of the primary self, extending out and relating to the environment while still maintaining a relationship to the whole. The taking in and digestion of food corresponds to reintegration.

A model of the primary self at its most primary state – at its 'very beginning' – is of a less developed amoeba. This can be pictured by imagining the reversal of the development of the amoeba as though looking at high-speed film shown in reverse. The amoeba will then be seen to become smaller and smaller, its ectoplasm shrinking to become part of the nucleated mass until the whole of the organism becomes quite simply a dot, 'like a point which has position but no magnitude' (Fordham 1985, p. 33).

Another picture of Fordham's 'ultimate', which views it from the inside, so to speak, has been supplied to me by the conscious vision of a patient in her late twenties. This vision occurred at the outset of a period of considerable change in the patient's life. I understand this experience to belong to a state of integration, in which deintegrates came together momentarily into a state of oneness, expressed through an image of 'the ultimate'. This experience is relevant to my subject because states of integration in individuating adults are very similar to primary states of integration in infancy and thus to the primary self. As Fordham commented:

> It follows that in normal development the 'delusional' state of primary identity or unity-with the mother can only be transitory and the formation of a new integrate, a new dynamic equilibrium within the infant, corresponding to, but more differentiated than, the original self unit.
>
> (Fordham 1985. p. 110)

In this vision the patient is an infinitely small speck – 'a point with position but no magnitude' – in an infinitely large universe of blue sky which is a pure nothingness. She 'knows' that this is the moment of death. Around and before her is timeless eternity, in which she is suspended in an eternal pause of beginning. This seems to be what Fordham described as the 'pregnant absence' of 'the ultimate' (Fordham 1985, p. 33).

The dynamics of the primary self: deintegration and reintegration

For Jung and Klein, the contents of the mind, whether they are called archetypal images or internal objects, are autonomous internal realities, relating to one another, to the ego and, via projection and introjection, to the external world. But how does the primary self relate to the environment if it has no contents to project? In answering this question, Fordham offered a unique contribution to our ideas about psychic dynamics as well as about individual development. He wrote:

> I considered the self as a dynamic system that acted not only as an integra-tor of psychic and physical elements bur also as a system that spontaneously could divide itself up into parts. For that I coined the term 'deintegration' which did not disrupt the integrity of the organism as would be implied by dis-integration. I postulated a rhythm of integration and deintegration that leads to growth. Deintegrates are new experiences, either predominantly affective or cognitive, which can then be digested and integrated into the whole.
>
> (Fordham 1987, p. 334)

It is important for an appreciation of Fordham's theory to understand that the concepts of deintegration and reintegration are designed to describe the dynamic of inner with outer, without necessarily referring to mental mechanisms and con-tents, although the dynamics of the self can give rise to them. Initially, the self is a structure of potentials and predispositions without contents and without char-acteristics: structures without images, the word processor's template without the print. Although deintegration is similar to projection and reintegration to introjec-tion, they are different in a significant way. Neither projection nor introjection can occur until there are internal objects – internal, initially, to the self – because pro-jection and introjection necessitate a content. Deintegration is the inherent action of the primary self and is a way of relating that occurs before objects have been internalised as well as after. Because deintegration means relating to an experi-ence, whether it is internal or external, early deintegrates are the same as Bion's beta elements, which are the primary instrument of the baby's relating. Beta ele-ments represent the facts of experience, that is, sense impressions and very primi-tive emotional experiences (Bion 1962). Therefore, like early deintegrates, they are physiological as much as mental; they are, to use Bion's term, 'proto-thoughts' or, to use Fordham's, 'proto-mental' (Grinberg et al. 1975, p. 38; Fordham 1985). This means that primitive mental processes have a psychosomatic, mind-body quality. One can observe how an infant's physical actions, such as sucking, elimi-nating and crying, are imbued with emotions and how they enable the baby to manage various states, like getting rid of discomfort, as well as to communicate with another through projective identification. This runs contrary to Stern's con-clusion that projective and introjective processes are not operative until the baby is capable of symbolisation, because he presumes that these dynamics are mental rather than mind-body (Stern 1985; Davies 1989).

Deintegration begins in utero and accelerates at birth, when the infant must adapt to extra-uterine life. About this Fordham wrote:

> Suppose that when a new 'adaptation' is required the self responds by deinte-grating optimally followed by a new integration. Birth is such an experience. A massive deintegration would occur causing fears of a very primitive kind

recorded later on as experiences such as catastrophic chaos, nameless dread, dropping into a black hole, etc. A reintegration would follow provided the suitable environment were made available.

(Fordham 1993, p. 71)

Commenting on the massive deintegration following birth, Hobdell described how when the infant is sleeping this is a time for integration. All but 6 hours of an infant's early life is spent in sleep expending psychical and physical energy on deintegration (Hobdell 1988).

The point I should like to make here is that the massive deintegration at birth may affect subsequent deintegrations, such as those at the breast, and that the relationship to the breast may be preceded by other experiences which have been taken in and organised by the self archetypally. That is, when the infant is put to the breast, the infant's response to it may not be, strictly speaking, an innate response, but rather the result of the interplay between the infant's self and the environment. The process that begins with the facts of experience, that is, sense impressions combined with primitive emotions into a psychosomatic, mind-body experience, quickly goes on to develop in complexity. In interactions with the mother, the baby takes in not only the physical contents of the breast which are assimilated into his body through milk, but proto-mental contents that are also assimilated. The baby's actions and the mother's actions interrelate, so that the baby's experiences of the mother also come back into the baby's self and are reintegrated. Experiences of the mother are taken in again and again through repeated deintegrations and are processed again and again through repeated reintegrations.

Once the baby has related to an experience, whether external to him, like the breast, or internal, like a pain in his stomach, the deintegrate withdraws and takes something in from the experience that will form a content. Actions of the self will form the contents into an internal object that is primarily archetypal. This means it is universal, unconscious, typical and combined with intense emotional 'meaning'. Being imbued with the self, these objects are felt to be omnipotent, have an all-or-nothing quality and thus seem to be of one extreme or its opposite.

As the process unfolds, 'bits' of experience, via actions of the self, coalesce in such a way that the contents of these experiences acquire characteristics. Stern concludes that initially the characteristics are 'global' (that is, archetypal) and are of 'intensities, shapes, temporal patterns, vitality affects, categorical affects, and hedonic tones' (Stern 1985, p. 67). In this way the baby gets 'an idea' of what the mother is like. Mother/infant observations show that babies can have this 'idea' soon after birth. Foetal studies which demonstrate deintegration also support this. Verney, drawing upon the results of such studies, vividly describes how the unborn becomes an 'active participant in intra-uterine bonding' and con vincingly supports the idea that 'bonding after birth . . . [is] actually the continuation of a bonding process that [begins] long before, in the womb' (Verney 1981, pp. 61–62).

This, then, is what Fordham means by reintegration; as experiences (that is, dein-tegrates, which can be construed as similar to beta elements) get withdrawn into the self, they become integrated into the self and then take on various forms which eventually acquire clearer definition. As cognitive and emotional development gains in complexity, the self begins to reveal its structure, much as the fertilised egg develops to reveal physical characteristics, such as individual facial features. As this development occurs, the infant can experience objects as having an inside and an outside. As this happens, and as the mind – now experienced as having an inside and an outside – develops contents, something can be done with the inner objects. Relationships come into play, and objects can be identified with, projected and introjected. This allows for further development of the inner world and its objects.

With continued deintegration and reintegration comes the capacity for a quali-tative change in the nature of inner contents. Stern and Trevarthen indicate that there are discrete, qualitatively different surges of change during infancy and childhood (which Fordham has described as 'deintegrating optimally'), but Stern is careful to distinguish them from developmental stages or phases (Stern 1985; Trevarthen 1974, 1987; Fordham 1991). Fordham too makes this point:

> Many psychiatric constructions and theories about infancy refer to states that may lead to psychic damage. Many of these can be described and/or inferred with considerable certainty, yet the impression given that they are more or less continuous and so defining stages in development is questionable.
>
> (Fordham 1987, p. 358)

With the gradual separating out of mind and body and the development of sym-bolisation, objects, through inherent actions of the self, can take on an increasing correspondence to their correlates in the external world. As that happens, it can be said that some contents refer mainly to reality and some refer mainly to the self.

In summary, Fordham's theory of deintegration and reintegration makes explicit the interplay of the archetypal and the external, which occurs from before birth. The primary self, initially without contents and characteristics, deintegrates and reintegrates as the infant adapts to extra-uterine life. The breast is an early object that the baby reaches out to and then assimilates, whereupon it becomes a percep-tion imbued with meaning and organised in a particular archetypal way to create an inner object. Experiences are taken in time and again and 'recorded' time and again. There is a change in the nature of inner contents as the primary self unfolds through deintegration and reintegration, leading to growing complexity and the enrichment of the mind.

According to Fordham, inner contents are initially internal to the self and not, at least until representations have been built up in the mind, to the ego. This view contrasts with that of Klein, who, drawing upon Freud's structural model, pos-tulates an ego from birth (Hinshelwood 1989) because the id has no organising or containing function. Thereby the concept of the ego is extended beyond that which would be understood by Fordham. This also contrasts with the viewpoint of Stern, who runs into a conceptual difficulty when trying to account for the early organising phenomena observed in infants before the ego (that which 'senses' the various 'senses of the self' that he describes) has become established (Stern 1985).

Early deintegration and reintegration: an infant observation

The most vivid way of describing early deintegration and reintegration is to turn to infant observation. The first three observations of Toby show him reacting to varying degrees of discomfort and seem to indicate the gradual coming together of experiences into what becomes a bad object.

> First visit (4 days old): His mother pointed out the line of a bruise across his brow, which she thought was from a contraction. . . . I watched him while he slept. I noticed him extend his arms forward from the shoulders and put his head back, in a single twitched movement. It seemed as though he was resisting something and pushing and moving against it. For the most part he lay with his arms crossed at the forearm in front of his face. . . . The baby twitched a couple of times, extending his hands forward and his head backward, but was otherwise still throughout the visit.

In this observation Toby's only movement during sleep is a reflexive forward pushing out of his arms and a simultaneous pulling back of his head. In the expression of resistance there is a suggestion of something unpleasant, but it is not much more than a suggestion.

> Second visit (1 week, 6 days old): Toby lay on his right side with his hands held outside the covers. During the whole of the observation he slept. . . . His brow occasionally knit into a frown, and the skin twitched along the temple between the outer corner of his eye and his ear. The eyes themselves moved beneath the closed lids, giving the impression that he was 'seeing' despite the fact that the lids were shut. . . .
> *He moved his head backwards and his arms stretched forward.* . . . His cheeks moved with the movement of his mouth when he drew it back at the corners as if he were going to cry. . . . Toby made one or two little monosyllabic crying noises. . . . At one point he screwed up his face as if he were going to cry and then farted quite loudly. His face then relaxed and he became still.

The same movement observed in the first visit – the head moving backward and the arms stretching forward – is also observed in the second. However, in the second visit, the experience is more clearly uncomfortable and is accompanied by crying noises and facial expressions that more than suggest discomfort. There seems to be evidence of an inner object; it has qualities (discomfort) and location (inside him), so that something can be done with the object. What is done is that it is evacuated through a bodily response, despite the fact that the experience is not entirely bodily because it also has something of emotion. In both observations, Toby is sleeping, and it is evident that it is not relevant to talk in terms of Toby being either conscious or unconscious; the distinction does not matter at this point.

> Third visit (2 weeks, 2 days old): Toby slept propped up in his chair. (He had had some milk from his mother's breast, but the full feed was postponed.) He occasionally stretched his legs, straightened and raised his arms and hands, and stretched and reached out, *as if pushing away from something in front of him.* . . . His face occasionally screwed up, and he knit his brow. Occasionally his eyes opened, but when they did he closed them quickly before they focused on anything. After a while he became more awake and stared at the side of his chair.
>
> Once he had awakened (although he shut his eyes for intervals), he began to screw up his face. He tensed his hands and wrists, quickly drawing them up towards his face and quickly taking them away. . . . Once or twice he pulled his hands to his face and sucked on the cuff of his Babygro. His noises became more disturbing. (On the mother's instruction) I picked him up. He moved his head from side to side and then quietened, relaxing into a half-sleep. Then he screwed up his face again and made repeated half-cries. . . . I lifted him against my right shoulder. His temple was against my right cheek, and he moved his head, which I supported with my hand, toward and away from my face. His left hand flexed and clenched, and his right hand firmly grasped the neck of my pullover. *He pushed against and away from me, a push that was from his shoulders with his head back and arms forward.*
>
> I patted his back with my left hand, and he was quiet and then became distressed again. I noticed that he was making a kind of clicking noise, and it seemed to be coming from the back of his mouth. It became increasingly distressing to see him so upset. . . . He went from his restless discomfort into a loud, open cry: long throaty aaaaahs. I gave him to his mother and as she took him Toby continued crying. . . . She raised her pullover over her left breast and directed his face toward the nipple. He took the nipple into his mouth and sucked with closed eyes, rapidly and rhythmically.

The same pushing movements observed in the first and second visits are again evident and observed with feelings of discontent. However, there are clearer indications of distress and discomfort; that is, there is increased intensity in body movements and crying. Over the course of the three visits, the experience in the first observation has been combined, via actions of the self, with subsequent experiences (deintegrations) of unpleasantness and discomfort to coalesce (reintegrate) into a more clearly defined bad inner experience, or object. Initially the experience does not have an 'all-or-nothing' quality because actions of the self have not by that point shaped it archetypally, although this happens within a short period after birth.

Fordham's postulate of a deintegrating and reintegrating primary self is supported by observation. In fact, while infant observation has here been used to illustrate the concept of deintegration and reintegration, one can equally say that the concept of deintegration and reintegration illuminates infant observation.

This also applies to the concept I am studying in this work. Infant research attests to the 'elaborate innate machinery' of the primary self (Trevarthen 1974, p. 231). For instance, Stern concludes that 'Infants are not lost at sea in a wash of abstractable qualities of experience. They are gradually and systematically ordering these elements of experience' (Stern 1985, p. 67). He also describes deintegration and reintegration. 'Development occurs in leap and bounds, qualitative shifts may be one of the most obvious features. . . . Between these periods of rapid change are periods of relative quiescence when the new integrations appear to consolidate' (Stern 1985, p. 8).

Clinical material

As clinicians, we know that actions of the self that shaped Toby's inner world archetypally and enabled his inner development can also result in the failure of maturation. What Fordham calls defences of the self serve to protect the integrity of the personality yet can also stand in the way of psychic growth (Fordham 1947; Davies 1991). This can come about as follows.

Deintegration is the way the self divides up and differentiates. 'The most primitive (differentiation) is the distinction between a good and a bad breast, and development follows from the reintegration of these experiences' (Fordham 1987, p. 357). But

> If, for instance, a baby is submitted to noxious stimuli of a pathogenic nature (either in utero, during or after birth) a persistent over-reaction of the defence-system may start to take place: this may become compounded with parts of the self by projective identification, so that a kind of auto-immune reaction sets in: this in particular would account for the persistence of the defence after the noxious stimulus had been withdrawn. Not-self objects then come to be felt as a danger to or even a total threat to life, and must be attacked, destroyed or their effect neutralized. The focus is therefore on the not-self and little or no inner world can develop.
>
> (Fordham 1969, p. 93)

In the following clinical example I hope to describe how these defences affected the patient's deintegrations and reintegrations, what the consequences were for his internal world, and how treatment brought about change. The material is that of a boy whom I call Ricky, and it was the supervision of his sessions with Dr. Fordham that started me thinking about how the self acquires contents.

Ricky attended a special school because of his difficulties in relating and learning. In some cognitive respects, Ricky was precocious: he could read well and was particularly good at arithmetic. However, he read with a flat, robotic quality that was detached from meaning, and his mastery of numbers was obsessional. For instance, he repeated over and over again in sessions a 'numbers game', in which he did nothing more than make a chart of the multiplication tables. Initially he made little eye contact with others and talked in an echolalic manner, unable to speak spontaneously. He confused personal pronouns, referring to me as 'she' when he meant 'you' and to himself as 'he', for instance, 'He wants the key' when he meant 'I want the key'. His sessions opened and closed with an obsessional ritual, and if he had to depart from it he became very upset. Despite his extreme cut-offness, he had a strong wish to fit in and be accepted by others, and often tried to do this by playing the clown.

When he began treatment his mother told me that he had been breast fed but failed to develop a good relationship with the breast and was a difficult feeder, with frequent vomiting, diarrhoea and crying. At 2 ½ he developed asthma, which for a period was life-threatening. His family, which included both parents and an older sister, was a loving one with many strengths. My picture was that he had undermined his parents' confidence, leaving them feeling intimidated by his odd behaviour, which they did not understand, and frightened by his asthma attacks. Thus he tended to control them, preventing them from helping him in areas where they might have done, like providing firmness for his silliness. He was not quite six years old when he came to his first session:

> Once in the consulting room, Ricky became rather nervous. I said that there was a box on the table with some things in it at which I thought he would like to look. He answered mechanically and with false enthusiasm: 'Game, it's a game!' and circled me as I sat in my chair. He ended up standing beside me on my left and touched his head against mine. . . . He stood away and said cleverly, 'Elizabeth, your name's Elizabeth'. As he walked around me, I said he wondered who I was and what I wanted to do with him.

He went through the contents of the toy box and, with exaggerated emphasis, recited what each object was, reading, when he could, what was on the manufacturer's label. Then

> He stood in the middle of the room and said to himself, 'Your name's Elizabeth Erminella', and laughing to himself, softly repeated, 'Erminella'. I said that Erminella was close to Urban, but not quite the same thing; perhaps it was his word for me which was different from my word for me. He came close to me and stood next to me, looking intently at my mouth. I said that he was curious about me and wanted to know who I was, so he wanted to look inside me – inside my mouth – to see where the words were coming from. As I said this, he peered – at a distance of less than an inch – into my mouth

and then – from the same distance – into my ear and my nose and then moved behind me, his head remaining only an inch from mine. I continued that he wanted to look into all my holes to see what was inside me.

Towards the end of the interview,

> He came and couched my left ear, very gently, whereupon my earring came off. He looked in wonder at the earring, and I pointed out that it was shaped like a hole and that he was interested in my holes – my mouth, my ears, my nose and my bottom hole. He tried to replace the earring and I helped. He laughed to himself, saying, 'Ostrich'. I asked what an ostrich does, and he said excitedly, 'It's got an O!'

What Ricky understood as a game seemed to involve our matching wits against one another. He expressed this concretely, so that matching wits, presumably located in one's head, was represented by putting his head against and touching mine. He knew very little of me, and this aroused his anxiety. Who I was – what kind of person I was inside – could only be explored by attempting a close examination of my physical inside, or what he could examine of it through my orifices. Holes, through primary thought processes, were linked with my round earrings, and then to 'ostrich' (O). This was not because of the meaning of 'ostrich' as a large, flightless bird, but because of the way the word itself looks. Thus, Ricky's inner objects had only flat, sensate qualities, and what was outside the sensate, or concrete, was beyond his ability to take in.

The flat, unidimensional quality of the 'O' deserves comment. It strikes me that the 'O' in Ricky's material held the potential for being a container, or self-representation, but was instead felt as a hole. This is reminiscent of Tustin's autistic black hole (Tustin 1974), although I view this phenomenon from a different theoretical perspective. I have previously quoted Fordham on the 'massive deintegration' at birth. He is suggesting that the infant experiences fears of a very primitive kind involving a sense of catastrophic chaos (Fordham 1991). I should like to expand on this comment and consider that at birth there is an explosion of deintegrates reaching out to make contact with the new, extra-uterine environment. The deintegrates would carry with them inherent 'expectations' of, say, a breast, but if the environment does not respond or contain these deintegrates, the deintegrates meet with 'nothing', and 'nothingness' is then taken back into the self. If the 'nothingness' is felt to be overwhelming, the self would not be able to assimilate the experience, although some kind of processing might be done which combines it with colourings of, say, dread. The 'nothingness' would then be defended against in the way described by Fordham (Fordham 1947).

This could explain why Ricky so resisted what was experienced by him as 'not self' (whether this was the contents of his mother's breast or my interpretations) and how, in not letting 'not-self' inside him, he was unable to experience having an inside, internal world, that is, having a mind that is a container. The defence against 'not-self objects' involved splitting, including that between good-inan-imate-controllable objects and bad-animate-uncontrollable objects. Stern and Trevarthen demonstrate that neonates respond differently to people. Ricky drew upon his ability to manipulate inanimate objects in an attempt to 'relate' to people.

In the introduction to this chapter I described Ricky as having autistic features. From the material I have given, it is clear that he had something of an internal world, but it was highly defended against. In further discussion in my supervision, Dr Fordham clarified that no one is completely autistic; some deintegration has taken place in order for the individual to survive. However, as a result of split-ting, Ricky's deintegrations were primarily cognitive. For him, cognitive develop-ment had become defensive and served to replace affective development, insight and symbolic thought. He could relate cognitively to the toys that I provided and 'know' what they were by reading the labels, although he never played with them, nor did he come to know their emotional meaning for him by projecting parts of himself onto them. Only at the very end of treatment did he seem to become aware of the emotional meaning of some pictures he drew, thus indicating that the 'O' that so fascinated him at the beginning of treatment was becoming a container for psychic experience.

As his treatment proceeded, I could respond to Ricky's likeability, but typi-cally I experienced cut-offness, frustration, uselessness and exclusion. Some-times I felt driven nearly mad by his obsessionality because it made me feel so excluded and controlled. He spent one session reading out the changes of number on his digital watch, which – to my relief – his mother usually kept at home. At one point in his treatment, I tried an experiment, in which I made a point of sur-rendering to his control. What happened arose out of what was happening in the session and was at a time when I was interested in a particular infant study which drew attention to the impact on infants when they experienced themselves as efficacious (Broucek 1979).

The experiment began in a session 18 months into treatment. Coming to his ses-sion that day meant that he was unable to go out on the playground during break, and he responded to this by calling out, 'Therapy stop!' when I went to pick him up in his classroom. In the therapy room he followed his ritual of taking out the toys from the cupboard, then paced the room before lying down on the couch and asking, 'Is it time?' I commented on his anger at missing playtime, and this was met by a mischievous sparkle in his eyes. He became increasingly prankish and silly. After a bit he started whispering, and I could make out that he was saying a children's rhyme – something about going to the zoo to see the elephants climb a fence so high it reached the sky. I repeated the lines in a whisper. Then he started rhythmically patting the back of the couch and softly sang 'Oh My Darling Clem-entine'. I joined in, singing as softly as he did. It took a moment for him to realise what was happening, and he stopped abruptly and turned and looked at me.

There was a pause before he settled again and started patting the back of the couch but not singing. I sang to the patting, following its faster or slower beat. When singing with him, I had sung at his pitch, but alone I sang at a lower pitch which was more comfortable for me. When I did this, he said, 'Higher', and I lifted my pitch; later he said, 'Lower', and I followed. His eyes sparkled and danced, and he giggled from deep within himself. When the session came to a close and he was making to go, he said, 'That's a lovely "Oh my darling" song.'

For the next several sessions he continued to co-direct my singing the same song by patting the back of the couch. Variations were introduced by my adding verses, so that he would direct me to sing 'In a cavern', 'Ruby lips', or 'Oh my darlin'', and he would be upset if I did not comply. I attempted to add interpretations by making up some verses, such as: 'Baby Ricky, Baby Ricky/ Wants Elizabeth to sing./ When she does he is delighted,/ She's the bride and he's the king.'

He seemed to enjoy the custom-tailored words, but their meaning had no interpretative impact. This play went on for several weeks, by which time I felt resistance towards his increasing bossiness, and also I began to question the value of what we were doing. This was because the treatment failed to include analytic thinking. I had abandoned mine and thus did not give my attention to the manic defence that Ricky felt to be so high that it reached the sky. I was also ignoring his heroic, large-as-an-elephant efforts to address this defence, a heroism that became clearer later in the treatment.

Ricky was understandably upset when I returned to more orthodox interpretations and resisted his attempts to control me. For my part, although I felt guilty that he had felt seduced by me, I had established in my own mind the value of offering Ricky my analytic thinking, a position which can better be explained after I have described the outcome of the treatment. Establishing this position resulted in my becoming more accepting of the slow pace of the work and the impression that there was no change.

This impression was, however, false. By the end of the second year of treatment, Ricky was accurately using 'I', and his pronoun confusion had disappeared. Although still quite inhibited, he was able to show some spontaneity, and this was reflected in his voice, which lost its mechanical quality. His echolalia disappeared, and he was able to speak from himself, although the results were sometimes baffling. I shall give an example of this, as it shows where he – and his family – had reached by the end of two years of treatment.

In the following excerpt, he had left the special school two months before, having reached the end of the period offered to pupils. At that time his family also moved outside London. Because special school provision would have meant Ricky being placed with children who were educationally subnormal, his parents arranged for him to go to a local school, which, although small, had classes far larger than Ricky had known at his special school. The parents valued Ricky's therapy and, concerned at the effect of their moving on their son, arranged to bring him to London for once-weekly sessions.

Initially I shared the concern expressed by the special school that Ricky's accomplishments would not be sustained, let alone increased, if he attended a mainstream school. In this I was underestimating Ricky's heroic quality and not understanding that it attached to his wish to be normal. I had only a faint awareness of this wish, when, during a session while he was at the special school, he was distracted by two boys outside, walking along the pavement. Teachers at 'normal' schools were on strike that day, while those at special schools did not take action. Ricky was aware of this because his sister attended a mainstream school and, like the boys on the street below, did not have to go to school that day. He looked at them long and hard, as if trying to understand what he was looking at. I also sensed a longing in his expression and commented that, although I knew that he liked his special school very much, he also wanted to be 'normal' like the boys.

I also had not appreciated the effect of the changes in Ricky in restoring his parents' confidence. They had become firmer with him when it was appropriate, and his mother could translate his sometimes peculiar statements. This is demonstrated in the following:

> Ricky and his mother came up the stairs and stood on the landing by the waiting room door. He said something that he had to repeat several times because it was not comprehensible, but eventually it became, 'Are you going go tell about her?' His mother translated back to him, 'Is there something you want me to tell Miss Urban?' 'Yes, about Cubs.' She then explained to me that he had started to go to Cubs. He was delighted and laughed in a giggly, convulsive way. He called out, 'Packs!', and went up the stairs to the consulting room calling this out. He went into the room ahead of me and shut the door (which was typical), and I could hear him inside, laughing and calling, 'Packs! Packs! Packs is normal!'
>
> I went into the room and sat down. 'I think that you're saying that your going to Cubs is what normal boys do and that going there makes you feel normal.' He continued to giggle in a manic way and then said loudly, 'Shhh! Don't talk! Be quiet! . . . Sit down and do your work and be quiet!' He continued to tell me to be quiet as I started to say, 'I think you're telling me now about going to a normal school, where your teacher tells you to be quiet.'
>
> Towards the end of the session he said to me, 'You're a therapist', and I answered that having therapy meant that he felt he wasn't normal. He asked when therapy would end.

The above session indicates Ricky's need to develop his capacity to think and express himself in a coherent manner. This is provided by his mother, who could understand and translate his rather odd communication and give it meaning, much as a mother does for her infant. His excitement about telling me that he was capable of joining in 'normal' activities was not contained, and he gave way to the feel of the plosive 'Packs!' (beta elements) rather than the more linguistically meaningful 'Cubs'.

The kind of thinking that Ricky's mother offered in the above example I have called 'translation', because his mother translated Ricky's sometimes idiosyncratic language into common parlance in order to give it meaning. Translation is different from interpretation, which is directed at the emotional meaning of what a patient says or does and is an expression of the analyst's symbolic thinking.

Interpretation, in contrast to translation, offers possibilities for a multiplicity of meanings and an opening up of ongoing related meanings, that is, an unfolding of meaning. For example, a toy truck with which a child plays can be interpreted in such a way that it is not only a toy but also a part of the child's self that is also part of an ongoing story about the child in relation to others and other parts of himself, including the range of emotions involved. When the child understands this, the toy has a number of dimensions and a depth of meaning for him, reflecting that his mind has multidimensionality and depth, that is, it has an inside which contains. However, the child needs to discover the inside of another's mind if he is to develop a mind of his own that is a container. Ricky seemed very close to this point by the time his treatment stopped.

A year after the session just described, Ricky announced that 'therapy is for babies' and wanted to stop. I considered his request, discussed it with his parents, and we agreed to an end of treatment. By that time Ricky had developed and maintained his capacity for self-expression. His heroic efforts to do what 'normal' children do resulted in a number of accomplishments, including moving into his second year at the mainstream school and managing a school weekend outing away from his family. I was concerned that, if his wish to end was not respected, his confidence would be undermined, added to which, I questioned what he could gain from a treatment for which he had little or no motivation. Moreover, by the time he had asked to stop, he had had a brief glimpse into what was for him a new way of thinking.

His parents drove to his sessions on the motorway and Ricky had become interested in the signs and what they meant; they had pictures, not words. In his sessions he began to draw the pictures he had seen on the signs, drawing them in three different sizes. I interpreted that he was drawing the Daddy Motorway, the Mummy Motorway and the Baby Motorway. What I said seemed to have some meaning for him and produced more pictures of the motorway signs. Although there was an obsessional feel to the repetitiousness of the drawings, there was also a sense of his trying to capture something, which I understand to be a thought. He expressed this once when drawing the motorway signs, telling me excitedly to 'Read that again!', meaning to repeat for him that his pictures were also meaningful representations to him of Daddy, Mummy and himself.

The reason I gave up my experiment in psychotherapy with Ricky was that it resulted in my not offering him symbolic thought. Only if it was offered to him, despite his not yet consistently being able to use it, would he have been able to achieve the awareness he did of the meaningfulness of the road sign pictures. I think that my opinion is confirmed by work with a profoundly deaf girl, with whom I used play therapy (Urban 1990). Although this kind of therapy brought about a dramatic change in her behaviour, it was limited in promoting her capacity for symbolic thought.

By persisting with my interpretations in my work with Ricky, I felt that I was able to offer him 'the mind of the analyst . . . [as] the breast, providing food for thought that is part of the experience of the analytic upbringing of our patients'

(Astor 1989, p. 17). In response, by the end of three years of treatment, Ricky showed signs of acknowledging and enjoying the symbolic aspect both of his analyst's mind and of his own.

Summary

In this chapter, I have tried to re-examine my understanding of early psychic processes and contents. This has involved comparing and contrasting the ideas of Jung, Klein, Isaacs and Fordham, with an emphasis on the contributions of Fordham. Fordham's postulate of a primary self that deintegrates and reintegrates is a model of the mind that combines structure and dynamics and which, moreover, helps to describe what is observed in infant observations and infant research. Infant observation has been used to illustrate these concepts, and clinical material used to show how the same concepts can be used to describe impairments to psychic development.

To pursue this study I have had to construct for myself models that describe and explain. I am aware that they are just as inaccurate as they might be accurate, because they imply that there is an answer to the questions I am asking and that there is a way of describing and explaining what 'the answer' is. 'Nature is always too strong for principle', wrote Hume (Hume 1751, p. 121), and this is particularly true of the ultimately unknowable self.

References

Astor, J. (1989). 'The breast as part of the whole: Theoretical considerations concerning whole and part objects'. *Journal of Analytical Psychology*, 34: 2.
Bion, W. (1962). *Learning from Experience*. London: Maresfield Library.
Broucek, F. (1979). 'Efficacy in infancy: A review of some experimental studies and their possible implications for clinical theory'. *International Journal of Psychoanalysis*, 3: 60.
Davies, M. (1989). 'Book review of D. Stern'. *The Interpersonal World of the Infant. Journal of Analytic Psychology*, 34: 1.
———. (1991). 'Defences of the self in a pre-adolescent boy'. *Journal of Child Psychotherapy*, 17(1): 2.
Fordham, M. (1947). 'Defences of the self'. *Journal of Analytical Psychology*, 19: 2.
———. (1969). *Children as Individuals*. London: Hodder & Stoughton.
———. (1976). *The Self and Autism*. London: Heinemann Medical Books.
———. (1985). *Explorations into the Self*. London: Academic Press.
———. (1987). 'Actions of the self'. In P. Young-Eisendrath and J. A. Hall (eds.), *The Book of the Self*. New York: New York University Press.
———. (1993). 'The model'. *Freud, Jung, Klein: The fenceless Field*. Edited by Roger Hobdell. London and New York: Routledge.
Grinberg, L., Sor, D. and de Bianchedi, E. T. (1975). *Introduction to the Work of Bion*. London: Maresfield Library.
Hinshelwood, R. D. (1989). *A Dictionary of Kleinian Thought*. London: Free Association Books.

Hobdell, R. (1988). 'Actions and defences of the self'. Paper read to the Israel Association for Analytical Psychology. (Quoted by permission of the author.)

Hume, D. (1751). *Enquiry into Human Understanding*. Quoted in F. Coplestone (1964). *A History of Philosophy*, Vol. 5, Part II. Garden City, NY: Image Books.

Isaacs, S. (1952). 'The nature and function of phantasy'. *International Journal of Psycho-Analysis*, 29.

Jung, C. G. (1911). 'Symbols of transformation'. *CW 5*.

———. (1919). 'Instinct and the unconscious'. *CW 8*.

———. (1921). 'General description of types'. *CW 6*.

———. (1927). 'Introduction to Wickes's "Analyse Der Kinderscele"'. *CW 17*.

———. (1955). 'Mandalas'. *CW 9, I*.

———. (1963a). *Memories, Dreams, Reflections*. Glasgow: Collins, 1977.

———. (1963b). 'Mysterium Coniunctionis'. *CW 14*.

Klein, M. (1952). 'The mutual influences in the development of ego'. In *Envy and Gratitude and Other Works*, 19, 16–1963. London: Hogarth Press, 1984.

Lichtenberg, J. D. (1983). *Psychoanalysis and Infant Research*. London. Analytic Press.

Stern, D. (1985). *The Interpersonal World of the Infant*. New York: Basic Books.

Trevarthen, C. (1974). 'Conversations with a two-month-old'. *New Scientist*, 2 May: 230–235.

———. (1987). 'Sharing makes sense: Intersubjectivity and the making of an infant's meaning'. In R. Steele and T. Treadgold (eds.), *Language Topics*. Amsterdam: John Benjamins.

Tustin, F. (1974). *Autism and Childhood Psychosis*. London. Hogarth Press.

Urban, E. (1990). 'The eye of the beholder: Work with a ten-year, old deaf girl'. *Journal of Child Psychotherapy*, 16(2).

Verney, T. with Kelly, J. (1981). *The Secret Life of the Unborn Child*. London: Sphere Books.

Chapter 2

Infant observation, experimental infant research and psychodynamic theory regarding lack of self/other differentiation

Introduction

In this chapter I am examining psychodynamic theory that attempts to explain early states marked by lack of differentiation between self and other. Concepts in psychoanalysis and analytical psychology that relate to these states include projective identification (Klein 1946; Bion 1962), primary identification (Sandler 1993) and primitive identity (Jung 1923; Fordham 1976). All are considered to operate from very early in life and refer to the lack of perceived differentiation between subject and object. Analysts agree that these processes, however they are conceptualised, persist into later life and are manifested in psychopathologies of varying severity, such as autism and borderline states. 'Fusion' and 'merger' refer to these states. However, it is unclear whether these terms refer to two people merged together in a combined mind or the experience of each – or one or the other – of being fused with another. In other words, these terms are ambiguous because each refers both to subjective states and to structures of the mind. In an effort to be clear I shall be describing these states in terms of lack of perceived differentiation, exploring how internal objects (structures) develop in one mind in interaction with another and trying to imagine how one (subjectively) experiences early objects in one's own mind. I shall be drawing upon what developmentalists have discovered about early infant perception and using this in a 'developmentalist informed' psychoanalytic infant observation. Following this I examine various theoretical perspectives about early states of lack of subject-object differentiation, and lastly comment on the thoughts that have struck me from this study. My work in this area makes me one of several, perhaps now many, analytically trained child therapists from different theoretical backgrounds who are attempting to assess and integrate various aspects of experimental infant research with analytic understanding of early processes and development (Alvarez 1992; Dubinsky 1997; Reid 1997; Urban 1998; Urwin 1987), to name a few in Britain alone). Although the work of developmentalists can be difficult to be assimilated into psychoanalytic models, their contributions are not antithetical to analytic thought and can add to its substantiality.

DOI: 10.4324/9781003215639-4

Infant experimental research

Developmentalists point out that in the first year there are two kinds of perception: amodal perception and feature-based perception. Feature-based perception is more developed than amodal perception and is the way we are ordinarily inclined to think of perception – through one or another specific sense mode. Amodal perception means not belonging to one sense mode or another; amodal perception is not of sights and sounds and touches, but of certain abstract properties. Newborns and young infants and foetuses (Bower 1982) perceive shape (contour), intensities (both absolute intensity and the contour of intensity) and temporal patterns (temporal beat, rhythm, duration). In other words, young infants perceive the 'thatness' and 'thereness' of something, its 'aliveness' and certain qualities of animation (rhythm and intensity). Amodal perception in newborns makes sense if one considers that the infant is required to relate to life, which is characterised by abstract properties. Stewart (1998), a mathematician, points out that life is a kind of abstract property of a system which involves various characteristics such as adaptability, reproduction and self-organization.

Human life is not only an expression of these properties. Infant minds with immature sense modes (especially sight) could not comprehend and recognise life-sustaining life forms in the external world if they did not have an inherent grasp of the abstract properties that identify aliveness. This comprehension appears to be innate and is evident in the newborn's grasp of abstract principles inherent in life – shape, unity, rhythms and intensities. These abstract qualities also apply to qualities of emotion; emotions have shape (the softness of tenderness, the sharpness of anger), intensity, and temporal patterns (duration, the slowness of calm and the quickness of excitement). Because these abstract properties do not belong to one sense mode or another (they are amodal) they can – and do – automatically translate from one mode to another. The translation across sense modes is known as 'transmodal'. Meltzoff and Bolton (1979) give an example of this. They studied three-week-old infants, who were blindfolded and offered two different teats to suck, one spherical and the other with nobbly protrusions. When the infants had had time to get used to the teats in their mouths, they began to show by increased sucking that they preferred one teat over the other. The blindfolds were then removed and the babies shown both teats they had previously experienced only through sucking. They consistently looked more at the teat they had preferred when sucking, indicating that they recognised by sight something they had previously only touched.

To relate this to the development of internal objects, I am turning to one of the developmentalists' great mysteries: newborn face imitation. How can an infant only a few hours old imitate another's face, despite having never seen another face nor his own? Bower (1989) understands this as an expression of amodal perception. He explains that the foetus builds up a primitive map of its body via touching its face with its hands and moving its face, mouth and tongue, which we know foetuses do (Piontelli 1992). After birth, when the infant looks at his mother's face, say, sticking out her tongue, the infant will respond in kind because the seen face is perceived to be the same as the touched and viscerally felt face – a transmodal perception in which there is no distinction between one sense and another. However, the experience is not only transmodal; it is also transpersonal because there is a yoking of two people into one perception. As the focus, so to speak, of the perception is on an abstract quality – shape – the perception is one in which the distinction between self and other is not relevant. That distinction is based more on lasting features (such as specific facial or vocal features) that distinguish self and others, and featured differences are not distinguished and internalised until months later. The perception of emotion would also be transmodal and transpersonal. An infant directly perceives, say, the mother's feeling of lovingness and goodness when she talks to him, and apprehends the perceived goodness in her voice to be the same as his own experience of goodness. What is relevant to the infant is what the developmentalists call the categorical affect (in this instance, the quality of goodness) and its contour and intensity. It is irrelevant to the baby that two people are experiencing it. This does not represent a confusion between self and other, nor is it the result of projective processes; it is simply the way young infants perceive experience.

The infant can produce an 'imitation' for a short time after the other's face has gone (Gergely 1992), and this suggests short-term memory and that the perception has been represented. However, more is needed to understand how the representation becomes a durable mental content. This appears to be done via the infant's capacity to identify the invariants of experience, which amounts to an ultra-sophisticated computer 'search and find'. Stern (1985) details how the mother offers her infant complex behaviour marked by theme and variation. From behaviours that are both familiar (the theme) and interestingly novel (the variation), the infant performs an automatic search and find, and seeks out those parts that are just the same as similar past experiences which always go along with that particular kind of experience. For instance, thumb-sucking is always accompanied by a number of 'invariants': volition ('I want to suck my thumb'), motor activity (thumb raised to mouth), proprioceptive feedback (hits target and lodges inside) and predictable consequences (sensations in both the thumb and the mouth). When the infant sticks his thumb into another's mouth, he may not be able to get it inside (the consequences are not predictable), and, if he does, he will not have sensations in his own mouth. Thus the baby groups together like experiences that relate just to himself and groups of experiences that relate just to his interchanges with others. However, unlike the word processor, the baby stores these collections of like experiences – and their emotional qualities – as representations and so, according to Stern, comes to have core representations of himself and of others. This appears to be how the baby develops a containing skin, as Bick (1968) described, based upon the baby's internalisation of the mother's capacity for containment. According to Stern's description, the infant has his own means and is quite active in forming his sense of his own skin, although it is of course formed within the relationship with his carer.

Stern describes how like experiences are grouped together internally via the infant's capacity to identify the invariants of experience. Gergely (1992) adds that affect can serve as an invariant, that is affects, like feelings of goodness or badness, can be the constants that link similar experiences together, which are then formed into representations. The result might be seen as the structuring of good and bad internal objects.

In contrast to amodal perception, featural perception is of constant, lasting features, say, the features of the mother's face, which are experienced through differentiated sense modes. The change from amodal to featural perception (and representation) does not occur until about five months. Bower (1982) found that infants under five months were not bothered when presented with multiple images of their mothers, and they interacted with each in turn: that is, the difference between different selves was not relevant. This contrasted sharply with infants over five months, who were distressed when shown simultaneously several representations of their mothers.

The development from amodal representations to featural representations demonstrates another astonishing capacity of the infant. The invariable features of, say, exchanges with a smiling mother are gradually worked out through repeated experience and become generalised into a prototype that is not identical to any particular experience. For instance the baby generalises a representation of his mother's smiling face made up of an average of all her different smiles. This prototype (of mother's smiling face) is then used as a model against which other prototypes (the mother's laughing, uninterested, troubled, worried faces) can be compared to establish invariable features and so on until a stable representation (of her face) is established. This example is of the organisation of visual perceptions, but prototypes would also be created around other sense modes as these gradually become differentiated (for instance, mother's loving, tired and angry voices). If one adds the emotional colourings of these different prototypes, say, the infant's love of the mother's warm, smiling face and anger or fear at the cross, disapproving face, then what is being brought together in the development of featural perception is not only 'pictures' but feelings. The result seems to be a description of the development of the depressive position. Interestingly, Klein (1935) dated the onset of the depressive position at midway in the first year, which is when Bower (1982) notes the change from amodal to featural perception.

To summarise, perceptual development in the first year shifts from amodal to featural perception. Amodal perception is linked to representations/objects in which the distinction between self and other is irrelevant. In later 'feature-based' representations the distinction between subject and object is of utmost relevance. Although featural perception through separate sense modes comes to predominate the way we perceive the world, amodal perception remains. It may be the way premature babies and children with autistic features perceive and, paradoxically, the means through which we appreciate music and poetry and the world directly perceived, uninterpreted by separate senses.

Psychoanalytic infant observation

I am going to trace in detail the interplay of mini-events and feelings between a newborn and his mother around a feed, when their respective feelings of anxiety shift with and against love and pleasure. Frames of reference are necessary for careful observation, and my way of seeing this infant and his mother is in line with psychoanalytic thinkers who feel that the very young infant does not have the maturity for projective identification (Bick 1968; Fordham in Astor 1995) and that identificatory processes are developmentally more fundamental than projective mechanisms (Fordham in Astor 1995; Sandler 1993). I shall be looking more closely at the theoretical framework in the next section of this chapter, while here my task is to describe how an infant, by means of identificatory processes, develops internal objects or representations in which there is no distinction between self and other.

The baby, whom I shall call Nathan, was a wanted baby and second son. He was two weeks and two days old at the time of the observation. When the observer arrived she was met by the mother and Nathan's 14-month-old brother. Together they took the observer to meet Nathan, who was lying in his bassinet alone in the parents' bedroom.

> He was lying on his right side with his right arm tucked under his body and his left arm bent up so that his hand was near his face. His head with its soft covering of jet black hair was touching the top of the bassinet and the mother said he had wriggled his way right up to the top. His eyes were open and he was moving his whole body slightly as if a little restless. His mother said he was probably hungry as it was nearing feeding time. He then suddenly quietened and for several minutes lay absolutely still with his black eyes staring at the side of the bassinet.

Nathan had been on his own in the bassinet, apparently making it familiar by moving up to the top so that his head was in contact with a surface, the way it was for him in utero. He became restless as, presumably, feelings of hunger started. He then settled, but I think it is unclear whether his sudden quieting and absolute stillness were due to hearing his mother's voice or 'playing possum' the way Broucek (1979) describes in small babies, because he heard the strange voice of the observer.

> His mother said the birth had been very easy. [She details the events surrounding the birth.] She said she just couldn't believe it was over so fast, particularly after her bad experience of giving birth to Nathan's brother. Nathan weighed 6 lbs. 2 oz. and after the birth he was put to her breast and sucked

vigorously. Since then he has fed hungrily and the feeding has gone very well. The day following the birth there had been some incident with the baby gasping and the mother had been very anxious and called the nurse, but the nurse told her that the baby had something that was quite normal for new babies.

When Nathan's brother was born, the mother had been in labour for three days, and this difficult experience shaped her expectations of Nathan's arrival. As Nathan's birth turned out to be just what she wanted, her love and gratitude toward him were evident, although her worry was also noticeable (the gasping incident).

> The mother picked up Nathan and they all went into the sitting room. The brother became demanding, and the mother handed the baby to the observer while she went to make coffee, taking the brother with her. Nathan laid in my arms looking intently at my face, often opening his mouth and making sucking noises. I talked to him and he responded by fixedly looking at my face. Several times he looked as though he was trying to smile and finally he gave a slight smile in response to my talking. Then he looked away as if exploring the room and, when I spoke he turned his head back to me looking in the vicinity of my face but not able immediately to focus directly.

Nathan's vision at 16 days was still immature. Presuming that he followed the norm, he could focus on objects at 10 to 12 inches but not over distances greater than that. That is, when the observer interpreted that he was 'exploring the room', this is unlikely. What Nathan saw would be contrasts (such as the hairline between dark and light), patterns and shapes. The observer interpreted Nathan's smile to be in response to her talking, which would enhance her good feelings towards him. It is hard not to imagine that she was smiling as she talked to him, and I suspect that his effort at a smile was a transmodal perception like that described by Bower (1989), in which the seen face (held in short-term memory) is experienced as a viscerally felt face which registers in his own facial musculature. Given his focal limits, when Nathan turned away from the observer's face as if exploring the room, he was, more likely, taking in his amodal perceptions of the shape and contour of her face and organising them according to the variants and invariants of his experience of faces. The fact that he did not readily re-engage with the observer's face was perhaps because its pattern did not match that of the mother's face which had been registered inside him.

The mother returned with the coffee but then the brother became so unruly that she left to put him down for a nap. The observer continued to hold Nathan until the mother came back.

> The mother talked to Nathan gently and lovingly, smiling a great deal at him and saying she just couldn't believe he was really here. Then she took the baby and put him to her right breast to feed. It took a few attempts for Nathan to get the nipple properly in his mouth, but he then sucked loudly

and greedily and hiccoughed. The mother said he often hiccoughs because he drinks so quickly and she laughed and said what a greedy little thing he was. Nathan has put on weight and is now 7 lbs. She commented she is losing weight but that is usual when one breast-feeds. She fed him for five minutes. Nathan sucked vigorously, occasionally stopping for a rest. At first his eyes were wide open looking into his mother's face but after a couple of minutes they shut while he continued to suck.

In the first part of the feed I think Nathan was responding as much to anxiety as he was to hunger. At the beginning he seemed un-together and uncoordinated, as indicated by the hiccoughs. Although the hiccoughs were interpreted by the mother and the observer as his being 'greedy', there is little indication that Nathan was very hungry. It makes more sense to me to think of his hiccoughing and sucking as perhaps being urgent because of being held by the observer, a stranger. Nathan then gradually settled.

Although this can be seen as his taking in what his mother mentally digested (Bion 1962), I do not think this hypothesis is necessary, nor does it take into account other important factors. Here I have in mind the oral anatomy of newborns. The moist surface of the lips is considerably more spongy than it will be in just a few months, indicating its vascularity and hence sensitivity to touch. Also in most newborns there is a narrow fold of erectile tissue along the outside base of the gum called the Magitot membrane. It swells during sucking and is thought to be an organ of sensation and, presumably, pleasure. This disappears by seven months (Middlemore 1941).

As Nathan settled into the pleasure of feeding from his familiar mother, he took little rests. Brazelton and Cramer (1991) note that infants feed in short bursts of sucking, five to twenty-five sucks to a burst, and then a pause. These rests occur more frequently with the breast than with bottle-fed babies. They suggest that pauses serve a social purpose by eliciting the mother's response to return to feeding, and, in turn, the baby comes to expect this. I would add that pausing not only allows space for the mother to react but also gives the infant space to integrate his perceptions and feelings. Hence the goodness of the experience is integrated in regular little intakes between bursts of sucking.

In this part of the feed I think what was being integrated were multiple perceptions and feelings into an early mental content, or object. At first Nathan fed while looking at his mother's face, and when he recognised its familiar shapes and patterns, his anxiety about being held by a stranger abated. Then his eyes closed, giving the impression that Nathan was giving himself more fully to the experience and experiencing wholeness. The sense of wholeness would include the pleasurable sensations in his mouth and the sound of his mother's familiar, loving voice. Given the nature of young infant perception, I picture that the regularity of the rhythm of his sucking, her familiar facial shapes and voice patterns settle with the goodness of the experience to register as an amodal perception, or early good object, in which the distinction between self and other is irrelevant.

While Nathan seemed to be putting together a good object, his mother seemed to be in a different state of mind.

> The mother explained that she had learned a new way of getting the baby to release his hold on the nipple. She had been told to press his chin and that the pressure would stop the sucking action. She said that before she had just tried to pull her breast away but that that had been very painful because Nathan would continue sucking and this method seemed much better. She demonstrated and the baby released his grip easily. She then sat him up holding him under his chin. His head flopped to one side and his eyes closed. He suddenly brought up some milk and then yawned widely. The mother talked about a yellow spot she could see at the back of his mouth and wondered about the possibility of thrush, but dismissed the idea as unlikely. She then lay him on his side on her lap, while she got ready to feed him from the other breast. Nathan usually feeds every three to four hours. She said she finds the 7 pm feed difficult because Nathan doesn't seem to get enough and she feels as though her breast is empty.

When Nathan settled into his feed his mother interrupted it. This may in part have been done for the sake of demonstrating her parenting to the observer, but I feel it is more fundamentally due to her anxiety about the pain that can accompany closeness. She also repositioned him, whereupon he posseted some milk. This affected her and seemed to make her anxious about him (her reference to the spot in his throat). His being emptied of some of her milk resonated, in what follows, with her own feelings of being emptied of milk (that is, seeing Nathan emptied of milk was the same as feeling emptied of milk).

> She put him to her left breast and he sucked vigorously with lots of little grunts and noises, looking intently upwards. I thought he was trying to see his mother's face, but she said he was looking at her red jumper. He then fell asleep and stopped sucking. The mother went to remove her breast and Nathan immediately started sucking again. After a couple more minutes the mother removed her breast without any resistance from Nathan, who was now fast asleep. She held him for some time in a seated position, with the baby slightly leaning forward and his mother supporting his neck. He burped loudly without opening his eyes. Then she lay him back in her arms and he looked very serious holding his hand close to his mouth. His mouth gradually fell open and she pressed his lips together telling him to breathe through his nose else he'd take in too much air. She said she likes to hold him after a feed but she can't if his brother is around because the brother doesn't like it.

Consequent to the interruption Nathan had a renewed sense of anxiety, the intensity of which probably accorded with the redness of the jumper. Once again, he settled and seemed to restore the goodness of the experience, with evidence of some anxiety as he seemed to need to cling onto the nipple to help himself hold on to these sensations when his mother tried to remove the breast. He was apparently asleep when he did this, and this raises the question of consciousness in babies. Fordham (1987) believes that it is not helpful to apply the concepts of conscious and unconscious to small infants, and his view is useful here. Still sleeping, Nathan was able to give up the breast a few moments later and sink into a sleep in which, presumably, he was taking in the experience and integrating it. During this integration, he seemed to attempt to hold onto the good feelings in his mouth with his hand, which neurologically is closely connected to his mouth (Trevarthen 1989). He gradually relaxed into deep sleep. The mother enjoyed the intimacy, possibly helped by projecting her impulse to rupture the closeness on to Nathan's brother (who must be absent if she was to enjoy this intimacy with Nathan). However her feelings of closeness gave way to deciding she must change Nathan, although it is not clear from the observation whether Nathan needed it. She lay Nathan down and went off to get a fresh nappy.

> She returned and showed me a mild rash on his bottom saying it would be much worse if he wasn't being breast fed. She commented that his scrotum was big because his testicles were filled with fluid but that the nurse said there wasn't anything to worry about. She showed me his long back and how long his legs were, commenting, 'He's going to be tall like me'. She said he loves his bath which he has every second day in the evening and that in a year's time he and his brother will be able to enjoy it together. She looked at Nathan in wonder, commenting on his heartbeat and gently touching his fingers saying how little they were and how perfect he was. She said that her husband is still rather scared to hold him because he feels he is so very fragile.

The changing seemed to help the mother restore confidence in the goodness of what she had to offer, and she expressed her belief that her milk mitigated Nathan's discomfort. Her feelings of closeness came up against her anxiety about the difference between them – he was male (had testicles) and she was female – but the anxiety soon subsided and she expressed a felt identity with him: they both had the same long back and legs. The goodness of the experience began to include her love of her other son and the pleasure they would all have when the boys could share bathing. This intensified into a loving wonderment at Nathan's perfection, while her anxiety about Nathan's vulnerability and dependency was projected onto her husband.

Theories of early object development: psychoanalysis and analytical psychology

I shall begin this section with psychoanalytic theories of early object development that refer to lack of differentiation between self and other and shall briefly review the theories of Klein, Bick, Bion and Sandler.

For Klein (1958), the infant at birth has a primitive means of distinguishing self from other, and it is this premise that underlies her belief that the infant is object-related from the beginning of life. According to Klein, infant feeding is the prototype for the first dynamic introjection, by which the infant takes in experiences that the infant innately recognises as good or bad. Good objects which are formed from good experiences and accompanying phantasies about them come to support the fragile ego in getting rid of bad objects. Bad objects are derived from 'bad' experiences and the phantasies of annihilation that are part of the death instinct which accompanies the experience. Getting rid of bad objects is done via a form of projection by which parts of the self as well as the bad object are eliminated into an object. Because parts of the self are involved in this process, the result is a projective identification. Another way of putting this is that the infant manages the early death instinct by identifying the unwanted part of himself with an object via projection. The resulting subjective experience of projective identification is that the object is not 'felt to be a separate individual but an aspect of the self' (Klein 1963).

Bick (1964, 1968) observed infants repeatedly falling into states of disintegration amid fears of annihilation, then recovering coherence through the ministrations of the mother. She questioned whether the young infant's fragile ego could initially recognise self from other or be able to internalise or externalise good or bad experiences. Bick concluded that the first object was necessarily a containing object, passively introjected from the prototype experience of the nipple fitting into the mouth during feeds with the mother.

Bick had taken her ideas about containment from Bion, who extended Klein's concept of projective identification by understanding it to be an 'interpenetrating contact' (Hinshelwood 1989), that is, of one thing inside another in such a way that the former is contained by the latter. Bion (1962) considered that projective identification operated from birth and initially was a primitive means of communicating. As communication, projective identification was 'normal', although later it could be used in the defensive and pathological way described by Klein. Bick disagreed with the notion that projective identification was a very early dynamic on the basis that the infant needed a firm boundary between self and other for this to happen, and this occurred only after the internalisation of a containing object, which develops into the experience of having a containing skin (Hinshelwood 1989).

There are significant differences between Kleinian and non-Kleinian understanding of early objects and processes. For Kleinians the term 'object' refers to subjective experiences, such as pain or pleasure, whereas for non-Kleinian ego-oriented psychoanalysts, objects are unexperienceable structures. For example Sandler, a Freudian, sees the earliest objects in terms of representations of self and other.

Sandler bases his thinking on Freud's concept of identification. Freud thought that the first form of an emotional tie was identification (1921) and suggested that it took place earlier than any object cathexis (1923). For Sandler the phenomena persists throughout life, so he terms it 'recurrent primary identification' (1993). He first discovered the idea from his own experience:

> I was walking along a crowded street in London, along the edge of the pavement, when suddenly a man who was walking a yard or two in front of me slipped off the edge of the pavement. I immediately righted myself, just as if I were about to stumble into the street. In thinking about this experience I became aware of how, when we are not on our guard, we mirror the movements we perceive in others.
>
> (Ibid., p. 1101)

Here Sandler is describing a primary form of identification which is passive, automatic and reflexive and is associated with perception. It includes communication through a kind of resonance, including emotional resonances, and suggests that it is this empathy which binds animal societies together (ibid.). Besides empathy, the concept also accounts for aesthetics and some states of oneness.

For Sandler, primary identification is an ongoing fundamental state closely linked to perception and one in which representations of self and other, although established, become lost until one actively disidentifies with the other. For instance when one listens receptively to another, one momentarily experiences the thought as one's own until quickly disclaiming this, thus moving from thinking with to thinking about.

For Sandler, states of fusion can be understood to come about through primary identification or projective identification. Sandler distinguishes between the two and defines the latter according to Klein's original description (1946), of which a significant element is the intention on the part of the subject to thrust an unwanted content into the object. Primary identification is, he stresses, a 'basic and automatic mirroring process' (Sandler 1993).

I shall now turn to theory in analytical psychology which relates to the earliest objects and their development. Whereas Freud believed that the personality was comprised of the gradual assimilation of identifications, Jung believed that the individual personality, the self, was a given to be discovered in the course of life, and identifications with others compromised the true self. Paradoxically – or contradictorily – Jung considered that the child's personality emerged, or rather e-merged, from an unconscious, fused state of oneness with the mother's unconscious, during an initial stage of identity, which lasted for the first four to five years. Unlike his theory of adult personality, Jung's theory of early development was not well researched, and the Jungian study of infancy and childhood fell to Michael Fordham. Fordham's work with children led him to conclude that from conception the child was an individual apart from his/her parents. Fordham postulated a primary, psychosomatic ingrate which he termed the primary self. The concept of the primary self assumes an initial organic wholeness (integrate) which then unfolds and unpacks (deintegrates) in order to relate to the environment. What is experienced is then assimilated into the personality in a process called reintegration. Deintegration and reintegration are biologically (or archetypically) determined. Early deintegration is very similar to Bion's (1962) innate preconception and is a means of relating before structures are built up and before objects have become internalised as well as after. These dynamics underlie projection and introjection but differ from them in an important way, because projection and introjection require a content and a separate object into which to project and from which to take in (Urban 1992).

For example, in my Jungian frame of reference, the unity or infant amodal perception is an expression of the wholeness of the primary self. Whereas Maria Rhode understands amodal perception from a Kleinian framework and looks to how the infant links together the different senses (Rhode 1997), I see it as something that is initially integrated but which through experience becomes de-integrated and separated into differentiated sense modes.

Although Fordham considered that projective and introjective identifications could result in lack of differentiation between self and object, he concluded that 'At first an infant has not enough structure for projective identification to occur without an earlier period in which identity between subject and object predominates. Out of that state enough structures form to make the theory of projective identification useful' (Astor 1995). The earlier period to which he refers is only when primary identity predominates. However, Fordham is careful to say that primary identity refers to temporary and fluctuating states and is not a stage in development as Jung saw it.

During this initial period the infant, via deintegrative and reintegrative processes, creates states of identity with the mother. Out of these states the first objects are produced, which Fordham termed self objects, as they are shaped largely by the primary self (and the archetypal patterning that goes with it), in contrast to reality. These are understood to refer to objects in which there is little difference between self and object.

Fordham said little more than Jung about the dynamic of primary identity, except that it does not involve projection (as Jung implied) and that it did not refer to states of either consciousness or unconsciousness (Fordham 1995).

Comments

Theoretical considerations

As an analytical psychologist I tend to use a Jungian conceptualisation of the development of early objects which are marked by the lack of differentiation between self and other. That is, I am addressing this development by attempting to describe the dynamic of primary identity. From this study I understand states of primary identity are a kind of sum of complicated interactions between an infant and his mother, interactions which are a series of mutually regulated, purposeful 'reachings out' to each other that are attempts by each to match up feeling states in such a way that each enjoys and is fulfilled from what is 'matched up'. The matching up involves 'work' and a certain amount of hit and miss. For instance, at the beginning of the feed, Nathan's efforts were first affected by his own anxiety about being held by the observer (not something which normally occurs during infant observations), and then they came up against his mother's anxieties which interrupted the feed. For the mother's part, she was working through her worries about closeness and whether she could be a good mother to him. By the end of the observation, each seemed to have 'matched up' to the good feelings inextricably associated with the other, with the overall effect that they shared the goodness of the feed. The overall effect seems to be comprised of 'mini-matchings up' between mother and baby. My picture is that the matchings might include a psychosomatic element, matching not only feeling but also somatic states, such as happens later in life in the matching up of body postures or of rates of heartbeat after sexual intimacy. These mini-matchings are similar to Sandler's idea of primary identifications in that they are basic, automatic, related to perception and refer to emotional resonances, but they are different in that they do not occur passively, nor are they sustained, except that they contribute to the overall sense of being together with someone in a particular way. This overall sense, which is the result of all the 'mini-matchings up', is a state of primary identity in a Jungian framework, that is, a feeling of being together in a shared experience. This state arises out of specific but frequently occurring episodes. By drawing upon his capacity to organise the invariants of the good aspects of this complex feeding experience, such as the one described here, the infant can bind them together internally into an early good object. Because these experiences are amodally perceived, they register internally as objects in which the distinction between self and other is not relevant and are (probably) experienced subjectively as being together in a fused and loving togetherness, the consciousness of which is not relevant. Thus a state of primary identity becomes an internal object in which there is a lack of differentiation between self and other.

Here I need to acknowledge that I have used 'object' and 'representation' interchangeably when in fact they have rather different connotations. Perlow (1995) has written a very thorough and helpful conceptual analysis of the psychoanalytic concept of mental object. There he points out that the Kleinian idea of the concept is irreconcilably different from that of ego-oriented non-Kleinians. A similar conceptual analysis needs to be carried out within the framework of analytical psychology, although one has been attempted by comparing Jungian ideas to Perlow's analysis (Knox 1997). On the whole, I join Anne Alvarez when she calls for a modified object relations theory that includes what she calls 'pre-objects' (Alvarez 1992).

The development toward projective processes

If primary identity occurs prior to projective processes, when do projective processes begin? The answer, I think, would depend in part upon when objects are formed, in other words, when there are contents to be projected. This seems to happen quickly and may vary from one infant to another.

The following is from the second observation of Nathan, a week later (when he was three weeks old).

> While we were talking Nathan gave a big smile as if in response to the familiar sound of his mother's voice even though she was out of his line of vision. . . . I talked to him and Nathan looked at me for a long time, at one point giving me a very wide smile. Then his eyes dropped and he looked at the side of the bassinet. He seemed restless and a little uncomfortable and his body was straining slightly. Then he made sounds as if he had defecated.

What strikes me in this second observation is that Nathan's good objects seemed more consolidated, and he smiled readily and broadly. He studied the observer's face and seemed to conclude that it was friendly, although perhaps worryingly strange, but he had a capacity to manage the anxiety by getting rid of the experience by evacuation. That is, he now had objects inside and he could project them.

Amodal perception, pathology and technique

One cannot assume that, theoretically, early contents and structures follow an uninterrupted line of development into more complex objects and structures. The early objects formed from amodal perception may be qualitatively different from later objects based on featural perception. With amodally formed objects, it is in the nature of the perceptions on which they are based that the distinction between self and other is irrelevant. With feature-based objects, difference between self and other is the hallmark.

Although part of normal development, amodally shaped objects appear to underlie pathological conditions, such as autism. Fordham (1976) considered that autism is an instance in which the individual's inner world remains fixed by self objects, which are distinguished by the lack of self-other differentiation. Alvarez (1992) appears to be considering a similar kind of object, or objects, when she refers to 'pre-objects' that predate objects in which the differentiation is evident. She has altered her technique with children with autistic features in order to help them create an enlivened object and in doing so conveys an appreciation of amodal perception.

To explain, I shall turn to an example from my own, much more limited experience with children who show autistic behaviour. Tim, aged 7, was being asked questions by my psychiatrist colleague about what others might think, in order to assess whether he had a theory of mind, as Hobson (1993) puts it. Tim couldn't do this and seemed to feel intimidated and angry. He took the toy he was holding and repeatedly thrust it towards her face. Without thinking, I matched what I said with the amodal properties of his actions, that is, its rhythm, contour and categorical affect (the aggressive thrust): 'Tim! doesn't! like – it! when – he! can't! answer! questions!' When I did he looked directly at me with sparkling eyes, turned and did it again to my 'accompaniment'. It is important to add that this kind of response is only one aspect of the considerable expertise needed to work with these children.

Experimental research and psychoanalytic infant observation

I should like to make a plea for the further incorporation of experimental studies into the way we observe babies. Although they have different aims, both psychoanalytic infant observation and experimental infant research involve observation and are valuable research tools (Miller et al. 1989). Experimental research draws upon technology that makes possible microanalysis of the observable. However, as Stern (1985) points out, what is omitted from experimental studies are inferences about what is happening in the baby's internal world and emotional life. Important sources of information in the making of psychoanalytic inferences are the observers' subjective responses. Davison (1992) remarks that observers' and mothers' subjective responses are valid for humans are programmed to be sensitive to social cues and processes present in the infant's emotional life.

Psychoanalytic observation can, I believe, be fairly criticised on the grounds that it is used to confirm existing theory rather than investigating and questioning it. My efforts here may be seen in that light, although I hope it is also evident that I am attempting to explore and experiment with theory rather than to prove it, which psychoanalytic infant observation cannot do. Although infant observation has not provided new knowledge in the way that experimental research has done, Michael Rustin (Miller et al. 1989) points out its research value in describing phenomena discovered by developmentalists and others using a more empirically based methodology. My position is that these methodologies are complementary, and both are necessary for understanding infant development.

Acknowledgements

I want to express my gratitude to my child analyst colleague who has allowed me to use her unusually fine observations of 'Nathan'.

References

Alvarez, A. (1992). *Live Company: Psychoanalytic Psychotherapy with Autistic, Borderline, Deprived and Abused Children*. London: Routledge.

Astor, J. (1995). *Michael Fordham: Innovations in Analytical Psychology*. London: Routledge.

Bick, E. (1964). 'Notes on infant observation in psycho-analytic training'. *International Journal of Psycho-Analysis*, 1: 558–566. Republished (1987) in *The Collected Papers of Martha Harris and Esther Bick*, ed. by M. H. Williams. Perth: Clunie.

———. (1968). 'The experience of tile skin in early object relations'. *International Journal of Psycho-Analysis*, 49: 484, republished (1987) in *The Collected Papers of Martha Harris and Esther Bick*, ed. by M. H. Williams. Perth: Clunie.

Bion, W. (1962). *Learning from Experience*. London: Heineman.

Bower, T. (1982). *Development in Infancy*. San Francisco: W. H. Freeman

———. (1989). *The Rational Infant: Learning in Infancy*. New York: W. H. Freeman

Brazelton, T. and Cramer, B. G. (1991). *The Earliest Relationship: Parents, Infants, and Drama of Early Attachment*. London: Karnac.

Broucek, W. (1979). 'Efficacy in infancy: A review of some experimental studies and their possible implications for clinical theory'. *International of Psycho-Analysis*, 60(3).

Davison, S. (1992). 'Mother, other and self -love and rivalry for twins in their first year of life'. *International Journal of Psycho-Analysis*, 12: 359–374.

Dubinsky, A. and Bazhenova, O. (1997). 'Moments of discovery, times of learning'. In S. Reid (ed.), *Developments in Infant Observation*. London: Routledge.

Fordham, M. (1976). *The Self and Autism*. London: Academic Press.

———. (1987). 'Actions of the self'. In P. Young-Eisendrath and P. Hall (eds.), *The Book of the Self*. New York: University Press.

———. (1995). *Freud, Jung, Klem – The Fenceless Field*. London: Routledge.

Freud, S. (1921). 'Group psychology and tire analysis oft/re Ego'. *SE 18*.

———. (1923). 'The ego and the ID'. *SE 9*.

Gergely, G. (1992). 'Developmental reconstructions: Infancy from the point of view of psychoanalysis and developmental psychology'. *Psychoanalysis and Contemporary Thought*, 15

Hinshelwood, R. (1989). *A Dictionary of Kleinian Thought*. London: Free Association.

Hobson, R. P. (1993). *Autism and the Development of the Mind*. Hove: Lawrence Erlbaum of Associates.

Jung, C. G. (1923). 'Psychological types'. *CW 6*

Klein, M. (1935). 'A contribution to the psychogenesis of manic-depressive states'. In M. Kahn (ed.), *Love, Guilt and Reparation and Other Works 1921–1945*. London: Hogarth.

———. (1946). 'Notes on some schizoid mechanism'. In M. Khan (ed.), *Envy and Gratitude and Other Works 1946–1963*. London: Hogarth.

———. (1958). 'On the development of mental functioning'. *International Journal of Psycho-Analysis*, 39: 84–90

———. (1963). 'On the sense of loneliness'. In M. Klein (ed.), *Envy and Gratitude and Other Works 1946–1963*. London: Hogarth. (1975) date publication of book in which 1963 paper is found.

Knox, J. (1997). 'Internal objects: A theoretical analysis of Jungian and Kleinian models'. *Journal of Analytical Psychology*, 42(4): 567–722.

Meltzoff, A. N. and Borton, W. (1979). 'Intermodal matching by neonates'. *Nature*, 282.

Middlemore, M. (1941). *The Nursing Couple*. London: Hamish.

Miller, L., Rustin, M., Rustin, M. and Shuttleworth, J. (1989). *Closely Observed Infants*. London: Duckworth.

Perlow, M. (1995). *Understanding Mental Objects*. London: Routledge.

Piontelli, A. (1992). *From Fetus to Child: An Observational and Psychoanalytic Study*. London: Routledge.

Reid, S. (ed.) (1997). *Developments in Infant Observation*. London: Routledge.

Rhode, M. (1997). 'Psychosomatic integrations: Eye and mouth in infant observations'. In S. Reid (ed.), *Developments in Infant Observation*. London: Routledge.

Sandler, J. (1993). 'On communication from patient to analyst: Not everything is projective identification'. *International Journal of Psycho-Analysis,* 74: 1097–1107.

Stern, D. (1985). *The Interpersonal World of the Infant: A View from Psychoanalysis and Developmental Psychology.* New York: Basic Books.

Stewart, 1. (1998). *Life's Other Secret.* London: Penguin.

Trevarthen, C. (1989). 'Development of early social interact ions and the affective regulation of brain growth'. In C. von Euler, H. Forssberg, and H. Lagercrantz (eds.), *Neurobiology of Early Infant Behaviour.* London: Macmillan.

Urban, E. (1992). 'The primary self and related concepts in Jung, Klein, and Isaacs'. *Journal of Analytical Psychology,* 37(4): 411–432.

———. (1998). 'States of identity: A perspective drawing upon Fordham's model and infant studies'. *Journal of Analytical Psychology,* 43(2): 261–275.

Urwin, C. (1987). 'Developmental psychology and psychoanalysis: Splitting the difference'. In M. Richards and P. Light (eds.), *Children in Social Worlds.* Cambridge: Polity.

Part II

Developments

Chapter 3

Out of the mouths of babes

An enquiry into the sources of language development

Introduction

This chapter is about the quest for what I call here the mother tongue. It is both my quest and that of a language-deprived, 10-year-old deaf girl. Both require an investigation into the developmental origins of language, and this is elucidated by infant observation and research. My model of early development is based upon that put forward by Michael Fordham, whose postulate of a primary self derives from Jung's concept of the self.

The self and the primary self

Jung's concept of the self developed out of his idea of the transcendent function (Fordham 1985a). In 'The Transcendent Function', written in 1916, Jung describes the psychological function which mediates between opposites and produces a 'living, third thing' when opposites confront one another (Jung 1958a, p. 90). Over four decades later, in his prefatory note to 'The Transcendent Function', he recalls the essay as being among 'the first attempts at a synthetic view of the psychic process in analytic treatment' (Jung 1958a, p. 67). The 'synthetic view' refers to Jung's discovery of the integrating function of the self. The 'self' in this context is 'the total personality', that is, 'conscious and unconscious', mind and body (Jung 1921, p. 460). Fordham draws upon this definition of the self when he postulates a primary self. The primary self is a psychosomatic integrate that contains the potential of the organism. From before birth the primary self has the functions of both integrating (Jung's 'synthetic view') and dividing up (Fordham's contribution). Development occurs through the dynamic of the dividing up in order to relate to the environment, or deintegrating, and the coming together again to assimilate experience, or reintegrating (Fordham 1976, 1985a). Archetypal, that is, instinctively human, processes regulate the patterns of deintegration and reintegration. Early deintegration and reintegration can be seen in the typical and organised way very young babies approach the breast and feed (deintegration) and then assimilate the experience in sleep (reintegration). According to Fordham, initially the baby experiences the touching, holding, feeding and other

DOI: 10.4324/9781003215639-6

components of its relation to the mother's breast as a single, 'whole' experience; that is, for the infant the breast is the centre of the world. In time, the 'whole' experience of the mother and her breast will deintegrate into experiences of increasing complexity and differentiation. The mother's face, voice and touch, initially perceived as all-in-one, develop into perceptions of different and distinct qualities. The first distinction the baby makes is between satisfying and frustrating experiences, which the infant self organises into 'good' and 'bad' experiences. Rudimentary awareness accompanies early experiences, and over time these 'bits' of consciousness coalesce into an ego. When the ego is established, the way is open for individuation to occur. Thus, the primary self is the developmental source of the self that Jung studied.

Infant studies and the work of Trevarthen

Fordham first hypothesised a primary self in 1947 (Fordham 1947, 1957). However imaginary or visionary the postulate is – and it is both – Fordham was aware that it 'hung fire' until supported by data (Fordham 1985b, p. 3). He has explained how 'systematic observations of babies and their mothers in emotional interaction', in the natural environment of the baby's home and family, later confirmed his ideas (Fordham 1987, p. 356). The infant observation at the end of this chapter is an example of this kind of confirmation. In addition to 'home observations', 'laboratory observations', such as those done by Stern and Trevarthen, confirm and fill in Fordham's intentionally abstract, 'empty' concept (Stern 1985; Trevarthen 1974, 1980, 1987a, 1987b, 1989a, 1989b, 1990; Trevarthen and Marwick 1986).

Trevarthen's findings are easy to integrate with those of 'home observations' because, first, both acknowledge the primacy of feelings over thought processes in early infant development. Trevarthen argues against developmental psychologists who, like Piaget, focus on the baby's cognitive development to what Trevarthen feels is the exclusion of the emotional underpinning that motivates later learning. He holds that the infant is innately endowed with personal motives, emotions and powers that soon after birth intimately affect his or her caretaker, leading to an interpersonal, interactional relationship. Infants learn about objects because there is someone specially cared for and caring to share them with; children learn how to talk because there is someone specially interested and interesting to talk to. Second, Trevarthen's studies, too, are longitudinal and describe behaviour that is observed at home and not just in laboratories (in contrast, for example, to experiments which show the infant's preference for the smell of the mother's milk by use of milk-soaked pads presented to the infant, which would not be observable in the ordinary home). There are important differences between 'home observations' and Trevarthen's. Selecting a particular behaviour for study and experimentation, Trevarthen focuses on very early patterns of communication between mother and infant, but only while the infant is in an alert state. If the baby needs feeding or comforting the observation stops. The emotional intensity between the mother and infant is therefore moderate, leading Trevarthen to describe the mother as the baby's 'favourite companion' (Trevarthen 1987b, p. 365). A 'home observation', in which the observer would attempt to minimise his or her intervention, would include as much as possible of whatever happened during the observation, with the observer particularly noting expressions of intense feeling. Trevarthen's observations were made in a laboratory 'studio', where what happened was videotaped, filmed and audio-recorded for later frame-by-frame microanalysis, showing details of mother-infant interchanges not available to 'home observers'. The results of Trevarthen's studies show a patterned development of communication over the first year, which can be summarised as follows: Although at birth infants can discriminate between people and objects and show means of orientating to each in distinctly different ways, these capacities are rudimentary and not developed until later – weeks later in regard to humans and months later in regard to objects. At six to eight weeks the infant has a noticeably improved ability to focus visually and to exert control over the direction and duration of the focus. The focus of the infant's eyes is most drawn to the mother's hands, face and, especially, eyes. By making, maintaining or breaking eye contact, the infant regulates a feelingful connection with the mother. An exchange of smiles that serves to match and express their respective feelings leads to 'a dialogic "proto-conversation", a cooperative exchange made up of complementary utterances with gestures' (Trevarthen 1989b, p. 193). The patterns of behaviour of both infant and mother are characteristic and universal. When engaged with the mother, the infant coos and makes elaborate lip and tongue movements that Trevarthen has recognised as efforts to articulate speech.

Pre-speech, as he terms these efforts, is accompanied by raising one or both hands and a variety of finger movements. The right hand moves more frequently than the left, indicating activity in the left hemisphere of the brain, which is where the language centre of the brain is located (Trevarthen and Marwick 1986). For her part, the mother synchronises regular and exaggerated head, eyebrow and face movements, accompanied by a particular pattern of vocalisation that Trevarthen calls 'intuitive motherese'. 'It is characterized by short, evenly spaced utterances with gently "breathy" voicing and undulating fundamental frequency in a moderately high pitch range' (Trevarthen 1989b, p. 198). These exchanges can best be described as an intricately arranged duet for eyes, face and hands, 'as tightly organized as the performance of well-matched and highly practical dancers or musicians' (Trevarthen 1987a, p. 179). Microanalysis of recordings of proto-conversations reveal astonishing comparisons between infant and adult rhythms in expressiveness. For instance, mother and infant are drawn to join in with one another on a shared 'beat'. When mother and baby attempt to synchronise their vocalisations, the duration of the pause to 'catch up' with the other and establish the 'beat' is the same as that 'of a wide variety of "pre-beat" signals – the article before a noun, prefixes, the up-beat of a conductor's baton, etc.' (Trevarthen 1990, p. 700). Each infant utterance lasts about the same time that an adult takes to say a short sentence, and the rhythm of turn-taking of utterances is a slow adagio: one beat every 0.9 seconds or 70 per minute (Trevarthen 1990). In these interchanges it is the baby who takes the lead and the mother who follows. If the mother fails to hold her attention on the baby's face, the baby will stop the proto-conversation, avoid the mother's gaze, show signs of distress that arouse the mother's sympathy or withdraw. This changes at three months. Conspicuous body growth, rapid increase in strength and control of arm, leg and head movements, and a maturation of binocular vision all contribute to an increased capacity to locate and manipulate objects. Trevarthen notes that the interest in objects competes with the interest in people during this period. The baby prefers objects to people, focusing not so much on the mother as on the animation she gives a toy. The mother naturally coordinates with the baby by using more vigorous approaches, but not only with toys. She also introduces games, such as tickling games, along with baby chants, like 'This little piggy went to market', and baby songs. The patterns of the mother's songs and chants, like 'intuitive motherese', are unconscious and universal (Trevarthen 1990). By the tenth month the infant has established distinctly different ways of orientating to people and objects; there is 'communication with persons and "doing" with objects' (Trevarthen 1974, p. 230). Bringing together the distinction made between people and objects, the baby begins to regard the mother in a significantly different way. There is 'a new form of spontaneous play, one that is more explicitly a joint enterprise in the managing of experiences and manipulation of objects' (Trevarthen 1980, p. 330). At this point, and not before, play becomes a shared activity, and the baby begins to cooperate with the mother, anticipating her motivations and learning from her the purposes of certain objects, for instance, what to do with a comb. 'Changes in the infant's cooperation as "receiver" or "listener" lead to large transformations in the mother's behaviour as "utterer". . . . She replaces questions and invitations with imperatives and directives' (Trevarthen 1990, p. 725). The unconscious and universal reactions of the mother give way to patterns of behaviour established by particular cultures and social class. When people and objects, which have been differentiated, come together in cooperative play, the object becomes a potential symbol because the meaning of the object can be shared with a person (Trevarthen 1980). At the same time, utterances, termed 'proto-language', are used to 'talk about' the objects and events of shared interest with another (Trevarthen 1980). Trevarthen concludes that 'The evolution of the infant's expressive behaviours, coordinating movements of the whole body, but particularly face expressions, visual orientations, head movements, vocalisations and hand gesticulations, confirms the existence of a central patterning of expression' (Trevarthen and Marwick 1986, p. 287). The 'central patterning of expression' is, in my opinion, a reference to the influence of the primary self, and the 'evolution' which Trevarthen describes in remarkable detail is the unfolding of deintegrative and reintegrative processes. When Trevarthen defines infant 'motives' as 'mental structures underlying perception and action', consisting of 'images' and schema that do not necessarily reflect experience (Trevarthen 1980, pp. 325–326), he is also defining archetypal structures underlying deintegration and reintegration. Both Trevarthen and Fordham view the way mother and infant interact as well as the overall developmental pattern of their relationship as shaped by archetypal (characteristic and universal) processes.

Incorporating Trevarthen's research with my understanding of deintegration and reintegration relating to early communication between a mother and her infant, I offer the following summary. Initially the infant experiences the breast as a whole, in which the qualities of 'good' and 'bad', and animate and inanimate, are combined. First 'good' and 'bad' experiences are deintegrated and reintegrated, and then, when the infant is about six weeks old, experiences of animate persons deintegrate out of the initial experience of wholeness and are reintegrated following repeated protoconversations with the mother. At three months, experiences of inanimate objects are deintegrated out and then reintegrated, so that by nine months the infant differentiates between people and things. At around 10–12 months, towards the end of the weaning process, the baby is able to combine in a new way what is animate with what is inanimate by sharing objects with others. When objects have shared meanings, they can serve as symbols. This marks a significant point in the development of the mind. Trevarthen notes that Klein dates the depressive position at this period, and Fordham has pointed out that the depressive position 'constitutes the first step in the lifelong process of individuation' (Trevarthen and Marwick 1986; Fordham 1989, p. 68).

Clinical material

The deaf girl I call Virginia stole various things, such as money from her mother and small items of school equipment from her classroom. Consequently I saw her weekly over her last four terms at primary school, from Easter until July of the following year. In what follows, I should like to examine what it was Virginia was trying to steal, or, as I was led to conclude, to retrieve. By the time she had reached the age of 10, Virginia's impulsive bad temper and stubborn defiance made her a target for criticism from her classmates, unfortunately all boys, who made a point of excluding her. Her teacher and her parents were concerned about both her stealing and their inability to manage her, as at times she became exasperatingly belligerent and obdurate.

Before either her stealing or her behaviour became matters for concern, the school for several years had been worried about her lack of language development, which lagged noticeably behind that of her classmates. According to her audiogram, she was one of the deafest children in the school, yet, from the time she had started school, there had been an ambiguity about the degree of her deafness. From her voice and lack of response, she seemed to be very deaf, yet – as will be seen – there were times when this conclusion seemed questionable. Although the cause of her profound perceptive (nerve) deafness was unknown, she was presumed to have been deaf from birth.

Virginia was the second of five children and the only member of the family who was deaf. Her parents believed that she should be taught lip-reading, because they felt she would be excluded from the usual advantages and opportunities available to those in the hearing world if she were taught sign language. Virginia seldom used her voice and communicated through gestures, which her mother and older brother seemed to understand.

She had two younger sisters and a baby brother. She had been quite involved with the care of the second sister when the latter was a baby, and their closeness remained until the sister began talking, whereupon the sister preferred to be with others who spoke. When her little brother was born, Virginia was also involved with looking after him. There were times when he screamed at such a pitch that the mother could not stand to be near him, and Virginia would turn off her hearing aids, pick him up, and patiently comfort him.

Virginia started school at the end of her second year, at the beginning of a period of considerable change in deaf education. Until a year before I became the social worker there, the school, then typical of schools for the deaf in the UK, taught lip-reading and discouraged sign language. This was done with the genuine conviction that it was damaging to deaf children to isolate them from the world in which the majority use spoken communication. The year I began work at the school, in 1977, a select number of pupils were being taught sign language as well as lip-reading. Originally this was done in an effort to reduce the behaviour problems of these children, which to a certain degree it succeeded in doing. Six years later, by which time Virginia had been taught lip-reading for four years, there was a major shift in deaf education, and sign language was taught throughout the school.

At the time I started to see Virginia, which was only a few months after sign language was incorporated into the curriculum. I was impressed by the impoverishment of her language. She was like the deaf boy of the same age who is described by Oliver Sachs in *Seeing Voices*. 'He perceived that something was "going on" between us, but he could not comprehend what it was – he had, as yet, almost no idea of symbolic communication, of what it was . . . to exchange meaning' (Sachs 1989, p. 39).

In regard to our communicating, to begin with, there was as much lack of understanding as there was presence of it. Virginia could not speak discernibly, save for a very few words, and although she was being taught signing, she had, as I have explained, limited understanding of language and what it is about. Added to this, she was uncommonly clumsy, and what signs she did use were conveyed in a sloppy manner. For instance, rather than point to herself to mean 'I', she limply patted the hearing aid harnessed across her chest. I had some signing skills, but basically it was a foreign language to me. Gradually Virginia and I developed a 'good enough' way of communicating based upon a kind of pidgin sign language, gestures, mime, drawing and simple written messages. In our painfully unpropitious first session, I understood virtually nothing of Virginia's communications, either analytically or in terms of signing. The feelings of being misunderstood and rejected which this evoked then became acted out. For the next two weeks, she refused to see me in my room, although I was able to persuade her to go to the shops with me during our second meeting, and in the third I joined her in her classroom. There she rebuffed me by refusing to look at me and by moving away if I started to approach her. I made it clear that I knew she did not like me, but it was equally clear that this did not provoke my retaliation.

As the fourth session approached, I felt a strong sense of failure when I considered that she would yet again refuse to come. This was followed by a sense of relief that I would no longer have to suffer her lacerating rejections, which left me with feelings of thorough worthlessness and intense pain, the nature of which I had never been aware of experiencing before. I was very dependent on my supervisor, Dorothy Davidson, who taught me how to rely upon projective identifications – the thoughts and emotions that Virginia aroused in me – to understand Virginia's feelings. When I could see that the rejection I felt had its source in Virginia, I could develop a way of understanding her.

To my surprise, she came willingly to the fourth session and rejected me in pretend. This was the beginning of a regular pattern of play; soon after the session started, she would feign a superior attitude and march haughtily into the medical room adjoining my office, slamming the door behind her. I would then jiggle the door handle in lieu of knocking and attempt to stick my head just inside the door, whereupon she would shriek one of her few understandable phrases, 'Go 'way!' I would retreat behind the closed door and wait for a few minutes before trying again. Occasionally she would allow me to stand in the open doorway, and I would pretend to beg her to let me play with her. She turned me away repeatedly – sometimes six or seven times – before eventually letting me in.

During the time she was alone in the medical room, she would be arranging the furniture and equipment to suit her play or going through the contents of the box of toys I provided, studying each object as if she were taking inventory of a treasure. When I was allowed in the room, she would play teacher, order me to pick up paper she scattered on the floor and direct me to do impossible homework. Later she became a doctor, isolating me beneath blankets and behind screens and leaving me until she returned to administer 'medicine' from a urine specimen container. She would also give me anxiety-provoking medical examinations, including eye tests in which I was expected to identify individual letters her ruler whisked past on the wall chart. When I failed to keep up, she became exasperated and critical.

As I have described elsewhere (Urban 1990), Virginia tended to expect others to look upon her with criticism and scorn. I found it difficult to watch her, say, examining the toys I provided without her feeling unbearably criticised. When she felt criticised, it was impossible to direct sign language to her; she would scream and turn away or refuse to look. I discovered that she was in fact interested in what I had to say because she watched me indirectly. When I became aware of this difficulty and how she managed it, I found alternatives to direct communication, such as using the mirror in the room or signing to a space next to her, rather than straight at her.

The endings of the sessions were characteristically disruptive, initially because she wanted to take something from the toy box away with her. Only later did I understand that her behaviour had a bearing upon her language deprivation. For instance, at the end of the fifth session, she stubbornly insisted upon taking the entire box of toys with her, and I tried without success to dissuade her. As she was leaving the room with the box determinedly tucked under her arm, I asked feebly if she was going to bring it back the following week. She answered yes. This she did, thus making what might have been stealing – or confiscation – into an exchange; she took something from me and then gave something back. This exchange was marked by ruthlessness (on Virginia's part) and intense anxiety (on my part). The anxiety that I experienced was related to dependency, because I felt that if she took all the toys and did not return them, we would not be able to continue to meet. This feeling was not based upon reality, because her play with me did not involve the toys; it involved playing school and hospital. But the toys were a means of exchange that served as a fundamental link between us.

Within the familiar pattern of play there were significant changes. She used her increasing communication skills to tell me to wait, rather than slamming the door shut and leaving me out. We worked out ways of accommodating one another that allowed for moments of good will, such as moving furniture together to make the arrangement she wanted. At our last meeting of the term, she wrote me a note: 'Elizabth not play. Sad not play Eliizabth [sic]'.

By the end of the term, Virginia had shown considerable changes outside her sessions as well as within. Her behaviour both at home and in class had improved. Her parents told me that she had changed '100% in her attitude'; she was more relaxed in herself and was more interested in joining in activities with others. Her communication skills had developed, and she was confident enough of her ability to communicate to have occasional chats with the speech therapist. Also, I had looked through the school accident book, where her name had previously been logged more than any other child's for regular falls, cuts and bruises. There was no entry for her during the term from Easter to the summer break.

To the best of my or anyone else's knowledge, she had not stolen from home or school since the first time she saw me. However, when I took Virginia's toys home with me over the long summer holiday, I happened to look inside. There, along with the small toys I had provided, was a strange toy I had not seen before. It was a tiny, soft cushion, probably part of the furniture for a doll's house, that only Virginia could have put there. Something had been added to that which stood for our means of exchange, that is, she had contributed something of her own to what passed between us. Granted, this was done surreptitiously, but it conveyed by its size and texture an element of tenderness.

When we resumed meeting the following autumn, Virginia's play continued to reflect change. The emotional intensity of the sessions in the first term became more moderate and her reactions to me less volatile. Her relationship to me shifted from one marked by controlling/being controlled to one of mutuality. She confided to me her need for help with her homework and drew a picture of a 'beautiful rainbow' to express the feeling of togetherness that existed between us. A new pattern of play developed; she played that she was my friend. The development of this play reached a climax in our last session before the Easter break, just a year after we had started to meet.

At the start of the session, she pulled out some disused speech therapy equipment that had been stored in my room. Using some of this equipment and the procedure with which she was familiar, she pretended to give me a hearing test. She put the headset on me and made various vocalisations behind me. Pretending to be deaf, I raised my hand when I 'heard'. She reversed our places, and I gave her the 'test', saying one of three names that she knew. At one point she turned, looked at me and smiled. Pointing to her ear and nodding affirmatively, she clearly indicated that she had heard me. Startled and pleased, I said that I thought she was deaf, adding that the headset would make hearing even more difficult. She removed the headset and turned away, asking me to repeat the names. Again she indicated that she could hear. I asked her what word she heard me say, and she answered correctly, 'Virginia'. When I asked what the second name was, she wrongly answered, 'Elizabeth'.

The subsequent session picked up from where this one had left off, despite the four-week Easter break between the two. She pulled out the hearing test equipment, darkened the room and administered the hearing test. She then insisted that I go with her into the school hall, where she directed me to pick a song from several that were written on posters hung on the wall and to copy it, while she did the same. When we returned to the darkened therapy room,

> She places me in the comer in front of the lamp and turns it on. She wants me to sing the song I chose, which I do with the spotlight on me, while she holds the music and, after a fashion, directs by signing the words. When we finish my song, she switches our positions so that she stands in the comer in the spotlight. She tells me to sign the words of her song, which I do. Together we perform the song with my inarticulate signing accompanying her flat yet enthusiastic tones, the words of the song being all but indiscernible; 'red and yellow and pink and green . . .'
>
> She intently watches my hands while I sign, and sings wholeheartedly, swaying rhythmically back and forth from one foot to the other. When we finish, she turns and stands opposite to where she stood to sing, and applauds, and has me do the same. There is enthusiastic appreciation in the applause – and a curtain call.

Comment

The feelings that were aroused in me by Virginia during these last two sessions helped me to understand what was happening not only in these two particular interviews but also how they represented a culmination of something that had been developing all along. What I felt during, and following, these two sessions was an intense humility at the unique privilege of being 'heard' by this deaf child and an exquisitely painful tenderness at being allowed close to what felt at the time like her 'primal wound'. These feelings of idealised specialness and closeness were opposite to the rejection and worthlessness I experienced at the beginning. These important clues enabled me later to consider how Virginia's play expressed phantasies she had about communicating.

These thoughts can be summarised as follows: At the time I started seeing her, Virginia identified with being deaf (patting her hearing aid to mean 'I'), and this to her meant being unable to communicate and being rejected. By the end of the first term, there was evidence in the tiny cushion that the foundations of communication had been established between us, and this was accompanied by an improvement in her communication skills. The primary means of communication had shifted from projective identification to play and semiotics (signing).

When the autumn term started, the development of her phantasy not only continued but gained momentum. It can be described as the unfolding (deintegration) of a complex phantasy of idealised good communication, in which there is a close and special togetherness with another, without the pain of not understanding or of being misunderstood.

In Virginia's phantasy, ideal communication could only occur if one were hearing and, by implication, speaking. Thus, she could only 'really' communicate while in projective identification with an idealised hearing (and speaking) object. From the feelings I experienced at the time, she was clearly in this state of mind in the two sessions involving the hearing test equipment. As she had undergone actual hearing tests many times, I think that she responded as she did because she knew what to expect and not because she could actually hear – that is, beyond some residual hearing, which may have come to have more value for her. So when she said she could hear, she meant she was projectively identified with me as a hearing person and felt that she could hear. She also felt that she could speak, and this was expressed in singing together with me, while in projective identification with an idealised speaking (singing) object. In that feeling state, she could both watch (my signing) and be watched (by me and an imaginary audience).

In summary, I think that in achieving a state of mind in which she felt that she could hear me and that she could speak to me, Virginia had been able to acquire 'honestly', that is, by hard work, what previously she had only been able to attempt to get by stealing.

I have so far described Virginia's quest as one for the experience of being in communication with another. However, at this point a new question arises: If Virginia was deaf from birth and without a visual language until she was 10, how did she know what she was missing? Or, put differently, was Virginia stealing something that she did not have or retrieving something she once had but had lost? To address this question I am turning to infant observation.

Infant observation

In what follows I am drawing upon notes I made of an infant and his mother and other family members during weekly visits to their home. At that time I attended a seminar with other infant observers, where my notes were discussed. Several years later I studied my notes again under Dr Fordham's supervision, and it was during this re-examination that Dr Fordham offered the reflection, which I shall point out in due course, which provides the central theme of this chapter.

In the following excerpts from my observation notes, I am focusing on early exchanges between the baby Toby and his mother. In the first observation Toby was two and a half months old, the age at which infants and mothers engage in proto-conversations. By this time, Toby had established a good relationship to the breast, which, I think, is clear in the observation.

> He sucked heartily at the breast for several minutes, making throaty noises and moving his cheeks rhythmically. He fed for several more minutes before his mother sat him up to wind him. She turned him around with his head resting on her right elbow, his eyes watching her. She looked at him intently and talked to him, her face occasionally breaking into a broad grin.
>
> Toby resumed vigorous sucking. After about five minutes, he pulled away from the breast and looked at his mother's face. He began to suck again, but more slowly than when he first fed. He then stopped sucking, and she asked if he had finished. She pulled him toward her right nipple and held him there for a minute. Although he had taken the nipple into his mouth, she told me that he wasn't sucking. She turned him around and sat him on her leg to wind him. He looked at me and smiled. I noticed again this time, as I had the last visit, how he seemed to play with his tongue. It seemed to move within his mouth causing his cheeks to move, and occasionally he stuck it out as if savouring it. She turned to him and said, 'There now, time to have your nappy changed'. Her tone to him was very affectionate and when she talked to him the questions she asked were spoken as if he might really answer. She undid his babygro and talked to him. He began what she called his 'conversation'. He made a series of noises which had the rhythmic inflection of someone speaking. His mother looked down at him and smiled, and talked back to him, asking him to 'Say that again?' As she spoke, he smiled and looked at her and then away and waved his arms. Then he held them out in front of him in the air, first suspended, then moved up and down. While he was 'talking', his face changed expression; he knit his eyebrows together with an intent expression, he smiled, and he just looked around with raised eyebrows, as if expecting something. These expressions added to the sense of his having a 'conversation'.

In this observation, Toby's relationship to the breast was intimately linked to the proto-conversation he had with his mother. The mutually satisfying feed included not only taking in milk but also touching, 'talking to' and looking at one another. Toby lingered at the breast after feeding and held the nipple in his mouth. When he was taken from the breast, the nipple was replaced by his tongue and, a few moments later, by vocalisations. Thus, for Toby a good feed of various components was located in his mouth, first as a nipple in his mouth, then as his tongue in his mouth, and later as vocalisations in his mouth. The vocalisations were part of a 'conversation' with his mother, the 'topic' of which seemed to be their mutual enjoyment of one another.

Influenced by Fordham's model of deintegration and reintegration, I view what was happening around Toby's mouth as an early step in development. That is, the nipple-in-the-mouth of a good feed is a proto-phenomenon which separates out (deintegrates) into a number of later discrete phenomena, such as container-contained, a good intercourse and, as I hope to show, a word-in-the-mouth. Thus, this proto-phenomenon is like a simple bud which gradually unfolds into an intricately complex flower.

I shall now turn to an observation when Toby was six months, three and a half weeks old. Earlier in the observation, Toby was in the kitchen playing with various utensils, and I noted that his main preoccupation had shifted from people to things. Later his mother left temporarily and, when Toby protested, I held him on my lap, which quieted him (not usual for infant observers to do).

> He sat on my leg and leaned forward and dug his fingers into a hole in the chair covering. I noticed that his mouth was pulled in as it is when one forms the letter 'B'. I spoke to him, and he looked up at me and then away again. I turned him around to face me. He leaned forward and reached out for the front of my sweater and breasts, feeling the texture of my sweater. After a while, he lay back a bit, half-upright, resting against my body and arm. A couple of times he turned his head against my shoulder and breast, as if expecting to suck. I talked to him, and he relaxed. I felt I was running out of conversation but that my voice was soothing to him, so I began to sing a little lullaby. His lids lowered as he watched my fingers rub his tummy, and then he looked away at nothing in particular, seeming to concentrate on listening to my voice. He seemed relaxed and pulled his right arm around so that he could suck on his fingers and waved his left hand in the air. He watched his left hand as he moved it around. He looked up at my face and then at my mouth, and then reached for my mouth and touched it as it moved when I sang, still sucking on the fingers of his other hand.

As in the first observation, there was an experience at the breast (reaching for it) followed by an exchange with another. However, there were developments in this observation beyond those which were noted in the first. His interest had shifted from people, especially his mother, to things, which he could manipulate through developing fine motor control. This is consistent with Trevarthen's finding that in the middle of the first year the baby, if in the company of the mother, prefers objects to people. Increased muscular control also applies to Toby's tongue and labials, as his infant cooing, which was made up of primarily vowel sounds, developed to include consonants (the 'B' mouth shape). Parallel to this was an increased awareness of inside/outside, and fingers were used to explore this dimension, for example, the fingers into the rip in the chair covering and into his own mouth and then my own. (I shall comment later on the developing awareness of inside/outside.)

Dr Fordham's reflection was on Toby's interest in the song/word in my mouth, for which he looked and tried to touch. Dr Fordham's comment carried the understanding that for Toby the word was a thing. Toby reached for this thing with one hand while simultaneously sucking on the fingers of his other hand, so that one can hypothesise that there was a link between the fingers-in-the-mouth (which derived from the nipple-in-the-mouth of the good feed) and the song/word-in-the-mouth.

The subsequent visit supported this formation. Once again, the mother had temporarily left.

> He sat on the mat on the floor and started to cry. I picked him up and held him on my lap and talked to him. I began singing to him, and he stopped crying and looked up and watched for a long moment. He then made agitated movements before becoming quiet again. He started to 'talk' as if commenting on something that was going on, and reached for my mouth. He then made sucking movements in his mouth.

In this observation, my song/word-in-the-mouth was linked, by Toby's reach, to his vocalisations-in-the-mouth and his sucked tongue-in-the-mouth. Thus, what became the song/word-in-the-mouth can be traced backward, via vocalisations-, fingers-, then tongue-, to its source in the nipple-in-the-mouth of a good feed. All of these thing-in-the-mouth experiences are inextricably bound up with emotionally coloured, that is, meaningful, exchanges with another. This describes the mother tongue to which I referred in my introduction.

In order to follow the forward development of the thing-in-the-mouth, one needs to keep in mind that Toby's growing awareness of inside/outside (exploring the tear in the chair covering and the insides of my and his own mouths) occurred alongside the gradual discovery of things (the kitchen utensils). Referring to a series of observations of children between 18 and 30 months (at least a year older than Toby in the previous two observations), Meltzer writes about the 'Buccal Theatre for Generating Meaning' (Meltzer 1986, p. 181). He describes the way one child seemed to be playing with the sounds in his mouth in a way that paralleled his play with objects, 'not merely as commentary on that play but as an alternative theatre of phantasy manipulation' (Meltzer 1986, p. 179). Meltzer concludes that 'the physical space of the oral cavity is utilized as the theatre of phantasy and play, a mid-point between external play and internal thought . . . [where] the sounds can be manipulated as concrete objects' (Meltzer 1986, p. 179). To show what had happened to Toby's language development by the time the word was in his own mouth, I am skipping almost 20 months to the time when he was two years, two months, two and a half weeks, to complete the picture.

> Toby smiled when he saw me. His mother asked him, 'Who is it?', and Toby, having been able to identify me by name for at least a month, said, 'Frances'. His mother said it wasn't Frances, and Toby said 'Elizabeth'. He said something I couldn't understand about a story, then repeated, 'Less read a story'. I followed him into the sitting room and sat down while Toby brought me

a book. He and I read it as he stood by my knee. He repeatedly pointed to pictures of mice and said, 'Dassa rabbit', but after a bit conceded, 'Dassa mouse'. There was a picture of a fly on one of the pages, and I asked him what it was. 'Dassa spider,' he answered. I said I thought it was a fly. 'Issa beliocopter', he declared authoritatively. Later he changed this; 'Dassa fly'.

By 26 months Toby had come to know a lot about language. Not only did he have a good vocabulary, which he could will to use accurately or not, but also he knew about statements, questions and imperatives. He knew about verbal one-upman-ship and that his 'heliocopter' outmatched my 'fly'. He was thus able to use words as part of a game. Knowing that at that time he was terrified of spiders, I think he was also using the word in his mouth as a toy with which he played, helping him to develop a means of managing a powerful phantasy and to differentiate internal from external reality, similar to the way Meltzer describes.

I have tried to show how the origins of what eventually became the richness of Toby's language can be traced to an object (the thing-in-the-mouth) that was simultaneously a relationship (a good feed). I believe that it was this 'mother tongue' that Virginia was trying to steal or, more accurately, to retrieve. Before this conclusion can be accepted, there is one more point to add. To do this, I would like to compare the part of the first observation that describes the post-feed proto-conversation Toby had with his mother during his nappy change with that of a baby girl just the same age as Toby (two and a half months):

> Amy looked at me and smiled, waved her arms and legs, and made 'eh' noises and raspy syllables in the back of her mouth. I could talk to her when she fin-ished her vocalization, so that we had a 'conversation'. In this 'conversation' she made single syllable 'ooh', 'eh', and 'ee' sounds and some multi-syllable sounds that in my imagination I could make into 'hello' and 'how are you?'. That is, she had in her voice the same song, or inflection, of someone saying this. There were a series of waves of smiles, crescendoing with her sounds. These crests were accompanied by vocalizations of a variety of human speak-ing sounds. She 'talked' in the crest of the wave, and I talked in the fall.

The proto-conversations between Toby and his mother and between Amy and me are virtually identical; each infant is in relation to an adult via alternating vocali-sations accompanied by facial expressions and arm and hand movements. In nei-ther case does it matter whether words are being used or understood. What does matter is that there is a meaningful exchange of expression. The only significant difference between Toby and Amy is that Toby is hearing, and Amy is deaf.

Conclusion

I would now like to return to Virginia and her quest, in which she was trying to get for herself the object that is the thing-in-the-mouth which is also a relationship in which there is a purposeful exchange and a feeling of being together with another in shared understanding. In infant proto-conversations, which deafness does not preclude, it makes no difference whether the utterances have specific meanings; it is the emotional quality – the meaningfulness – of the exchange that counts.

It could be argued that Virginia's loss of her mother tongue was inevitable. Not untypically, her deafness was not diagnosed until she was in her second year. This is well beyond the second half of the first year when babbling develops and when the mother helps her child to establish a preference for certain babbled sounds which become phonemes, the 'alphabet' of the sounds of a language. It is clear that the baby must be able to hear in order to establish which of his or her vocalisations have meaning when he or she babbles. This might have been Virginia's first step towards language deprivation and, to her, the loss of the mother tongue.

A more convincing view is that Virginia, for unknown reasons, was severely deprived. Most of the other children at the school also had hearing parents and late diagnoses of deafness, but they did not have her difficulty in understanding that language, whether signed or spoken, is fundamentally about the exchange of meaning. Hence Virginia's deprivation was not simply one of language because of her deafness, although I think that in both my and Virginia's minds that was where the deprivation was located. It was in the area of deafness (play referring to her experiences at the school for the deaf and at the hospital audiology department) that feelings of hurt, rejection and being excessively controlled could have a place, and it was in the area of hearing and speaking that feelings of hope could develop.

Also, Virginia was very like the severely deprived children described by Alvarez (Alvarez 1992). Alvarez's view is that these children are burdened with despair of attaining what is meaningful, and she argues that the therapy of these children needs to be directed to helping them with 'the new hopes and the new development of idealization' (Alvarez 1992, p. 126). Certainly this was the way Virginia used her therapy.

What Virginia did with her therapy can be described using Trevarthen's framework. When Virginia developed a way of managing her feelings of rejection and being excessively controlled, she started to play that we were friends. I understand this to be her way of working towards an attitude that could lead to the fulfilment of an unmet longing. What I think she hoped for and temporarily achieved was the experience of what felt like a post-feed proto-conversation. What happened following the play with the hearing test equipment had marked similarities to just that: a duet for eyes, face and hands in an emotionally coloured exchange with a special person. The parallel with infancy is that only after the infant's hunger and discomfort have been allayed (Toby's feed and nappy change) and there is a good object in the infant's mouth (a nipple, then musical vocalisations) can there be a mutual, pleasurable interchange with a 'favourite companion'.

However, this description is not complete without an analytic understanding of the content of our exchanges. Jung likened the transcendent function to 'a language which is eloquent enough for one who understands it, but which seems like deaf-and-dumb language to one who does not' Jung 1958, p. 89). The feelings Virginia aroused in me served as such a language. Only if I experienced, contained and understood the feelings Virginia stirred up in me could there be a relationship in which the fundamentals of communication were re-established and developed. Because this happened, Virginia was able to retrieve an experience of the thing-in-the-mouth that is also a relationship of shared meaning. This developed alongside her acquisition of sign language, whereby a word-in-the-hand, which derives from the gesture-in-the-air, could come to serve the same purpose as a word-in-the-mouth.

Summary

The clinical material in this chapter is drawn from the treatment of Virginia, a profoundly deaf 10-year-old, who was referred for treatment because she stole things from home and school. This chapter attempts to address the question of what it was she was trying to steal. In formulating an answer, I draw upon the infant research of Trevarthen and my own infant observation. I attempt to comprehend the clinical material and the infant studies within Fordham's model of early development. My conclusion is that Virginia was attempting to retrieve, rather than steal, an experience that lies at the source of a number of later developments, including that of language and friendship.

References

Alvarez, A. (1992). *Live Company*. London: Routledge.
Fordham, M. (1947). 'Integration and disintegration and early ego development'. *The Nervous Child*, 6(3) (1957)
——. (1957). 'Some observations on the self and ego in childhood'. In *New Developments in Analytical Psychology*. London: Routledge & Kegan Paul.
——. (1976). *The Self and Autism*. London: Hodder & Stoughton.
——. (1985a). *Explorations into the Self*. London: Academic Press.
——. (1985b). 'Abandonment in infancy'. *Chiron*.
——. (1987). 'Actions of the self'. In P. Young-Eisendrath and J. Hall (eds.), *The Book of the Self*. London: New York University Press.
——. (1989). 'The infant's reach'. *Psychological Perspectives*, 21.
Jung, C. G. (1921). 'Psychological types'. *CW 6*.
——— (1958). 'The transcendent function'. *CW 8*.
Meltzer, D. (1986). 'Concerning the perception of one's own attributes and its relation to language development'. In *Studies in Extended Metapsychology*. Pitlochry: Clunie.
Sachs, O. (1989). *Seeing Voices*. Berkeley: University of California Press.
Stern, D. (1985). *The Interpersonal World of the Infant*. New York: Basic Books.
Trevarthen, C. (1974). 'Conversations with a two-month-old', *New Statesman*, 2 May.
——. (1980). 'The foundations of intersubjectivity: Development of interpersonal and cooperative understanding in infants'. In D. Olson (ed.), *The Social Foundations of Language and Thought*. New York. Norton.

————. (1987a). 'Sharing makes sense: intersubjectivity and the making of an infant's meaning'. In R. Steele and T. Treadgold (eds.), *Language Topics.* Philadelphia: John Benjamins.

————. (1987b). 'Mind in infancy'. In R. L. Gregory (ed.), *The Oxford Companion to the Mind.* Oxford: Oxford University Press.

————. (1989a). 'The relation of autism to normal socio-cultural development: The case for a primary disorder in regulation of cognitive growth by emotions'. In G. Lelord, P. Muh, M. Petit, and D. Sauvage (eds.), *Autisme et Troubles du Developpement Global de L'enfant.* Paris: Expansion Scientific Franaise.

————. (1989b). 'Development of early social interactions and the affective regulation of brain growth'. In C. von Euler, H. Forssberg, and H. Lagercrantz (eds.), *Neurobiology of Early Infant Behaviour.* London: Macmillan.

————. (1990). 'Signs before speech'. In T. A. Sebeok and J. UmikerSebeok (eds.), *The Semiotic Web.* Berlin: Mouton de Gruyter.

Trevarthen, C. and Marwick, H. (1986). 'Signs of motivation for speech in infants, and the nature of a mother's support for development of language'. In B. Lindblom and R. Zetterstrom (eds.), *Precursors of Early Speech.* Chineham, Basingstoke: Macmillan.

Urban, E. (1990). 'The eye of the beholder: Work with a ten-year old deaf girl'. *Journal of Child Psychotherapy,* 16(2).

Chapter 4

'With healing in her wings . . .': integration and repair in a self-destructive adolescent

Introduction

One of the most important of Jung's concepts is that of the self. Although he used the term in a number of different ways, the one that predominates is Jung's definition of the self as the totality of the personality: mind and body, conscious and unconscious, ego and archetypes (Jung 1917). As a phenomenon, the self is characterised by totality and wholeness, and is the source of meaning. Functionally it is an organiser and integrator, bringing together and structuring the inner world. Because the self is the totality of the personality, it contains or, rather, transcends opposites.

For Jung, meaning and the pressure to become whole are the motivating drives behind development. From his work with adults in mid-life, he conceived development as a process, termed 'individuation', in which the individual becomes more deeply and truly himself. Individuation is ongoing; one individuates but is never individuated. Technically, it is a process by which the ego, the centre of perception, time and again confronts conflicting and opposite forces, say between good and evil, or being dependent and being separate. The consequence of the conflict between opposites is – and here is Jung's optimism (Fordham 1985a) – a new resolution, symbol or insight arising in the ego. Individuation thus involves the ego and a pair of opposites, and this triangulation is a cornerstone in Jungian understanding of development (Jung 1955–6, 1959; Fordham 1985b).

Fordham's model

Drawing upon Jung's concept of the self, Fordham postulated a primary integrate at or before birth, which he termed the primary self. Taking Jung's concept of the self as a psychic integrator and organiser, he added his own original concept, that the primary self divides up, or deintegrates, in order to relate to the environment. The self then assimilates the experience by reintegrating it (Fordham 1976, 1994).

Freud used the protozoa amoeba as an analogy for the ego (Laplanche and Pontalis 1973), and it can also be used as a model for the deintegrating and reintegrating primary self. The pseudopod of the amoeba reaches out into the environment

DOI: 10.4324/9781003215639-7

and takes in food (deintegration). What is taken in is then assimilated into the nucleated endoplasm (reintegration). The pseudopod does not become detached from the rest of the amoeba but remains part of it, just as deintegrates remain part of the primary self. If the deintegrate (experience) becomes cut off from the self, then splitting occurs. In other words, according to Fordham, splitting refers to experiences that have pathologically become detached from the self (Fordham 1987, 1993).

Fordham cites a typical example of deintegration and reintegration in infancy. An infant wakes up from sleep, a state of integration, and relates to the breast during a feed. Following the feed, the baby sleeps again, assimilating, or reintegrating, the milk and the experience (Fordham 1987). A fuller description, which takes into account the interactive dimension of Fordham's model, would be as follows: The infant wakes from a state of integration, having an archetypal predisposition. Only in the course of development, that is, as the self deintegrates and reintegrates, a stable ego is formed.

The unfolding of the personality proceeds in surges, which can be understood as periods of massive deintegration. The findings of experimental researchers indicate surges within the first year occur at birth, at about two months, to a lesser degree at three to five months, and again at 10 to 12 months (Stern 1985; Trevarthen 1980; Trevarthen and Marwick 1986).

I should now like to focus on three corollaries of Fordham's postulate of a deintegrating and reintegrating primary self, which pertain to whole and part objects and the depressive position. I shall attempt to expand upon each by drawing upon infant studies.

First corollary

Whole objects precede part objects

For Fordham, the primary self begins before birth. Unlike Freud's primary narcissism with its libidinous and destructive energies, the energy of the primary self is neutral. Interaction between archetypally (biologically) determined expectations and the intra-uterine environment produces the first objects, which Fordham terms 'self objects' (Fordham 1994). These are pre-image and pre-symbol and, as I understand them, are what Alvarez is describing when she refers to the pre-objects of autistic children (Alvarez 1992).

Self objects are imbued with the self, that is, with feelings of wholeness, at-oneness, altogetherness, together-with-me-ness. At the beginning of life, these qualities pervade experiences, thus creating states of fusion via the processes of projective and introjective identification, early processes that initially are probably very close to one another. Foetal swallowing provides a picture of how the experience of being at one with that which one is inside (projective identification) can be very close to that of being at one with that which one has inside (introjective identification). According to Milakovic, the foetus 'at will' swallows amniotic fluid in order to regulate the imbalance of fluids in its body (Milakovic 1967). It is easy to imagine that, because what provides relief is of minimum texture and the same temperature as the foetus, what envelops and what is taken in is experienced by the foetus as being part of itself.

After birth, early feeds (deintegrations) are typified by the infant's total absorption in the experience, eyes closed, body still and mouth sucking rhythmically, as if the breast were the whole of his universe and he was giving himself entirely to it. Visual, aural and tactile aspects of the mother become incorporated into the wholeness characterising early self objects. From the observer's point of view, the baby is relating to parts of the mother, but from the infant's point of view, the part is the whole (Fordham 1987; Astor 1989).

Earlier, I stated that when the infant assimilates an experience (reintegration), he adds something to it. An example is amodal perception and cross-modal fluency. Because the newborn can fluently translate amodal experiences towards that which fills his need (cf. Bion's preconception [Bion 1962]), he gives signals, such as crying, to his mother. The mother takes these signals into herself, does something with them and then responds to her baby, such as putting him to the breast. The baby feeds and takes in not only the milk but something of the mother's way of feeding and responding. In assimilating the milk and the experience, the baby adds something of his own, such as meaning, the way the mother added something of her own, such as alpha function, when she took in the baby's signals. What is done within the baby is the result of actions of the self. I shall return to this.

The organising functions of the self differ from those of the ego. It is the self that accounts for the overall, archetypally shaped unfolding of the personality and for the organisation of the infant's personality. However, infants also exhibit rapidly fluctuating states, which Fordham understands as evidence of the fragile and unstable infant ego. There are bits of ego at birth. Because early experiences (deintegrates) include bits of perception or awareness from one sense into another, Stern concludes that the 'seen' breast is experienced by the infant to be the same as the 'sucked' breast (Stern 1985). In Fordham's model, the global, whole nature of the infant's perceptions is an expression of actions of the self that make them so. According to the infant's experience, self objects are whole objects. However, even in infancy, self objects come and go, and so do experiences of wholeness and fusion (Fordham 1985b).

Second corollary

Part objects are a result of deintegration and reintegration

Self objects arise out of and represent the satisfied needs of the foetus and, later, the infant and quickly develop into good objects. Early on, other concurrent sense data, for example, commotion from an older sibling, do not become integrated (Stern 1985; Brazelton 1991) or are experienced as not-self. If not-self objects are felt to be frustrating or unpleasant, they initially are rejected, attacked or evacuated (Fordham 1976) and can later become bad objects. The intensification of and differentiation between 'good' and 'bad', which can be observed in young infants, is a result of early actions of the self, creating parts out of the whole.

At about six weeks to two months, dramatic changes occur in the infant, indicating a new surge of deintegration. Trevarthen details the considerable changes that occur in the area of communication. He describes in fascinating detail the intricate, alternating behaviours of infant and mother that develop into proto-conversations. Later, at three to five months and given a secure relationship with a present mother, the infant turns away from face-to-face conversations in order to engage with an object animated by the mother (Trevarthen 1980; Trevarthen and Marwick 1986). Psychoanalytic baby observations show how babies this age explore objects on their own through mouthing and handling. Taken all together, these observations show how animate and inanimate become firmly differentiated.

Stern describes the gradual differentiation between self and other. He details how the infant sifts invariant from variant features of experience and organises them into clusters of experiences associated with self and experiences associated with another, resulting in the infant's sense of core self and sense of core other: 'Somehow, the different invariants of self-experience are integrated. . . . Similarly, [the different invariants of different experiences of the mother] all get disentangled and sorted. "Islands of consistency" somehow form and coalesce' (Stern 1985, p. 98).

In Fordham's model, the sorting of invariant from variant features and the organisation of them into discrete clusters are actions of the integrating and organising functions of the primary self. Fordham would consider Stern's description of the coalescence of 'islands of consistency' into a sense of self to be a description of ego formation. For Fordham, having a sense, a perception or an awareness – no matter how primitive – is a function of the ego (Fordham 1994).

The self not only shapes the ego, it also adds something to the clustering of perceptions. This means that there is a fundamental difference between Fordham's and Stern's concepts of the ego. This can be seen in their different views about self-representations, which arise in the ego. Stern's representations of interactions that have been generalised (RIGS) are mental prototypes of lived experience, that is, memories of actual experiences. For Fordham, the ego 'is born out of the self' and despite the gradual boundary that is built up between them, the self remains partially represented in the ego. Hence self representations contain aspects of the self, and are more than memories of actual experiences'(Fordham 1985b).

In summary, through deintegration and reintegration, the original wholeness of self objects divides up into parts, such as good and bad, inside and outside, animate and inanimate, and self and other.

Third corollary

Individuation begins with the depressive position

At about 10 to 12 months there is another surge of new developments, or deintegrations. In the period Trevarthen terms 'secondary inter-subjectivity', play between mother and infant becomes a shared activity. The baby begins to cooperate with the mother, anticipating her intentions and learning from her the purposes of certain objects, for instance, what to do with a comb. When the meaning of an object can be shared, the object becomes a potential symbol (Trevarthen 1980; Trevarthen and Marwick 1986). According to Stern, this is the period of establishing a sense of subjective self. As the infant discovers that inner experiences are shareable, he begins to relate to his mother's mind and acquires 'a "theory" of separate minds' (Stern 1985, p. 124). Thus, Trevarthen and Stern demonstrate the enormous potential for cognitive development that comes out of the bringing together of self/other, animate/inanimate and inside (the mind)/outside (behaviour).

Psychoanalytic baby observations during this period are usually concerned with the infant's final weaning from the breast. An example is from the observation of Edward, at 12 months, one week. I am grateful to the observer in the British Association of Psychotherapists training who allowed me to use the following extracts from her notes.

> Edward was completely weaned from the breast only a few weeks before. At the beginning of the observation, the observer watched him being given lunch from a bowl. When the bowl was emptied and taken away, Edward suddenly let out an intense wail, 'mouth open wide and crying bitterly so that he was just exhaling in bursts. He was inconsolable.' His mother offered him the bowl and then juice, which he refused. Then she tried to hold him. Each effort on her part to comfort or distract seemed to escalate his screams. Eventually the mother took him into the lounge and cleared a space for him on the floor, while she sat close by. 'For fifteen or twenty minutes, he rolled on the floor and screamed, [writhing] back and forth.' Throughout this time the mother remained close and attentive.
>
> Slowly the intensity of the screaming eased but did not stop, and Edward seemed able to tolerate his mother's soothing. The screams had changed into something more regular and rhythmic, but [eventually] they stopped altogether and at last he lay still and quiet. . . . He stared at the ceiling, exhausted. . . . His mother bent over him after a while and he smiled slowly in response. Within minutes he was smiling and seemed quite happy.

The seminar group found this observation quite upsetting and considered that Edward's loss of the bowl might be an expression of his loss of the breast. Nothing external in the observation accounted for the unreachable depth and intensity of his response; he was responding to something internal. In thwarting his mother's efforts to console or distract, he seemed to be 'true' to his experience of his loss and to show a depth of character. Eventually and of its own accord, the intensity subsided, then disappeared, and a good relationship with the mother was restored. When his mother went into the kitchen, he played happily with the observer, something he had never done before and which seemed to mark an increased awareness of reality and affection. These are hallmarks of the depressive position.

The classical Kleinian idea of the depressive position is that the infant comes to experience that the good, satisfying breast is the same as the one he recognises as bad and frustrating and which he attacks. Consequently he comes to feel that he has destroyed that which he loves most (Segal 1979). Fordham describes the sequence that follows:

> He pines and becomes absorbed in himself so that he is inaccessible to his mother. After a variable and distressing period of time, he gradually recovers; now he has reconstructed the breast internally. In short, he has accomplished a rather wonderful act of reparation. After this sequence, the baby's sense of reality takes a step forward and his mental life is enriched. The transformation is called the depressive position and, in my view, constitutes the first step in individuation.
>
> (Fordham 1989, p. 68)

When Fordham states that the depressive position marks the beginning of individuation, he understands that the opposites of good and bad and love and hate are brought together in such a way that a new symbol (an internal breast) is formed, thereby enriching inner life and, equally, leading to an increased sense of reality.

These three corollaries, taken in the order presented here, demonstrate the development of the internal world. The original wholeness of self objects divides up into parts, and then the parts come into relationship with one another.

Clinical material

The girl I shall call Ruthie was 13 when she was referred because of her excessive and irrational terror of pigeons. Ruthie could not walk from home to the nearby tube nor from school to the bus stop without being frightened that she might encounter a pigeon.

A psychoanalytic understanding of a phobia would usually include sexuality. Although treatment included the gradual understanding of emotional, cognitive and sexual aspects of what the pigeons represented to Ruthie, in what follows I shall focus on the aspects of the phobia that related to certain states of confusion. These states were not only the subject of much of Ruthie's treatment but also referred to her self-destructiveness and what stood in the way of her development. I should like to use Ruthie's treatment to describe how Fordham's model of development helped me to help Ruthie to integrate the experiences represented by the pigeons and how, therefore, splitting became deintegration.

When Ruthie and I first met she reported in detail how abhorrent and repulsive she found pigeons. I asked her to draw a picture of one, and she made an attempt but stopped short of completing the picture because it aroused such strong fear and revulsion. Closing her eyes and shaking her head, she shuddered and flapped her hands while expelling repeated 'oohs' of disgust. We established that what was unthinkable for her was that a pigeon would fly up on big flapping wings and rush into her face.

Once-weekly treatment started, and Ruthie eventually filled me in on some of the details of her external life. She had started to become frightened of pigeons after her family moved to London from a smaller community, when she was about 10. Unhappy and friendless, she remained the 'new girl' in school until secondary transfer.

Most of the sessions during the first months were detailed, repetitious accounts of her day-to-day encounters with pigeons, which left me feeling sleepy, cut off and useless. For her part, Ruthie found me cold and unfriendly. When I tried to offer an interpretation, she frequently would ask me to repeat it or to say more. When I tried to do so, I often discovered that I was unable to restate my thoughts coherently; my sentencing broke up into nonsense.

Eventually I suggested that she was frightened of getting into a flap. Having had some experience of her mother's anxiety and volatility, I felt I could picture what Ruthie might feel like when her mother was upset. I wondered if, when her mother got in a flap, Ruthie became frightened that the flap in her mother's mind would get into her mind. This line of thinking seemed to mean something to Ruthie. She became increasingly aware of her worry that my muddle or lack of understanding might become her mixed-upness and confusion. She told me dreams and then worried about the parts she could not remember for sure. What if I got the wrong idea about the dream and based my interpretation on a misconception? She feared that she would then have this wrong understanding in her mind and believe in it. This implied that Ruthie felt that knowledge and understanding needed to be linked to the truth.

After about five months, Ruthie left for an extended holiday abroad, and, when she returned, her mother stopped the treatment because there had been no change in the pigeon phobia. The mother arranged for Ruthie to see a behaviour therapist, and over a year passed before this broke down. The mother contacted me again, thus beginning a second period of treatment that, in retrospect, roughly corresponded to the school year prior to her taking her GCSEs.

Ruthie returned to treatment livelier and more motivated and with a positive transference to me. Mostly she spoke to me of her fear of failing her exams, and from week to week she faced one assignment or exam after another, fraught with an anxiety bordering on panic. She spent more and more time over her studies and turned down invitations to be with friends over the weekend, in order to do homework. She became exhausted from these efforts, which seemed her only protection against the dread of failure.

As her exams approached, any changes in my room were noted and treated with deep suspicion. For instance, during a break my consulting room was redecorated, and I moved a vase containing a willow branch from a position opposite to one alongside where Ruthie sat. She became frightened of this, frequently looking across her shoulder as she spoke. I made a number of interpretations, including that the spreading branches were felt by her to be the spreading wings of a flapping pigeon. Just saying this seemed to vivify and intensify her fears. The terror on the streets was now in my room.

This period of treatment came to an end when she passed her GCSEs with virtually all A's. The confirmation of the competence of her own thinking seemed to parallel her developing confidence in mine.

A-level developments

Soon after starting her A-levels, Ruthie's accounts of her anxiety about schoolwork began to include fights she had with her mother. The rows tended to arise when her younger sister got attention from their mother that Ruthie felt was her due. The fights usually occurred at bedtime, when Ruthie demanded that her mother see her to sleep. Arguments also arose from Ruthie's demand for a vegetarian diet, different from what the rest of the family ate.

Some of the fights became violent, with Ruthie furiously decanting non-vegetarian food from the fridge, throwing things and, occasionally, hitting her mother. The emotional violence could keep the family awake until the early hours of the morning. Just what occurred was difficult to ascertain because Ruthie got confused and forgot what happened. Gradually a pattern could be described. As the anger and hate escalated, Ruthie would tip into feeling out of control and screaming, hitting, crying, swearing and vomiting. Rage became violence which became chaos.

I did not appreciate the extent of Ruthie's destructiveness at home until the parents contacted me, asking to meet. Ruthie had anticipated this, saying she hoped I would see them because they were upset and needed my help to understand what was happening. After I heard the parents' accounts, I explained that Ruthie's pigeon phobia represented a condensation of intense emotions that were now beginning to break up and be experienced as feelings in relation to the family. We discussed how Ruthie needed boundaries in order to help her manage the violence of her feelings and to limit psychological, personal and material damage that she might inflict. By the end of the interview I was impressed with the parents' ability to work together to draw limits that, by the mother's admission, had not before been established.

When Ruthie and I next met, she was in a flap. Her parents had told her of the boundaries they were going to set, and she was overwhelmingly persecuted by the awareness that her parents were not under her control. At one point, she spluttered out through her tears, 'I can't stand being ordinary!' Tearful, frightened and outraged, she was reluctant to go home after her session. In order to restore her omnipotence, she threatened to cut herself. That night she carried out the threat, the first of several instances of self-inflicted wounding.

There was a long period of intense and turbulent emotion, as limits became set and tested both at home and in her sessions. But there was evidence of change. Her relationship with her father improved, she spent more time with her friends, and she used her therapy to avoid fights with her mother. From time to time she indicated that her fear of pigeons was subsiding. These changes happened along-side evidence of her increased dependency on her treatment and the thinking she associated with it. For example, there was a crisis during the summer break between her first and second years of A-level study. She had been given home-work to complete over the summer, but she got into such a state over it that the family holiday abroad had to be cut short. There was a very real question about whether she would be able to continue with her A-level work, and her sessions were increased to twice weekly. Her return to A-level studies was accompanied by heightened anxiety about failing because of the incomplete homework. She studied increasingly late into the night, which left her so tired after school that she had to sleep and then wake up in the late evening to begin her work. As this pattern became set, rows about her mother putting her to bed became replaced by arguments about whether the mother would wake Ruthie up in time for school in the morning. I pointed out how days and nights, holidays and term times were all mixed up.

When studying for her GCSEs, Ruthie had been compelled to check and recheck that she had gathered up all her papers when leaving class. She was deeply anx-ious that her papers would get all mixed up, and she spent considerable time sort-ing them. With A-levels, her 'obsessionality', as she herself called it, increased. If she threw away a wasted sheet of paper, she would spend long periods frightened that she was throwing away good work needed for class. Sorting out dirty laun-dry could take hours, because she repeatedly had to check that the pockets were empty.

I had taken a number of approaches to this material, but it became clearer that these yet-to-be-understood phenomena had to do with mixed-upness and confu-sion. My comments along this line seemed to produce relevant, guiding dreams. In one of the first, her mother was wearing Ruthie's swimsuit while diving into what I interpreted was their fused and confusing pool of emotional life. In another dream about the same time, Ruthie was in a house associated with mine talking on the telephone to me. I was in the house of one of her best friends. I interpreted that the Ruthie in me was talking to the me in Ruthie. Not surprisingly, the confu-sion the dream was describing spilled into our discussion, so that we both had to struggle to disentangle the muddle.

Following these dreams, new images arose expressing internal development. In one dream, two birds flew into her room, which was at the top of the house. They settled, one above her desk and one above her bed. Ruthie left and went into the room of her younger sister, whom Ruthie had described as a 'go-with-the-flow' kind of person. This was not long before a holiday break, and I understood it to be an expression of her worry about getting into a flap without her two sessions. What was important was that she had another state of mind to which to go. That was to the room of the easy-going, that is, unflappable, sister.

In another dream, I was visiting her in her room. She was pointing out that there were two piles: one a messy stack of schoolwork and the other dirty laun-dry. When she told me the dream, she said she had sorted this laundry over the weekend. What seemed significant was that she could take my thinking into her mind – her room at the top of the house – without the previous worry about being contaminated. Also, there was a sorting out of internal objects, between schoolwork done during the week and household chores done during the weekend. Because I was concerned about Ruthie's confusion, I focused on evidence of underdeveloped differentiation – the separate piles – rather than on what was in need of processing – the messy homework and the unwashed laundry.

Still another dream pictured her father showing her mother a series of lottery cards that looked like bingo cards. The mother commented that there were so many cards and so many numbers that it was confusing, and one could not tell them apart. I interpreted that 'lottery' referred to 'lots and lots' and that the dream was about having lots and lots of feelings about her parents and their relationship. In her father's hands the lottery cards and bingo cards were, upon discernment, distinct and separate items. Although for her mother these were overwhelming and confusing, there seemed to be a new thought – a Bingo! – namely, that there is a difference between a single mass of confusion and a plurality of distinct thoughts and feelings.

These dreams occurred alongside her increasing interest in my mind, which she found calm and settled. Her curiosity was evoked: How do I remember what she says? Do I keep notes on her? Are they in the filing cabinet across the room? Is that a dictionary on top of the table? Gradually we established that she perceived my mind as containing things that were organised. The filing cabinet was my mind with ordered contents, and the dictionary was my mind where everything had a meaning, all in order. Although these were rather sterile pictures of a mind, they were a development from the threatening chaos of misperception, wrong understanding and a mind in a flap.

After the Christmas break there were other views of my mind and thinking, which arose out of an emerging negative transference. Although the apparent trigger for the change in the transference was moving one of her session times, there were other factors. Deepening supportive friendships and other advantages of being 'ordinary' had begun to compensate for the loss of omnipotence over her parents. Also, as Ruthie began to see beyond her A-level exams, there was a dawning awareness that going to university meant that she would leave home and, of course, her therapy.

About this time there were two sessions in which her negative transference was evident. Each was followed by other events, and it was noticeable that those following the second session resulted in a state of confusion while those following the first did not. I should therefore like to compare these two sessions and their subsequent events.

In the first, Ruthie had been squeezing one of her fingers with a string, while talking in a teasing and manic way about clever people who knew things she wished she did. I interpreted that she wanted to squeeze information out of me that would explain why I was changing the session time. She agreed, and the jokey teasing and wheedling escalated, until eventually, in answer to her direct question, I said I did not intend to tell her why. The giggly mania abruptly became rage.

She attacked me with the criticism that I was just like her mother; I was inconsistent, sometimes I answered questions and sometimes I did not, and session times changed. She exclaimed, 'I never know what to expect from you!'

A week later, she briefly referred to what had happened in our session but was preoccupied with something that had happened at school the same day as the giggliness-turned-rage session. She had got into a similar teasing with a teacher, with whom, as with me, she had become friendly only after a difficult period. Although that school day ended in a spirit of high jinks, the atmosphere of the next day (the day after the session) was very different. She thought the teacher had become distant and disapproving and that their good relationship was damaged. Yet he also seemed still to be interested. Several times at school she burst uncontrollably into tears and yearned to talk to him to get the problem sorted out. Later at home she again experienced waves of intense pain and episodes of unstoppable crying. When I suggested that she was worried and hurt that she had damaged our relationship, she denied this, protesting that she was still angry at me.

Not long after, she again became angry at me, for what I thought was the changed session. Her anger in this session was expressed as criticism that I would not make up sessions she intended to miss over the summer because she planned to have two summer holidays after her A-levels. She told me that I was stupid not to make up important sessions and, in the same breath, that I was too intelligent to do so without a good reason. She demanded to know what it was, and when I did not offer one acceptable to her, she again attacked me for being inconsistent and irrational, like her mother.

Following that session, she was scheduled for some minor surgery with a doctor she admired. She had broken her toe at Christmas, and this required a brief hospitalisation. When she later told me about this, she was full of praise for the doctor and the hospital staff. She anticipated a similar good experience from the follow-up surgery, but at the last minute the day of the operation was changed. She had planned to stay in overnight, but this too was changed, in part because the experience had become so 'horrible'. Before going to hospital she had cleared up her room in a brief 20 minutes. When she came home, she returned to her old obsession of checking and re-checking what needed sorting out in her room. Worried, she wanted to know why this was.

I compared the two sessions I have described here. In the first, a clearly perceived bad, injurious me was experienced in contrast to a good but injured (by her) teacher. In the second, a similar bad me was experienced in contrast to what might have been a clearly perceived skillful and good doctor, but his goodness had become mixed up with badness because he had unpredictably changed the time. That was just what I had done to make me bad. The good and the bad had become all mixed up, and she was compelled to try and sort them out. This interpretation had a noticeably calming effect upon Ruthie.

As the end of school approached and as her exams were eventually taken and passed, Ruthie's material increasingly focused on leaving her family and her friends to go to university and drawing her therapy to a close.

Discussion

I have described the treatment of an adolescent girl, who was eventually able to integrate a split-off part of herself. What was split off held not only unwanted aggressive parts of herself but also projective and introjective identification with unprocessed 'bits' of an anxious maternal mind. Ruthie's fears about psychic contamination had therefore to be dealt with first. Ruthie then faced her anxieties about her own destructive phantasies, which were split off from both her loving relationships and a primitive form of guilt. I should add that I view her Herculean efforts to get good marks to be a way of warding off this primitive superego.

I have just suggested that Ruthie had split off 'bad' parts of herself from 'good' parts, but in another sense 'bad' and 'good' had not developed into distinctly differentiated qualities. It was as if the distinction between bad and good rested on a precariously held foundation. This foundation was an infantile state of fusion with a mother-in-a-flap, a state of projective and introjective identification analogous to the foetus swallowing some of its amniotic environment. When tested against the weight of change – of moving to London and of puberty – the foundation became split off and the pigeon phobia developed. Although her self-inflicted wounding could have become dangerous if not dealt with, I consider that it was of secondary importance compared to the destructiveness of splitting and states of primitive projective and introjective identification. Self-wounding was a conscious effort to punish her parents, while splitting and confusion were unconscious phenomena that interfered with Ruthie's mental processes and development and impoverished her internal world and her external relationships.

With treatment and consequent deintegration and reintegration, confusion developed into differentiated qualities of experience. When parts became distinguishable, they could then come into relation to one another, as I think they did when Ruthie's 'bad' therapist came into relation with her 'good' teacher. The pain, pining and remorse she felt in relation to him, and for which what actually happened did not fully account, are reminiscent of little Edward. I viewed my therapeutic role to be similar to that of Edward's mother: to allow space, to monitor the degree of persecution and to process the fluctuating states of mind, even if the process was sometimes unspoken.

I should now like to turn to the theme of my chapter, Jungian concepts relevant to integration and repair. First, although Ruthie was well defended against the part that had become split off, I also think that she was just as drawn to the pigeons as she was repelled by them. In being drawn to them, I think that she was seeking wholeness. According to Jung, wholeness is a characteristic of the self, and the pressure to become whole is the motivation behind individuation. It is out of my understanding that the self seeks to integrate that I have titled this chapter 'With healing in her wings'.

Second, what was integrated was a self-representation of what I consider to be something like a self object and thus referred to primitive aspects of Ruthie's experience. The image of the pigeons was characterised by wholeness, because they were totally bad. Ruthie was preoccupied by pigeons for a long time and spoke to me of little else, which indicates how much meaning they had for her. The image also included reference to states of projective and introjective identification with a mother who was in a flap and thus referred to states of fusion.

As with self objects, the representation contained enormous potential, which gradually began to unfold. What early on was experienced as chaos and confusion was acted upon by the self and organised into discernible objects and experiences that then developed and became more complex. My understanding and handling of the dreams of differentiation were informed by my understanding of how the self, in the Jungian sense, operates to differentiate and organise. I suppose that one could say that these were unconscious operations, but for a Jungian it is more meaningful to refer to the self.

This brings me to the concept of repair. Within a Jungian framework, 'repair' is seen as making whole. Ruthie's personality was 'repaired' when the split-off part became a deintegrate and experienced by Ruthie as a part of herself. In other words, to use a model I described earlier, the pseudopod got reattached to the amoeba. This is also what is meant by integration in a developed personality, like Ruthie's, in contrast to a small infant, for whom integration would refer to states of at-oneness.

As what the pigeons represented became a deintegration, Ruthie became more open to deintegrative and reintegrative processes. In this the ego is just as important as the self. As Fordham writes, 'the ego contributes and ensures that the dynamic sequences in the self (deintegration and reintegration) do not prove unproductive and circular, but are changed by ego activity, which in turn increases its strength' (Fordham 1994, p. 73). Hence, the treatment could be seen to have facilitated actions of the self that restored the dynamic processes of deintegration and reintegration, thereby enriching Ruthie's ego, her personality and her life.

I should like to make a distinction between 'repair' and 'reparation'. I understand 'reparation' to arise creatively out of guilt, born out of the conflict of opposites in the depressive position. With Ruthie, when feelings of persecution occurred alongside deep remorse and apparent pining in the 'bad' therapist/'good' teacher episode, her internal organisation seemed close to that of the depressive position. It is difficult to say whether reparation was involved. Fordham points out that in infancy the depressive position does not occur 'in a clear-cut form' (Fordham 1995, p. 72), and it is likely that the same applies to adolescence.

Finally, having distinguished deintegration from splitting, I should like briefly to comment upon 'disintegration'. Fordham holds that, in a fundamental sense, the self is indestructible, and he points to the persistence of the individual's uniqueness and continuity, which are expressions of the self. 'Disintegration' refers to the ego. It was Ruthie's ego, not her self, that from time to time disintegrated in the face of overwhelming fear, rage, persecution and confusion.

Note: The title of this chapter is taken from a quote: 'But unto you that fear my name shall the Sun of righteousness arise with healing in his wings; and ye shall go forth, and grow up as calves in the stall' (Malachi iv, 2).

References

Alvarez, A. (1992). *Live Company*. London: Routledge.

Astor, J. (1989). 'The breast as part of the whole: Theoretical considerations concerning whole and part objects'. *Journal of Analytical Psychology*, 34(2).

Bion, W. (1962). *Learning from Experience*. London: Heinemann.

Brazelton, B. (1991). *The Earliest Relationship*. London: Karnac.

Fordham, M. (1976). *The Self and Autism*. London: Heinemann Medical.

———. (1985a). 'Abandonment in infancy'. *Chiron*, 2(1).

———. (1985b). *Explorations into the Self*. London: Academic Press.

———. (1987). 'Action of the self'. In P. Young-Eisendrath and J. A. Hall (eds.), *The Book of the Self*. London and New York: New York University Press.

———. (1989). 'The infant's reach'. *Psychological Perspectives*, 21.

———. (1993). 'Notes for the formation of a model of infant development'. *Journal of Analytical Psychology*, 38(1).

———. (1994). *Children as Individuals*. London: Free Association Books. Revised and amplified edition of the 1969 edition, Hodder & Stoughton.

———. (1995). *Freud, Jung, and Klein: The Fenceless Field*, ed. R. Hobdell. London: Routledge.

Jung, C. G. (1955–6). 'Mysterium Coniunctionis'. *CW 14*.

———. (1959). 'A study in the process of individuation'. *CW 9 ii*.

———. (1917). 'Definitions'. *CW 6*.

Laplanche, J. and Pontalis, J. B. (1973). *The Language of Psycho-Analysis*. London: Hogarth.

Milakovic, I. (1967). 'The hypothesis of a deglutitive (prenatal) stage in libidinal development'. *International Journal of Psycho-Analysis*, 48.

Segal, H. (1979). *Klein*. Glasgow: Collins.

Stern, D. (1985). *The Interpersonal World of the Infant*. New York: Basic Books.

Trevarthen, C. (1980). 'The foundations of intersubjectivity: Development of interpersonal and cooperative understanding in infants'. In D. Olson (ed.), *The Social Foundation of Language and Thought*. New York: Norton.

Trevarthen, C. and Marwick, H. (1986). 'Signs of motivation for speech in infants, and the nature of a mother's support for development of language'. In B. Lindblom and R. Zenerstrom (eds.), *Precursors of Early Speech*. Basingstoke: Macmillan.

Chapter 5

Developmental aspects of trauma and traumatic aspects of development

Introduction: the developmental perspective

From its beginning psychoanalysis has held a developmental view of the mind. Analytical psychologists, on the other hand, have been ambivalent about taking a developmental perspective, for a long time eschewing it as 'reductive'. It was Michael Fordham who was the first Jungian to appreciate that 'if the archetypes are universal they must be demonstrable in childhood' (Fordham 1944, p. 5). Over more than 50 years of clinical experience and observation, he worked at shaping a model that centres on Jung's concept of the self and encompasses early development. This concept of the self, in contrast to the sense of self, is outside direct experience, expressed in individuality, the capacity to adapt and continuity of being (Fordham 1985a). It is the continuity of being, in particular, that makes a developmental approach a study of the self in the Jungian sense of the term.

Fordham postulated a primary self and its paired processes of deintegration and reintegration. He intended deintegration to describe the means by which the infant relates to the environment in an archetypally patterned way. Reintegration accounts for the incorporation of experience into the personality, which, in turn, triggers complexification and further structuring. Failures to reintegrate have an effect on the capacity to deintegrate and hence to develop. Trauma, which is an experience that cannot be assimilated, can thus be seen as a failure of reintegration that impedes further deintegration.

The primary factors determining trauma are the nature of the external event, the nature of the internal world and how the two interact. Trauma is thus subjectively defined, whether the external event is a major disaster, like war, or a more ordinary life event, like the breakdown of a relationship. In what follows I shall be linking archetypally laid-down developments in infancy that have failed to become reintegrated with later events in life that appear quite ordinary but are experienced as traumatic. I shall be drawing on analytic work with a man whose dreams and transference expressed a particular, but not uncommon, inner constellation of problematic object relations associated with a certain developmental period.

In taking a developmental perspective, I am not viewing the earlier happening as the cause of the later one, but rather looking at how the later resonates with

DOI: 10.4324/9781003215639-8

the earlier, intensifying and making more pervasive the effect of it within the personality. Put another way, I do not understand the difficulties within the highly complex adult to be 'really' or 'only' infantile phenomena; however, I do believe that experiences in later life trigger those in infancy and childhood. This can be seen particularly in analysis, which can help the patient with an understanding of these resonances and thereby extend and deepen the sense of self.

Having said this, the role of infancy in later mental life remains controversial (Green and Stern 2001). For those who do take a developmental view in analytic work, their understanding must take into account how infants actually develop. There are no commonly held conclusions about this. However, in the past few decades developmental psychology and, more recently, neurobiology have made significant advances in our understanding, although the implications for analytic theory and practice are still being worked out.

Early surges in development and the contributions of developmental psychology and neuroscience

Fordham most commonly described deintegration and reintegration as they occurred in daily episodes of feeding, bathing and play. Only occasionally did he refer to the archetypally programmed surges of deintegration and reintegration. That deintegration and reintegration occur in this way is clear from developmental psychologists. As Daniel Stern describes this,

> Development occurs in leaps and bounds. . . . During these periods of change, there are quantum leaps in whatever level of organization one wishes to examine, from electroencephalographic recordings to overt behaviour to subjective experience. Between these periods of rapid change are periods of relative quiescence, when the new integrations appear to consolidate.
>
> (Stern 1985, p. 8)

Developmentalists have clarified the endowments and limitations of infant capacities, especially perceptual ones, and have identified waves of development during which the infant constructs qualitatively different senses of self and of other. (In Fordham's model these 'senses' refer to the ego, so that these surges can be viewed as the way the ego emerges out of the primary self.) Firstly the infant senses perceptions and emotions occurring within him, which are probably experienced as 'happening' to him (birth to two months). Then he senses himself and others as being bodily different (two to six months), followed by the sense of himself and others as having different minds and purposes (nine to eighteen months). Lastly, with the capacity to symbolise, the baby can stand aside from himself and see himself not only as a subject, but as an other upon whom he can reflect (eighteen months to two years). These domains of senses of self and relatedness, what might be thought of as qualitatively different consolidations of consciousness, remain once established. However, until they are established, the infant's focus of operations is limited to the domain or domains in which he is or has passed. For instance, a newborn, experiencing and consolidating his direct awareness of his perceptual and emotional aliveness, perceives his mother as being separate, but that is not relevant to him until he enters the next developmental realm of experience.

This chapter will focus on developments that occur at the end of the first year, which produce revolutionary changes. These include what Stern calls the infant's sense of intersubjective self, the emergence of attachment proper (Bowlby 1969), the beginnings of a theory of mind (Bretherton et al. 1981; Bremner 1994) and significant shifts in self-regulating processes in the brain (Schore 1996). To this I would add a new level of awareness of the difference in status between self and other, that is, of the generational difference between self and parent.

In order to appreciate the vastly complicated nature of these changes, one needs to know something about what has gone on before. I shall briefly summarise some of the changes that are relevant to my subject.

Trevarthen has researched the foundations of language development, describing periods of change at two to six months and at ten to twelve months, which he terms the periods of primary and secondary intersubjectivity. During the first period, consequent to significant physiological, motor and neurological changes, the infant is drawn to his mother's face in a new way, concentrating on it, initially, with an awestruck expression. These intense and emotionally rich face-to-face engagements lead to carefully synchronised proto-conversations in which the baby takes the lead. The mother naturally softens her voice by lifting the pitch and making it slightly breathy, a universal response called 'intuitive motherese', her vocalisations alternating in a slow adagio with the baby's utterance of an undulating 'a-ghu'. These behaviours are hardwired, universal and innate, that is, archetypal. According to Trevarthen, the relationship between mother and baby during this period is marked by companionship (Trevarthen 1988). In other words, there is a quality of the relationship in which there is an assumed equality of status between the partners. This is because the mother's status as a 'superior' is not relevant to the infant's domain of experience; what is relevant is her awesome, fascinating, numinous otherness.

During secondary intersubjectivity this changes markedly. By the end of the tenth month the baby begins to regard the mother in a new way, and the mother senses this and changes her responses to him. At this point, and not before, the baby lets the mother take the lead, and she begins to teach and to become a socialising agent. 'Before the change, the infant has no interest, no comprehension of what is wanted' (Trevarthen 1988, p. 193). However with the surge of development at the end of the first year, the baby begins to anticipate his mother's motivations and 'to take a gesture and a spoken message as an instruction' (ibid., p. 193). For instance, if a mother points to something, a very young baby will look at her hand, while an older baby will follow the direction of the point, aware that the mother is making a gesture that conveys her intention that he looks at something. The infant's capacity to glean that the mother has an intention enables cooperation between them. This leads to new developments in play, in which there is a sharing of objects and through which the mother will introduce cultural elements, for instance naming toys as she and the baby play with them. Hardwired patterns of communicating that have existed prior to this, such as 'intuitive motherese', give way to expressions shaped by culture, such as the mother reinforcing certain babblings to 'teach' her child the phonemes of the mother tongue used in that particular family.

Thus an important element of the period of secondary intersubjectivity is the baby's dawning awareness that behind his companion's face is a mind with intentions, thoughts and aims that are different from his. The baby's newly developed capacity for what will become a 'theory of mind' combines with other developments, such as establishing an internal 'schema, a mental image of the mother, especially her face' (Schore 1996, p. 68), meaning that he becomes more sensitive to the subtlety of his mother's expressions. Accompanying the increased awareness of others is increased self-awareness. Trevarthen notes that by ten to twelve months the baby shows gender and age awareness (Trevarthen and Marwick 1986), so that the baby can recognise that he is like some who are his age and gender and unlike others who are not. At this point status becomes relevant to the infant.

Trevarthen points out the heightened, positive energy that accompanies the infant's growing sense of autonomy. He calls this *prestance*, from the French for having a 'commanding deportment', a subjective state that analysts might view as omnipotence. Schore, a psychoanalyst who also works within the field of psychoneurobiology, is particularly interested in this period because it is when the infant shifts from being dependent on the mother for the regulation of his internal states to beginning to acquire the capacity for emotional self-regulation. The 'highs' that are notable during this period need to be self-regulated by 'lows' that balance them. Schore states that shame, which is known as 'the primary social emotion' and which emerges later in this period at 14 to 16 months, plays a role in this: 'Shame, a specific inhibitor of the activated ongoing affects of interest-excitement and enjoyment-joy, uniquely reduces self-exposure or exploration powered by these positive affects' (Schore 1996, p. 69).

The experiments on which these discoveries are based have their limitations; for instance, they focus on particular areas to be tested, leaving out others, and many are carried out only when the baby is in a state of alert inactivity. The results, valuable as they can appear to be, must also be seen as having limitations, so that one must not assume that 'companion' or later 'teacher' are the only ways to describe the mother's relationship to her baby. Having said this, I think psychoanalytic infant observation supports the hypothesis that there are vast changes at the end of the first year, when, in my view, the baby begins to perceive differences in status between himself and his mother in a new way. One of the most common expressions of this change is when the mother starts telling the baby 'No'. It will have been experienced all along, for instance, in the implied 'No' of an interrupted feed and various stages of weaning, to which a baby can have very strong reactions. However, it is a very different experience for the infant when he becomes aware that his mother intends to oppose him, and to take this in he will repeatedly test her during toddlerhood to discover whether she means 'No' when she says it. This represents the emergence of a more complex, qualitatively different way of being, perceiving and relating.

An infant's experience of being told 'No'

In the following two excerpts from an infant observation, I shall contrast subtle changes in the way a baby girl reacted to an explicit 'No'. The first excerpt is at nine and a half months, just on the cusp of the vast changes that occur at the end of the first year. Baby Anna was interested in a set of keys, and the mother dropped them on the floor in order to show the observer how Anna could crawl. Anna did just that, clutching the keys when she reached them.

> With the keys in her grasp Anna shifted her weight back and by trial and error pulled one leg under her so that she could sit back. She immediately put the keys in her mouth after looking at them briefly. She took them out of her mouth, waved her arms up and down and bounced herself vigorously on her seat, banged the keys on the floor and put them back in her mouth. The mother said 'No' firmly, but Anna just looked at her with them in her mouth; the mother again said 'No' and gently and firmly pulled them away from her mouth. Anna did not protest but waved her arms up and down, bounced and put the keys back in her mouth, chewing and sucking them. Again the mother took them out and again after waving her arms and bouncing, Anna put them back.

In the second observation, just two weeks later, the mother once again set Anna on the floor.

> After sitting still for a few moments Anna set off to crawl to the back of the room but the mother quickly called out 'No' firmly, and indicated the other direction, which was towards Anna's area, her bookcase, toys, etc. Anna hesitated, looking at her mother, before starting again in the 'wrong' direction, and the mother again said 'No' and talked to her about why she had to go in the other direction. Anna hesitated again, then sat looking at the area just around her. She 'bounced' a bit, kicked and stretched her legs and waved her arms, touched the floor with both arms/hands once or twice, then without looking at her mother set off in the 'right' direction.
>
> Anna came towards me on the settee, looked up and sat nearby. Her mother gave her a rag doll baby. Anna took it and *threw it away* – about a foot away from her and within reach. The mother gave it back, and she *threw it away again*, reached forward to pick it up again and *threw it away again*. The mother gave it back and pressed it against Anna's chest as though suggesting that Anna should hug it. Anna tossed it up in the air lightly, looked at it

on the floor, picked it up and banged it on the floor once or twice, felt it and squeezed it, threw it away and picked it up again. But she would not hold it close. [My emphases]

In the first observation Anna seemed unaware of what her mother meant when she said 'No', even though the mother demonstrated by taking the keys out of her mouth. In the second Anna seemed to know her mother had an intention when she said 'No' and discovered by trial and error that her mother intended to prevent Anna from going in the direction she wanted to go. In response, Anna got cross.

I should now like to turn to Barnaby, who was six when he was referred because of behaviour problems. His difficulties started when his little sister was born, when he was one and a half years old. Being told 'No' made Barnaby not just cross but enraged. In contrast to Baby Anna, who expressed her crossness directly, Barnaby usually conveyed his anger by having the person who told him 'No' feel furious. I was to experience this on several occasions over the 12 brief therapy sessions I had with him, sometimes on his own and sometimes with other members of his family. Typically Barnaby would do something he knew I did not allow, like investigating the contents of my desk drawers. Then he would ignore my asking him not to do this, and I would feel angry, understanding this to be his anger. However, on two occasions, something else happened as well.

The first of these two sessions included his mother. He provocatively asked her if he could have a Happy Meal from McDonald's, something that for dietary reasons he knew would be refused. His response to his mother giving him a mild, almost kindly 'No' was dramatic. He slumped over the picture he had drawn, would not answer his mother's or my expressions of interest in him, and slipped down onto the floor and curled up in a ball. A moment later he slid under my chair. I spoke to him, saying when Mummy said 'No' it hurt him deeply and made him feel he was no good and just bad. I asked about his picture, which had disappeared with him, and a moment later a wadded-up ball flew across the room. I said he seemed to feel like rubbish when Mummy said 'No'. As we had previously discussed how his behaviour had changed at the time of his sister's birth, I linked his feeling of worthlessness to her arrival and his wondering why his parents wanted another baby when he was their baby.

Barnaby's behaviour was melodramatic, but I think there was something genuine in what Barnaby was enacting of his low self-esteem. It reappeared several months later, when Barnaby provoked me to say 'No'. After he had been given his own box of toys, he opened a toy cupboard and proceeded to empty what was visible onto the floor. When he ignored my request not to do this, I became firm, and he stopped. Barnaby then became withdrawn and sat at a small table and quietly drew two pictures. The first was of a large head with a large, long body, and the second was of a head only.

While he was drawing, I acknowledged that I had had to say 'No' and wondered how it made him feel. When he finished the pictures, he pushed himself away from the table, eyes cast downward and looking despondent. I asked who the pictures were of, and Barnaby pointed to the one with the long body and said it was Father Christmas [it was July]. There was a pause and I pointed out that the other was of a head but no body; it was a no-body. I said the Father Christmas was me because both Father Christmas and I had lots of toys for children, while the no-body was himself, who felt like a no-body when I told him 'No', that he could not take the toys out of the cupboard.

Barnaby makes it clear that being told 'No' can be not only infuriating but also painfully and despairingly humiliating. I have understood this to be his continuing struggle with his awareness of the fact that he and his parents, along with his teachers and therapist, live on different sides of a generational divide, a difference fundamentally marked by status, with expanding ripples of implications, such as his parents' sexuality and their capacity to create new life.

So far in this chapter I have described how at the end of the first year the baby moves towards a new awareness of the difference in status between self and other, about which there may be negative feelings, and illustrated this with Baby Anna. I then described Barnaby's reaction to the same realisation, pointing out not only feelings of anger, shared to some extent by Anna, but also feelings of shame, worthlessness and despair. I linked these feelings to what was for him the traumatic birth of his little sister, which I see as epitomising the difference in status between him and his parents.

Clinical work with an adult

I should now like to look more closely at trauma in my work with a depressed man, whom I shall call Charles, who was in his late thirties when he came for treatment. I shall try to show how Charles expressed, in dreams and in his transference to me, the dilemma that can accompany changes at the end of the first year, when a 'companion' becomes a 'socializing agent'. If the loss that is part of this change cannot be processed, then grief becomes grievance as one struggles with what are experienced as persecutory 'superior' objects.

It was loss that brought Charles into his first treatment, following the breakdown of a long-standing relationship. This occurred about the same time that his freelance work dried up, leaving him dependent on an unsatisfying part-time job in a large organisation. He saw a psychotherapist weekly for several months but stopped going following the first long summer holiday, during which the therapist had a new baby. About that time he became involved in a new relationship with a woman, Donna, falling into debt by taking her out to expensive places in order to impress her. They had started to live together in a more modest lifestyle, but by the time I first saw him this relationship was also failing. He acknowledged that Donna was disappointing when he compared her to the girlfriend who had left him. I had the clear impression that he felt he wanted to get out of the relationship because Donna was not quite good enough.

Charles and I concluded that as the non-intensive therapy had not worked, it made sense for him to have four-times-weekly treatment. He did not want to start until he had settled some matters, including separating from Donna and moving back into his own flat. When he did begin analysis, he surprised me by describing the breakup as if Donna had left him because he was not good enough. In particular, it was because of what he called his 'naivete', by which he seemed to mean a lack of mental manliness. He grieved for Donna for a long time in his analysis, but the grief was more like a stuck record than a process that developed and then allowed him to move on.

By his own account, Charles had been traumatised when his parents' marriage broke down when he was nine. Before this happened, his parents had been socially prominent, frequently leaving the children in the care of their nanny. They held high ambitions for Charles, the only son in the family, and had chosen a career for him. When they separated and the father went to live on the Continent, the mother and children were left in considerably reduced circumstances. Despite this, Charles started having private tuition to set him off in his career. Coming to see me sometimes reminded Charles of going to these lessons. It was, he explained, because my consulting room is close to where he went to see one of these teachers. Thinking of his inner situation, I understood him to be saying that coming to see me after the loss of Donna placed him in the same internal neighbourhood where he found himself after the loss of his father, left with the pain of his absence, resentful of the presence of a 'teacher' who limited and made demands upon him. This inner situation was conveyed in a dream he had early in the analysis:

> I'm walking along a high street with my mother and sisters, carrying a heavy burden. I asked them if we can take public transport or a car because the burden is so heavy. They wouldn't answer; they kind of teased me with not telling. I got angry and set the burden down and crossed the street, and as I was doing this, a man about 40–50 yards away threw a stone – a pebble – which hit me in the face. I got angry and went over to the man and said, 'If you're going to throw stones, don't hit people'.

Here I should like to focus on how Charles's loss of Donna resonated with the earlier crisis of the breakup of the parental relationship and, with it, family life. The burden he carried was experienced as the weight of his loss after his father left home. The help he asked for, I think, was having a family, complete with father, which Charles imagined to be the vehicle for his development, that is, growing up and feeling like a man. When his request for help was ignored, Charles got angry and set down the burden, as if he was unprepared to struggle with the pain of his loss.

Charles crossed the street to another internal position, where he became aware of a man who had projected something at him. I think this refers to Charles's sense of the ambitions his father had projected onto him and hence to the tutors to whom

Charles was compelled to go. It was as if the absence of a valued father became the presence of a rather persecutory teacher father. In the dream this figure wore thick glasses, like, as Charles explained, Mr Magoo in the comic – like, in fact, Charles, who wore similar glasses and felt himself to be similarly nearsighted or, as he called it, naive. Here we have the image of a naive, that is, baby-like, son mixed up with that of a teacher-father. I think this indicated that internally Charles had not differentiated his inferior, filial status from his father's superior paternal status.

Here I should like to recall what Trevarthen tells us about the period at the end of the first year, when the primacy of the baby's view of the mother as companion is lost to a more complex view of her as teacher and socialising agent. Charles's analysis indicated that he was struggling with just this adjustment and the loss it entailed. As this developed, his material took on Oedipal dimensions.

Charles continued to be full of grief over the loss of Donna, to whom he often referred as 'a kind of angel'. Six months after the Mr Magoo dream, over a weekend break, he had the following dream, in which, alongside his grieving, lay deep grievances.

> I was in a village by the sea, a village I've dreamt about before. The village is on a peninsula, by a hill and the sea. I am walking along with Tom, Donna's current boyfriend, whom I'm sure Donna was seeing before our relationship ended. Tom and I happen to look into a pub we pass. It reminds me of the pub in Islington where Donna used to meet with her friends, at the Angel. Inside the pub, Donna, who has her back to us, is talking with another man in an intimate way, and I know she is having a relationship with him. Donna is wearing glasses with gold wire rims. I'm so upset with Donna that I rush away from the pub, through King's Cross, and off in the direction where I live.

The setting of the dream was a familiar place, what I understand to be his traumatised internal world. However, the location for what was happening was on a peninsula, as if by this point in his analysis the feelings that had been split off were experienced as having some connection with the mainland of Charles's personality.

The dream can be seen to be about Charles's growing emotional awareness of the difference between himself and his parents. From this perspective it is significant that the figures referring to the internal mother and father each had dual aspects. The dual aspect of the mother was her ideal nature and her duplicity; she appeared to be an angel, while inside her angel mind she was having thoughts about another. Here was Charles's theory of mind in operation. The father had two aspects too. He was both a familiar companion, Tom, who accompanied Charles's awareness of his internal mother's duplicity, and also a rival, that is, the one with whom Charles feared Donna had a liaison and who provided the identity for the stranger in the dream who was having the intimate exchange with the mother. Equally important, the figures in the dream depicting the internal parents – Charles's superiors – were in external life his peers.

Despite the continued blur of generational boundaries, a distinction was beginning to be drawn between relationships in which there was no difference in status between self and other, and relationships in which this difference was of utmost importance. However, the dream depicted that this development was undermined. What Charles did see of the generational divide was unbearably painful, and this pain was masked by anger and omnipotence: the King's Cross, and it seemed a very cross, belittled king who returned to 'where he lives' in his internally fortified castle.

Spectacles featured in both dreams, Mr Magoo's in the first and the gold-rimmed glasses Donna was wearing in the second. I think both refer to Charles's theory of mind about his own and his object's insight and reflective capacities, and how their two minds related. There was little sense of sharing between them, in part because there was so much distance between them. Charles sensed his own mind to be diminished (short-sighted), while his object's was idealised (gold-rimmed). There was a transference link here as Charles openly confessed to feeling 'in awe' of the way he felt my mind worked.

Looking at a session in detail reveals more about Charles's theory of his object's mind. Charles occasionally referred to a male friend with whom he had an ambivalent relationship, and once, when they fell out, he had felt deeply upset. We discussed this over a number of sessions one week, and then the next, after a weekend break, the subject suddenly changed to what had been happening at work. One of his most important responsibilities had been shared with a colleague. However, Charles had recently been asked by his manager to undertake this work on his own. Charles felt 'paranoid', as he put it, that this would result in his being seen to be a fraud.

Just before the next session the following day and in anticipation of his arrival, I found myself thinking about Charles and feeling resentful because of how and what Charles paid me, which I need to explain. Charles could not afford to have private intensive treatment, and I was seeing him under the auspices of the C. G. Jung Clinic, which is a charitable clinic set up for those who need analysis but cannot afford it. The Clinic arrangement is that the analyst sets the fee with the patient, which due to Charles's circumstances was the minimum fee. The fees are then paid via the analyst, who passes them on to the Clinic. Ordinarily I would have billed Charles at the end of each month, but, despite the low fees, he wanted to pay at the end of each session in order to avoid getting into debt, as he had done when he started to see Donna. There was something of a ritual to the way he paid me on his way out of each session. He would get up from the couch, step toward me, then pause and dig deep into his pockets and pull out pound coins. Standing so close to a man of over six feet, I often felt dwarfed.

That morning I found myself feeling belittled by his height, and, while dwelling on that, it suddenly occurred to me I was being paid 'pocket money' for my professional efforts! In retaliation I wanted to raise his fees, remind him that I did not get paid anything for seeing him and demand that he pay monthly by cheque or banker's order. In short, I felt furious and retaliatory at what I experienced as Charles's diminishment, undervaluation and humiliation of me.

When he arrived he said that he had been so engrossed in a mental argument with his colleagues that he had missed my street. He was furious that the people who planned the change at work earned twice as much as he and that they wanted him to do this work all on his own. He wanted to leave his job; in fact, he thought he needed to leave. I mentally noted that if he did leave his work, he would also have to leave his analysis. He went on about how impossible the job would be single-handed and was clearly intensely anxious and struggling against despair.

I commented that he seemed to be dreading what he felt sure was going be a failure and how he felt singled out, as he may have done as the only son in the family, who was expected to achieve what seemed like impossibly high demands from his parents who gave him so little emotional support. He said he did indeed feel singled out, adding that he felt he would be watched. I said that he seemed to feel that his manager would be looking out for his inadequacies. Drawing on my transference experiences just before the session, I added how he felt frighteningly and humiliatingly small in comparison to his manager, while at the same time enraged that he was being undervalued by him. This seemed to settle Charles somewhat. In a less angry tone of voice he said he thought what might happen would be that he would stay at his job but become cynical and not take his work personally. I privately noted he had stepped back from his threat to leave and said out loud that cynicism would protect him from caring about what his managers thought of him.

He said he admired people who make something out of nothing, which he could not do. Some were given a lot. People had told him he was gifted and had been given a lot, and he could see that he just could not use these gifts. I sensed that the matter had shifted more into the transference and said that he felt I was giving him a lot because he was coming four times a week and under a special arrangement. I added that he appreciated this, especially when he experienced me as understanding how he felt, so he wanted me to know that he was aware that he was not using what was available to him in his analysis (which I too felt was the case). I continued that the reason for this was because he could not help feeling resentful that I seemed to have so much, like the managers who earned twice as much as he. In a tone of self-flagellation he answered that he turned this resentment against himself. I answered that when I just referred to how much he felt I had, he experienced this as me saying how much I felt I had. This made him angry because he felt I was flaunting what I had, but he took his anger out on himself rather than me.

Following this, toward the end of the session, he talked about another friend, Edward, describing their relationship as one of unequal dependency. In this he, Charles, was dependent on Edward, but Edward could not see anyone's wishes other than his own. Edward had lots of money but did not even repay Charles what Charles had loaned him. I commented that Charles felt he was in a similar relationship with me. Not only did he feel that I was more concerned with myself and my own needs, but also that I did not appreciate his good feelings toward me, like admiration, which from time to time he expressed. He felt I used his valuing of me mainly to make myself feel better about myself rather than fonder of him, and this made him feel exploited. I suggested that he might feel particularly sensitive to such feelings as the weekend was coming up.

This session contained the theme evident from early in Charles's analysis: grief over the loss of someone (the friend with whom he fell out), followed by grievance against persecutors associated with superiority and authority (his managers). However, in the course of the analysis there had been developments on this theme, such as a growing range of feelings about a more clearly delineated status-differential between Charles and his parental objects. These feelings included resentment, rage, envy and the pain of not having his good and idealising feelings reciprocated because his object was felt to be self-centred and narcissistic. In relation to his internal 'superiors' Charles felt not only naïve but humiliatingly inadequate, with persecutory fears that these inadequacies would be seen and he would be unmasked as a sham. This is more complex than what Barnaby described as being a 'no-body'; it is a no-body pretending to be a somebody and caught out at wishing to be so. It is a double shame.

Discussion

Charles's intense ambivalence towards his objects and the way they had become split into 'bad' and 'good' are the most noticeable aspects of his personality. The conflict between idealised good objects and persecutory bad objects is at the core of what Klein calls the depressive position.[1,2] This is a process beginning in infancy that can lead to a more realistic awareness and appreciation of other and self, a process that recurs throughout life (Klein 1935). Jung, too, referred to an on-going process involving the conflict of opposites which can lead to a more realistic sense of oneself and the other: individuation. Michael Fordham used Klein's concept, which applies to a process of mourning in infancy, to extend Jung's idea of individuation into babyhood, thereby integrating the depressive position into a Jungian concept of development that covers the life span.

Moving on from Fordham and combining analytic observation with contributions from developmentalists and neurobiology, I consider that there is another dimension to mourning in infancy which is an inherent part of early development. I consider that loss is involved in the shift from 'companion' to 'teacher'. Here I am using the two roles in a diagrammatic way to describe how one generalised way of relating can be experienced as lost to another in the course of development.

What I have in mind is related to, but not the same as, the loss in infancy with which Kleinians are concerned. Margot Waddell captures the nature of the loss to which I refer when she describes it as a 'nostalgia for a state of being which can never be "home" in quite the same way again' (Waddell 1998, p. 57). Ron Britton refers to this loss as that of an 'idea of a relationship' (Britton et al. 1989). That to which both are referring is the infant's 'idea', held separate from affectively quite different 'ideas', that he and his mother have an exclusive, mutually significant relationship which has an assumed primacy over all other relationships. Although this 'idea of a relationship' is not the same as Trevarthen's notion of early companionship, it does seem very similar, especially as Trevarthen also referred to this as being 'best friends'.

Britton and Waddell link the loss they describe to processes involved in the depressive position. Here the loss is the consequence of destructiveness and the developmental move from part to whole objects. In contrast, I associate the loss not only to the struggle to integrate affectively charged perceptions and experiences held, up until that point, in separate coexistence. I also associate it with the struggle to integrate new emotionally laden perceptions and experiences, when the mother starts to behave differently in archetypal response to her changing baby, and with how the new way of being threatens the loss of the old. These conceptually different losses may be linked if one considers that an infant may regard the changes in his mother as she subtly shifts from 'companion' to 'socializing agent' as her changing from being a good to a bad object. This is what seemed to be happening with Charles, whose mind shifted between grief and grievance.

Compounding factors may intensify the feelings. As the baby becomes more aware of his own intersubjectivity with another, he becomes increasingly aware of the intersubjectivity between others. This becomes the basis of the Oedipal conflict, which Klein emphasises 'develops hand-in-hand with the developments that make up the depressive position' (Britton et al. 1989, p. 84).

According to Klein, the struggle between loving and hating can arouse concern for the object and guilt at the destruction done by hate. Out of this arises the wish to repair. The infant's reparation to the mother helps to restore his sense of his own goodness, and this brings mourning to a close. With reparation in mind, I am returning to the observation of Baby Anna, which left her feeling cross and banging and throwing the doll her mother had given her. What happened next was that the mother gave Anna another doll, which Anna accepted and held. The mother seemed to know that Anna was upset with her and that she (the mother) needed to do something to repair matters. Here the mother seemed to be helping Anna with the 'idea' of reparation by being capable of being repaired.

The part Anna's mother took in this is an example of how Allan Schore regards reparation in infancy. In contrast to Klein, he emphasises the importance of the mother's reparative role rather than the infant's and holds the position that the mother's restoration of good feeling is necessary to the baby's development:

> Although re-regulating repair transactions begin in the first year, they are essential to emotional development in the second. Under the aegis of a caregiver who is sensitive and cooperative in this reparative process, the infant develops an internal representation of him/herself as effective, of his/her interactions as positive and reparable, and of the caregiver as reliable. . . . [They] permit the infant to develop the capacity for anticipation of relief and a sense of his/her own efficacy.
>
> The child's experiencing of an affect and the caregiver's response to this particular affect are internalized as an affect-regulating, symbolic (as opposed to earlier presymbolic) interactive representation.
>
> (Schore 1996, p. 71)

In the observation the mother was helping Anna's brain to self-regulate emotions by modifying a drop from 'high' – Anna's heightened sense of can-do – to 'low'. To repeat what was said at the beginning of the chapter, later on in the same developmental shift, the drop is accompanied by shame, a specific inhibitor of the 'highs'. Anna's mother, through her act of repair, can be seen to be offering a way for Anna to 'come down' softly that anticipates helping Anna manage later shame without too much humiliation. According to Schore, ordinary play such as this can establish lasting bridges both in the parent-child relationship and in the brain.

Barnaby and Charles did not seem to have internalised in a secure way this reparative link between companionable moments and brushes with a thwarting authority.[3] This left them vulnerable to overwhelming feelings of humiliation and affected their confidence in their own capacity for reparation, both of which inter- fered with recovering from the loss of their good objects. Britton links the inabil- ity to give up, or lose, the 'idea' of this very early relationship with 'the failure to establish a securely based good maternal object before encountering the vicissi- tudes of the Oedipus complex' (Britton et al. 1989, p. 94). When Barnaby was an infant his mother was depressed, and Charles's material indicated that his internal maternal object was narcissistic, a characteristic consistent with the picture he drew of his mother when he told me about his contact with her during the course of his analysis.

Both Barnaby and Charles experienced my analytic understanding as having reparative aspects. To show this in relation to Barnaby I shall return to what hap- pened after we had talked about his picture of the 'no-body'. He then drew a picture of me smiling, then a man with large feet, who he said was 'Daddy'. I told him that when he felt I was interested in the way he felt about my saying 'No', he felt as big and important as Daddy. This was followed soon after by Barnaby say- ing in a soft but very determined voice that he wanted to go to the lavatory. After only a moment he returned, lively and pleased with himself, with a toy from the waiting room. He opened the toy cupboard door and placed it with the set to which it belonged that he had discovered during his ransacking. The completeness of the set had been restored and a part reunited with the whole, although it was done in a spirit of making a power play; he had tricked me into believing that he was going to the lavatory when he intended to do something else. My comments had restored not only our good relationship and his esteem, but also his self-inflation.

Charles, like Barnaby, struggled against feelings of belittlement and shame, especially in the session I detailed, and my understanding of this helped to restore his self-esteem and re-establish a good relationship between us. As with Barnaby, the effect was not simply benign. It led onto an opening up of various aspects of what had been split off, what might be described as a persecutory inner relation- ship between humiliating insignificance and a rather grandiose superiority. Both were traits of Charles. His humiliation was clear in the session I detailed, and his inflated superiority was evident from early on, for instance, in his attitude of being too good for Donna. Although my understanding in the session went somewhere towards restoring a good internal relationship, as we have seen, Charles would not make fuller use of it because my having 'something' aroused his resentment and envy. Acknowledging this led to thoughts and feelings he had about being in a relationship of dependency with a narcissistic other who provoked resentment and envy. This object relationship seemed to be a vicious circle, but over time it was modified as Charles experienced my motives as benign rather than self-serving.

Klein has pointed out the important role of guilt in the achievement of the depressive position, and Schore has discovered the role of shame in the development of the infant's frontal cortex, which fundamentally influences the way the baby will experience himself and others. I have linked these two by bringing them together as aspects of a complex surge of deintegration at the end of the first year. It is then that the infant's dawning awareness of his status, like that of his newly acquired upright stature, is less than that of his parents. There is a sense of the loss of an earlier relationship in which these matters are irrelevant and so seemed not to exist. The loss fuels the intensification of ambivalence that can lead to guilt. Parallel to this, the baby begins to experience shame as his sense of his own 'size' oscillates like that of Alice in Wonderland, as does his sense of importance in the eyes of others.

If leading up to this the baby has not been supported by the sense of well-being that comes from an adequately sensitive and attuned 'companion', then he may not be able to bear the loss of an assumed 'equal' relationship, nor to work out a new relationship in which differences in status between self and other can be tolerated. The effect is considerable. There is a lasting sense of overwhelming shame and humiliation, which stands in the way of accepting the reality of the generational gap between self and parent and impairs the capacity for empathy, concern and self-reflection (Britton et al. 1989; Schore 1996). There are also lasting difficulties with the achievement of the depressive position and therefore with individuation.

I have drawn attention to clinical phenomena I believe are linked to developmental processes at the end of the first year. My understanding of the material draws upon psychoanalytic concepts, yet it differs in that I see the developmentally linked connections between such clinically diverse phenomena as the patient's grievance about my setting holiday dates independently of the patient, sensitivity to withholding information about my personal life in contrast to the patient's revelation of intimacies and jealousy when I am perceived as being with others. What each has in common is a heightened sensitivity not just to differences between patient and analyst, but to the patient's perception of differences in their status.

Conclusion

In this paper I have tried to show how emotional experiences that are the stuff of trauma are inherent in healthy development. Failure to reintegrate them means that they can serve as a resonating board for difficulties in later life, adding to their traumatic impact.[4]

Trauma involves a wound to both the self and the sense of self, and both must be addressed in treatment. The wound to the ego means the sense of oneself is susceptible to unbearably low esteem and to omnipotence that can mask not only helplessness but also humiliation, as clinical material with Barnaby and Charles illustrates. Helping the patient manage feelings of shame is essential to further development. The wound to the self, in contrast to the sense of self, is an impairment of reintegration, resulting in part of the self being split off from the personality, affecting further deintegration and therefore impeding the individuation process.

I have also tried to convey that development entails complexity; what for the infant was being cross, for the boy was being furious and humiliated, and for the man, furious, envious and doubly shamed. What they have in common are certain experiences arising out of a shared, archetypally shaped unfolding that they gather into themselves in their individual ways.

Notes

1 My definition of trauma is based on Freud's, whereby trauma is not viewed by objective standards such as childhood sexual abuse. Rather it is understood to be defined subjectively according to the individual's 'incapacity to respond adequately to [the intensity of an event], and by the upheaval and long lasting effects that it brings about in the psychical condition' (Laplanche and Pontalis 1973, p. 465).

2 Developmentalists disagree with Klein about early splitting, whereby isolating 'bad' from 'good' feelings is considered one of the earliest defences. Stern and Gergely conclude that the very young infant does not have the developmental capacity to split in this way (Stern 1985; Gergely 1991). However, they describe how feelings serve as invariants that bind experiences together into representations. This process can be seen to provide the structuring for the internal grouping of 'good 'and 'bad' experiences which Fordham considered to be part of normal development. Post-Kleinians call this 'normal splitting', whereas Fordham reserved 'splitting' for pathological states (Fordham 1985a).

   Klein dates the depressive position at six months, and Fordham seems reluctant to note that it was not evidenced in the observations he discusses. However, he describes aspects of the depressive position in a 13-month-old baby, and I have done the same using an observation of a similarly aged infant (Fordham 1985b; Urban 1996). My view is that the processes associated with the depressive position arise out of the surge of deintegration at the end of the first year.

3 It should also be noted that Anna was only entering into the deintegrative surge that begins at the end of the first year and continues, with changes building on one another, to the middle of the second. In relation to being told 'No', Schore writes: 'At 10 months, 90% of maternal behavior consists of affection, play and caregiving. The mother of the 12- to 17-month old toddler expresses a prohibition on the average every 9 minutes' (Schore 1996, p. 68).

4 Donald Kalsched describes how self-care defences can build up around trauma. Fordham refers to these entrenched, pervasive and 'rota!' defences as defences of the self (Fordham 1974). They are commonly linked to borderline psychotic phenomena, which is well-exemplified in Kalsched's paper.

   I consider that these defences are not established until after a period of development at the end of the first year. However, I believe there is an important link between this period, when the beginnings of what will become shame begin to emerge, and the development of defences of the self. Defences of the self serve to protect a vulnerable and unstable sense of self from overwhelming shame and the threat to an individual's sense of agency, which is a fundamental expression of the self. Interestingly, Steiner and Schore associate overwhelming shame with borderline personalities (Steiner 2001; Schore 2002).

References

Bowlby, J. (1969). *Attachment and Loss I*. London: Hogarth.
Bremner, J. (1994). *Infancy*. Oxford: Blackwell.
Bretherton, I., McNew, S. and Beeghley-Srnith, M. (1981). 'Early person knowledge as expressed in gestural and verbal communication: When do infants acquire a "theory of mind" '. In M. E. Lamb and L. R. Sherrod (eds.), *Infant Social Regulation*. Hillsdale, NJ: Erlbaum.
Britton, R., Feldman, M. and O'Shaughnessy, E. (1989). *The Oedipus Complex Today*. London: Karnac.
Fordham, M. (1944). *The Life of Childhood*. London: Kegan Paul, Trench, Trubner.
———. (1974). 'Defences of the self'. *Analytical Psychology*, 19 (2): 192–199.
———. (1985a). *Explorations into the Self*. London: The Analytic Press.
———. (1985b). 'Abandonment in infancy'. In Corina Peterson (ed.), *Chiron: A Review of Jungian Analysis*. Wilmette, IL: Chiron, 1–23.
Gergely, G. (1991). 'Developmental reconstructions: Infancy from the point of view of psychoanalysis and developmental psychology'. *Psychoanalysis and Contemporary Thought*, 14: 3–55.
Green, A. and Stern, D. (2001). *Clinical and Observational Psychoanalytic Research: Roots of a Controversy*, eds. Joseph Sandler and Rosemary Davies. London: Karnac.
Klein, M. (1935). 'A contribution to the psychogenesis of manic-depressive states'. In *The Writings of Melanie Klein*, Vol. I. London: Hogarth.
Laplanche and Pontalis. (1973). *The Language of Psychoanalysis*. London: W.W. Norton.
Schore, A. (1996). 'The experience-dependent maturation of a regulatory system in the orbital pre-frontal cortex and the origin of developmental psychopathology'. *Development and Psychopathology*, 8: 59–87.
———. (2002). 'Clinical implications of a psychoneurobiological model of projective identification'. In Shelley Alhanati (ed.), *Primitive Mental States, Vol. 2*. London: Karnac.
Steiner, J. (2001). 'Terror, trauma, revenge and repair: Reactions to 11 September 2001 and its aftermath'. Conference presented by The Psychoanalysis Unit, University College London, London: 14 & 15 December 2001.
Stern, D. (1985). *The Interpersonal World of the Infant*. New York: Basic Books.
Trevarthen, C. (1988). 'Sharing makes sense: Intersubjectivity and the making of an infant's meaning'. In R. Steele and T. Treadgold (eds.), *Language Topics*. Amsterdam: John Benjarnins.
Trevarthen, C. and Marwick, H. (1986). 'Signs of motivation for speech in infants, and the nature of a mother's support for development of language'. In B. Lindblom and R. Zetterstrom (eds.), *Precursors of Early Speech*. Basingstoke, Hants: Macmillan.
Urban, E. (1996). 'With healing in her wings . . .'. *Journal of Analytical Psychology*, 22(1).
Waddell, M. (1998). *Inside Lives: Psychoanalysis and the Development of the Personality*. London: Duckworth.

Part III

Extensions

Chapter 6

Fordham, Jung and the self

A re-examination of Fordham's contribution to Jung's conceptualisation of the self

Introduction

This chapter is about Fordham's contribution to Jung's studies on the self. He was well aware that the self is a 'special case' because the subject studying is also the object studied and, moreover, that the observing ego is only a part of the total subject of investigation: 'a concept of the totality is particularly difficult to construct', he noted; 'Indeed it is impossible' (Fordham 1985, p. 21).

Any study of the self presents fundamental dilemmas. In philosophy the self is included under the 'complementarity principle'. Here Heisenberg's uncertainty principle is extended beyond quantum physics to encompass philosophical situations involving properties that appear as particular pairs of opposites, termed canonical conjugates. 'Heisenberg deduced that when this relationship [of canonical conjugates] holds, . . . the more determinate or 'sharp' the value of one of the quantities, the less determinate (or more 'unsharp') its value for the other quantity' (Bullock and Trombley 2000, p. 893). In Michael Frayn's play *Copenhagen*, the character Heisenberg discusses the 'application of complementarity' to the self:

> Heisenberg [to Bohr] . . . Exactly where you go as you ramble around is of course completely determined by your genes and the various physical forces acting upon you. But it's also completely determined by your own entirely inscrutable whims from one moment to the next. So we can't completely understand your behavior without seeing it both ways at once, and that's impossible. Which means that your extraordinary peregrinations are not fully objective aspects of the universe. They exist only partially . . . as our minds shift endlessly back and forth between the two approaches.
>
> (Frayn 1998, pp. 69–70)

The *Oxford Dictionary of Philosophy* defines the self as 'the elusive "I" that shows an alarming tendency to disappear when we try to introspect it' (Blackman

DOI: 10.4324/9781003215639-10

1996, p. 344). Warren Colman referred to the elusiveness and endless shift he encountered in the course of his own study on the self:

> Trying to think about the self was like trying to grasp a jelly that keeps slipping out of your hand. Someone pointed out to me that mercury would be an apt image of this and I suddenly understood why Mercurius holds such a central position in Jung's thinking.
>
> (Colman 1999)

Another expression of the elusiveness is the way the concept – an abstraction – shifts easily into reification, and the self becomes a 'thing' rather than an idea. Jung had resisted this in his work on religion,

> by claiming that all he could know is that psychology could explain much of religion and denying that psychology could be used as an instrument to tell whether God really existed apart from man. This is not a psychological issue at all and could only be tackled by philosophy.
>
> (Fordham 1985, p. 179)

Fordham had tried to be clear that his and Jung's researches pertained to psychological theory and phenomenology, not ontology. However, as the reader may find, this distinction can easily be lost when studying the self.

Fordham's studies of the self

Fordham regarded himself as a scientist. Late in life he reflected, 'I never really wanted to become a doctor, but rather, after studying natural sciences at Cambridge, was interested in the application of science to medicine' (Fordham 1988, p. 7). Fordham entered child psychiatry in 1933, just as he was beginning to become involved in Jungian psychotherapy. His earliest papers (1937–1943) reflected his conviction that children are individuals rather than products of parenting and identified archetypal phenomena in the play, dreams and drawings of the children he treated. By 1947 he had observed clinically how alternating states of integration and disruption produced ego development in small children and, within ten further years, he had established a model of development based on a deintegrating and reintegrating primary self (Fordham 1957). Fordham's work on the self culminated in *Explorations into the Self*, published in 1985. The volume is a tour de force of comprehension, intellect and Fordham's particular kind of vision, and it is disappointing that the editing of this volume did not match the quality of the author's work. Following *Explorations* there were numerous papers and two other volumes; however, these were refinements to rather than major revisions of his model.

The first chapter of *Explorations*, titled 'The self in Jung's works', is probably Fordham's most condensed and complex paper. The chapter opens with a notable understatement: 'This first chapter is lengthy and somewhat heavy going' (ibid., p. 5). Essentially it is a research project attempting to clarify what Jung meant by the self. It originally appeared in 1963, not long after Robert Hobson had published his brief study of how Jung used the term 'archetype' (Hobson 1961). Fordham's study reveals inconsistencies in the way Jung used the 'self', and he sets out to explain how they arose and how they can be resolved.

In the introductory summary, Fordham contends that these incompatible definitions 'stem from the interlacing of primitive experience and the abstractions from them' (ibid., p. 8). Jung's data were subjective affective experiences, symbols and myths derived from clinical experience and comparative studies. When making hypotheses from this data, 'Jung kept his abstract formulations related to empirical affective experiences' (ibid., p. 25) in order for his theory to convey the wholeness for which it was supposed to account. To achieve this, Jung used metaphors. Hence his conceptualisation combined directed thinking (the logical form underlying theoretical thought) and undirected thinking (thought, like metaphors, influenced by archetypal processes). Added to this, over time Jung 'ran up against the lack of adequate [scientific] language' for expressing the wholeness of the self, so that later on in his writing he 'relied more and more on paradox' (ibid., pp. 8–9). Fordham criticises Jung's mixing myth with abstract statement because it devalues the role of theory, when 'theories have advantages over myths in scientific studies' (ibid., p. 8).

Fordham then reviews Jung's data and points out that the clinical population from which Jung had drawn was not representative. Rather, those involved tended to include exceptional individuals who were introverted, schizoid and some apparently mildly depressed. Jung's data also excluded references to relationships with the external world and internal objects. Lastly, he indicated that there was a lack of attempt t to bring in 'material related to childhood let alone infancy' (ibid., p. 17).

Fordham next considers Jung's theories of the self, first as it is defined as the totality of the personality and then as an archetype. The totality definition derived from references in Eastern mysticism to states of at-one-ness. However, using this as the datum for defining a concept of totality comes up against the epistemological dilemma to which I referred earlier. 'If the self is the whole psyche, then it cannot be observed intrapsychically' because the observing ego is only a part in the whole (ibid., p. 21). Furthermore, as much as Jung needed to base his theories on experiences, 'The difficulties in taking the primordial experience to represent the totality of the psyche are many, but the greatest so far considered is that experiences in solitude, however important in themselves, leave out the organism's adaptation to external objects whether personal or otherwise' (ibid., p. 22).

As for the archetype definition, Fordham notes that it accounts for a range of phenomena related to wholeness (archetypal images) and, in fact, is closer to the data than the totality definition. However, this data 'cannot also be the totality' because it excludes the ego, which Jung differentiated from the archetypes. For instance, in *Answer to Job*, Jung (1954) used God to refer to the unconscious (a totality), yet God needs humans (the ego, which is not an archetype) to become conscious. Fordham concludes that although 'this definition [self as archetype] is nearer the phenomena described, . . . the experience of wholeness is not a reliable basis on which to construct a definition of the self' (Fordham 1985, p. 23). Fordham comments that all the images associated with the central archetype suggest a 'powerful integrative influence', whether in schizophrenia or a well-developed individual (ibid., p. 26).

Fordham's conceptual analysis concludes by returning, full circle, to the introductory comments about Jung's methodology. He asks whether it is acceptable to run two incompatible theories alongside one another: 'Is it enough to say that it is effective [sic: affective], pre-logical experience that counts and then play down theory?' (ibid., p. 29). Fordham thinks not. While he appreciates Jung's efforts to maintain the links between the concept and the data it was intended to describe, Jung's 'often graphic word-pictures . . . are theoretically confusing' (ibid., p. 25).

In a highly condensed paragraph at the end of the section on 'General Psychology' (p. 30), Fordham disentangles Jung's 'interlacing of myth and model' (ibid., p. 7). To summarise it, I shall draw upon the distinction in logic between contradiction and paradox. A contradiction can be stated as follows: A is B and A is not B. It is unresolvable, inasmuch as true ontradictions indicate some conceptual (theoretical) error (1). In contrast, a paradox is an apparent contradiction, the resolution to which can be worked out. When Jung used paradoxes to capture the nature of experiences of the self, he was referring to contents within a whole, which includes opposites. From this position one can make paradoxical statements such as 'the whole (images and experiences of totality) is in the part (the ego, the observer)' and 'the part (the ego) is in the whole'. However, Jung seemed to regard experiences of wholeness as if they were actually of the totality, ignoring that the whole is beyond experience. Fordham's point is that the 'as if metaphor' (undirected thinking) blurs logical distinctions (directed thinking) that are necessary when defining concepts used in a theoretical model of the self. Theoretical models require clear definitions and logical consistency. In effect Jung was saying that the self is the totality and the self is not the totality (it is a part, an archetype). This, Fordham points out, is a logical contradiction within a theoretical scheme, not a paradox.

Having identified Jung's incompatible concepts of the self, Fordham asks, 'Can a hypothesis be formulated closer to the experiences accumulated and capable of being tested by or used to organize them?' (ibid., p. 31). Here lies Fordham's resolution to the dilemma. I shall develop this later on.

The model

The model as it stood in its most mature form drew upon several concepts: the primary self, deintegration, reintegration, self objects, self representations and individuation.

Jung had conceived of the self as a way of accounting for certain, particularly mystical, phenomena in adulthood. Fordham shifts the function of the self within the theoretical model so that it accounts for development, postulating a primary self as the starting point. Certain processes are defined as integral to the central postulate, which accounts for how development proceeds and contents and structures are formed. These processes, structures and the relationships between them are then used to account for subjective phenomena, including the states of integration for which Jung sought an explanation. Implied in what Fordham writes is that the primary self also refers to an overall developmental process.

Fordham's starting point is before and beyond all phenomena and hence refers to a phenomenon-less state. As a postulate, the primary self is a psychosomatic integrate, that is 'empty' of phenomena, so that it is 'nothing but' potential. Rosemary Gordon has described the primary self as 'a simple totality . . . a matrix of all those potential faculties of the organism which await the process of "deintegration" and "reintegration" in order to become operative and so actualize themselves' (Gordon 1985, p. 267). Mario Jacoby also associates the primary self with potential, describing 'the primary self as the original potential' (Jacoby 2003, personal communication). Elsewhere I have commented that the primary self might be seen as analogous to the egg at the instant (if there is one) of fertilisation, at a moment conceptually held in time (Urban 1992). Astor describes it as 'somewhat analogous to the potential in DNA but probably without its hereditary constituents' (Astor 1995, p. 50). Unlike the egg at the moment of fertilisation but like the cosmic egg to which Fordham had earlier associated it (Fordham 1957), the primary self is a mystical concept, referring to the 'nothing that is everything'. Although the primary self has no representations, there are subjective states associated with it, such as those in early infancy following a satisfying feed, as well as later on, such as mystical states that refer to the 'pregnant absence' expressing the potential that is the essence of the primary self.

The concept implies that the infant is an individual from the start and that development begins from within, given of course an adequate environmental background. A physiological analogy is the onset of the embryo's heartbeat. As the embryo's first observable activity, at about three weeks, the heartbeat 'initially originates within the heart itself . . . it is not a response to an external stimulus' (Bremner 1994, p. 25).

Inherent in the concept of the primary self is its dynamic, the complementary processes of deintegration and reintegration that, taken together, Fordham terms actions of the self. Both concepts refer to processes that underlie development. The alternating disruption and stability of deintegration and reintegration can be recognised in a summary hypothesis offered by Thelen, as quoted by Bremner, from her studies of motor development in early infancy:

> in order to understand development we have to understand that complex systems are self-organizing: they 'prefer' states of equilibrium. However they can be pushed towards new states of equilibrium by particular forces, acting from within the organism or from the external environment. Thus development is understood as a progression through a series of stable states.
>
> (Bremner 1994, p. 47)

As the earliest period in development, the primary self is assumed to operate from before birth. This is substantiated by, amongst others, Piontelli, who made ultrasound observations of foetal development. Her studies show fetuses exploring their intrauterine home, playing with the placenta, touching themselves and, in twinships, their foetal sibling through the membranes that separate them (Piontelli 1992).

Fordham conceptualised deintegration and reintegration in order to account for developmental processes before structures and contents become established. For example, internalisation is development of deintegration and reintegration, involving repeated engagements with an experience (deintegration) and assimilating these time and again into the personality (reintegration). He held that initially these actions of the self create a particular state, termed primitive identity, which is meant to account for states of fusion. Recent neuroscientific studies into right brain function have contributed to an understanding of how this state comes about.

Researchers have discovered that it takes 30 milliseconds for infant to appraise facially expressed emotional cues, 100 milliseconds to detect and carry out complex processing of change within a human face, and 300–400 milliseconds to mirror and synchronously match the affect of an emotionally expressive face. The same applies for recognising and matching the emotional qualities of voices (termed 'prosody'). Within this split second, what is perceived by the infant triggers affect and concomitant bodily responses that are innately connected to expression. So " 'reading" another's emotional expression' entails decoding by 'actual felt [somatic] emotional reactions to the stimuli' (Schore 2002, p. 27, quoting from Day and Wong 1996, p. 651). Schore emphasises how instantaneous perceiving and matching are occurring within both mother and infant engaged together. This results in a mutual mapping process comprised of a 'very rapid sequence of reciprocal affective transactions [co-constructed] within the intersubjective field' (Schore 2002, p. 19). These are experienced subjectively as a state of fusion.

Deintegration and deintegrates are conceived as processes, structures and experiences that remain part of the self. An analogy is the relationship of the pseudopodia (deintegration and its contents, deintegrates) to the amoeba (the primary self). Early deintegrates are structured within the self via reintegration, which shapes experiences along archetypal lines, that is, within universal human patterns. In time, these proto-structures, which are made up of fragments of similar kinds of experience such as good, bad, 'I' and 'not-I', coalesce into more stable structures that develop into archetypal forms and the ego. As they all begin as deintegrates, they maintain a fundamental link with the primary self. The neurological understanding behind this is that experiences provoke firings in the brain that over time become wired together, and these wirings, if repeated often enough, become patterned, that is, integrated within the brain into generalised phenomena.

As I have noted, the subjective experience of states of identity is a state of fusion with the other, producing an object Fordham termed a self object. Self objects contrast with 'reality' objects:

When the object is mainly a record of reality, it may be called a reality object; when it is mainly constructed by the self and so records states of the self, made out of exteroceptive and introceptive sense data, then it may be called a self object. . . . It appears that self-objects increase in affectively charged states, whilst in quiet contemplative exploring activities real objects predominate.

(Fordham 1985, p. 56)

Conceptually, self objects are closely related to self representations, and Fordham's use of each has become confused with how other theoreticians have used these terms. Stern describes the infant's developmental experience from the point of view of the emerging ego, beginning with the sense of emergent self. Over time a more coherent sense of self begins to emerge, indicating that the ego has taken on some preliminary form and that mental representations of the self are becoming established. Fordham's position contrasts with developmental theorists who hold that the baby's self representations are derived fundamentally from internalising the experiences of and with the mother (Stern 1985; Fonagy et al. 2002). In Fordham's model self representations are understood as expressions (representations) of the wholeness of the primary self occurring in the developing ego, that is, conscious awareness. Because it is a product of deintegration and reintegration, the infant's sense of self derives from the infant as well as from interactions with the mother. To give an example of what is meant by the emergence of self representations in the ego I shall turn to a brief observation. It is of two babies about the same size, although one was five months old and the other eight months. They were sitting near one another on the floor when a large doll was placed between them. Each explored it simultaneously, and it began to topple from one to the other. Occasionally when the younger one had the doll, the older one seemed to want it and pulled it his way. The younger one did not get distressed but seemed perplexed that the doll was 'going away' and watched it go with some surprise, clearly unaware that another person was removing it. The younger one never tried to pull away the doll when the older one had it, while the older one did this several times from the younger. The impression is that the older one had a stronger sense of himself, his agency, his wishes and what he felt to be his, while the younger one had not yet reached this point of self-awareness.

Fordham links the infant's developing sense of himself with individuation. He holds that the infant is an individual from the start, so that 'individuation becomes realization of his condition through the development of self representations' (Fordham 1985, p. 54). This is another way of saying that the infant's ego is developing a gradually more discriminated sense of his individuality and wholeness, realised through evolving expressions of the primary self. These expressions are not directly of the self, but via representations of a psychosomatic unity beyond experience, let alone consciousness. In this process the infant's experiences involving various senses of himself are incorporated around a sense of having a centre. Fordham links this centredness back to the original state, re-experienced during early infancy in the sense of wholeness that occurs with, say, pleasurable feeds.

As deintegration and reintegration continue, more stable internal structures and processes develop, leading to greater complexity. For example, at the end of the first year, the baby begins to understand that when the mother points, she intends for him to look at something. This is the beginning of what developmental psychologists term a 'theory of mind', whereby the baby is able to perceive that the mother has her own motives, intentions and thoughts, in short, a mind behind her face, and this matches a growing sense of his having a mind of his own.

Discussion

Although Fordham's work is based in Jung, some elements diverge from Jung. Fordham 's developmental approach often reconciles apparent differences, as I hope to explain.

The definition of the self concept totality or archetype

Fordham had pointed out (1963, 1985) Jung's 'incompatible definitions' of the self. Fordham consistently defined the self as the totality of personality. I shall try to give an example of what Fordham meant by the infant being a psychosomatic totality by giving a brief observation of a baby, whom I shall call Jake.

> Jake and his mother had been referred for parent-infant therapy and I saw them when Jake was just over a month old. Throughout the session Jake was asleep while his mother and I were talking. From time to time I noticed Jake and what he was doing, which gave the impression of a progression, or unfolding, of development in relation to what was happening around him.
>
> Just as I was entering the room to join Jake and his mother, the door slammed behind me with a loud bang. Jake was asleep in his sling cot on the floor in front of his mother, and he startled at the noise. His whole body jerked forward reflexively as if to curl up protectively, although he did not wake up. A bit later I noticed Jake begin to squirm and buckle forward – a variation of the reflexive curling into himself – after which he stretched out with his arms raised in front of him. He slept soundly again and then wriggled a bit, his face puckering as if working up into a cry, his head gently turning from side to side as if expressing 'no'. He then stretched his arms forward and upward, his fingers extended with palms outward. It appeared as if he was pushing something away, what I presumed was the 'badness' of the noise.
>
> A bit later, as he drifted again into lighter sleep, the pushing away movement was clearly directed toward me, and what I guessed was the 'badness' of my felt presence, which might have been linked with the bang followed by my unfamiliar voice. Still later I observed him making similar yet quite different motions toward his mother. He stretched his arms out toward her but with his fingers extended and palms held downward rather than up, so it

looked as if he was reaching rather than pushing away. As I watched, his gestures seemed quite different depending on the direction of his arms; toward me, he pushed away and toward his mother, he reached out.

Here we see a baby relating to what is happening around him in spite of being asleep. It is difficult to say what level of awareness he has, but he is certainly not conscious in the sense we ordinarily mean it. In fact the distinction between conscious and unconscious is irrelevant, and it is useful to consider what is happening in terms of the self. Jake's self is a psychosomatic self, whereby bodily actions convey that experiences are being internally organised, or differentiated, into 'me' and 'not-me' and 'good' and 'bad'. It is however not an observation of the primary self, only of its expressions via deintegration and reintegration, functioning in a unified way within a separate 'unit' responding to what is going on externally and internally. Furthermore, the experiences are of sensations rather than of mental images.

I am trying to show how Fordham recognised a unity and personhood of the infant. However, might this observation also be seen as an example of the self regarded as an archetype? I shall come to this later in the chapter.

The mind-body relationship

Jung seemed divided on the issue of mind and body. Fordham notes, 'At one time Jung conceived the archetype as the psychic representation of instinct only, but he often writes as if they were purely psychic forms' (Fordham 1985, p. 162). In *Psychological Types* Jung defines the self as the psychic totality; 'the self is the subject of my total psyche which also includes the unconscious' (Jung 1971, para. 706; my italics). Also, Jung considered psyche and soma as opposites: 'Mind and body are presumably a pair of opposites and, as such, the expression of a single entity whose essential nature is not knowable either from its outward material manifestation or from inner, direct perception' (Jung 1926, para. 619, p. 326).

Undoubtedly Jung was aware of a mind-body link because his experimental researches depended on this. These researches drew upon the James-Lange theory of affect, which distinguished between 'emotion' and 'feeling':

> I take emotion as affect, it is the same thing as 'something affects you'. It does something to you – it interferes with you. Emotion is the thing that carries you away: You are thrown out of yourself; you are beside yourself as if an explosion had moved you out of yourself and put you beside yourself. There is a quite tangible physiological condition which can be observed at the same time. So the difference would be this: feeling has no physiological or tangible physiological manifestations, while emotion is characterized by an altered physiological condition.
>
> (Jung 1935a, para. 6, p. 25)

Jung's statement is in line with the thinking of the contemporary neurologist Anthony Damasio, whose research has drawn upon the same theory of affect:

> In a typical emotion, then, certain regions of the brain, which are part of a largely preset neural system related to emotions, send commands to other regions of the brain and in almost everywhere in the body proper. . . . The result of these coordinated chemical and neural commands is a global change in the state of the organism. The organs which receive the commands change as a result of the command, and the muscles, whether the smooth muscles in a blood vessel or the striated muscles in the face, move as they are told to do. But the brain itself is changed just as remarkably.
>
> (Damasio 1999, pp. 67–68)

According to Damasio, the brain spontaneously makes a primary mapping of these 'changes in the body state that are induced in myriad organs' (Damasio 1994, p. 139). In contrast to emotion, feeling is the imaging of these changes, called secondary mapping. Just how this happens is unknown, although secondary mapping (feelings) might be said to be more clearly psychic than psychosomatic. If the self is considered the psychic totality, then by logical extension the concept would exclude emotions, and this makes no sense. If emotions are included in the notion of psyche, then the body is necessarily involved. According to Damasio, to 'feel the feeling', consciousness as well as primary and secondary mapping are required, that is, consciousness is based on psychosomatic elements.

Fordham addresses the mind-body question developmentally. He regards the self as a psychosomatic entity, which over time deintegrates and reintegrates into mental and physical functioning. 'In treating these twin concepts, psyche and soma, as deintegrates, their origin in the self is not lost sight of, nor is their adaptive value left out of account' (Fordham 1985, p. 170). When Jung states (in places), and other Jungians imply, that the self is 'only' psychic, it may be because they work primarily with adults. Throughout Fordham's career he worked with children and was aware of how bodily their expressions are – touching, running, stroking, climbing, biting, hitting and spitting. His developmental model was intended to cover the continuity between childhood and adulthood, and the bodiliness of the mind throughout life was integral to his thinking.

The 'ultimate'

Both Jung and Fordham commented on a state to which they referred as 'the ultimate'. Jung's reference is in *Memories, Dreams, Reflections*, when he is describing his experiences following the breakup with Freud. He wrote, 'Only gradually did I discover what the mandala really is: "Formations, Transformations, Eternal Mind's eternal recreation". . . . In them I saw the self – that is my whole being – actively at work . . . [in them]. I had attained what was for me the "ultimate"' (Fordham 1985, p. 12, taken from Jung 1963, pp. 187–188).

Fordham's comment on 'the ultimate' is as follows:

> a reflection on 'the ultimate'. I take it to represent a state in which there is no past and no future, though it is present like a point which has position by [sic: but) no magnitude. It has no desires, no memory, no thoughts, no images but out of it by transformation all of these can deintegrate. There is no conscious ness so no unconscious – it is a pregnant absence.
>
> (Fordham 1985, p. 33)

The 'ultimate' described in each quote refers to mystic states, which both Jung and Fordham studied. Jung's work was extensive and well-known, while Fordham's lesser-known studies focused on the experiences described by St. John of the Cross. As Astor describes, Fordham saw similarities (as well as important differences) between the process described by the saint (the *scala mystica*) and individuation (Astor 1995). Noting that 'the past never disappears, it is transformed', Fordham traces 'ultimate' union with God to its sources in infancy (Fordham 1985, p. 197). This primitive object relationship involves an experience of a good feed leading to the image of a good breast. This occurs developmentally before the infant's capacity for differentiation, thus involving projective and introjective identification. This account explains the subjective experience of union and views the mystical state as a transformation of the earliest state of infancy. Fordham notes, 'That state is nearest to the whole self' (ibid., p. 198).

Fordham's comment on the 'ultimate' comes at the end of the first chapter of *Explorations into the Self* and seems tacked on to what precedes it. In fact, the paragraph was not included in previous editions of the paper (Fordham 1963; Fordham et al. 1973). Why did Fordham add it? I believe that he did so because states of integration were central to Jung's conceptualisation of the self and Fordham wanted to include an equivalent state associated with his model. Drawing upon Bion, Fordham refers to a phenomenon-less state, a 'pregnant absence', which presents a contrast to Jung's idea of the 'ultimate'. For Jung, the 'ultimate' is the individuated self experienced as a unity that transcends the multiplicity of object relationships. For Fordham, the 'ultimate' is the primary self, which precedes but contains the potential for and predisposition to develop a multiplicity of objects and relationships with them.

The 'origins' of the archetypes

The old conflict between nature and nurture for a long period divided psychologists into opposing camps of 'nativists', who came down on the side of innateness, and 'empiricists', who came down on the side of the environment. Within the nativist camp, distinctions were made between 'preformationism', whereby "structures underlying behaviour are there from birth, and 'predeterminism', in which structures develop during childhood through a predetermined sequence of differentiation and elaboration"' (Bremner 1994, p. 5). Although Jung and

Fordham held that both nature and nurture played a role in development, the distinctions between preformationism and predeterminism may help to clarify a difference between them regarding the 'origins' of the archetypes.

Jung had stressed that the archetypes were *a priori*, as was the archaic substrate of the collective unconscious. To use Barbara Wharton's metaphor (personal communication), archetypes are there from the beginning like a dry riverbed ready to receive water and then flow. Jung wrote,

> So far as I know, there is no inheritance of individual pre-natal, or pre-uterine, memories, but there are undoubtedly inherited archetypes which are, however, devoid of content, because, to begin with, they contain no personal experiences. They only emerge into consciousness when personal experiences have rendered them visible.
>
> (Jung 1935b, para. 846)

Here it is implied that the archetypes and the collective unconscious are conceived to be 'there' as innate, 'pre-formed' endowments.

In relation to Jung, Fordham can be seen as a 'predeterminist' (although only in this specific sense). He holds that structures, including body, mind and the structures and processes of each, unfold out of the primary self via deintegration. He writes, 'in infancy the archetypal forms are derived from the self through its deintegration' (Fordham 1985, p. 45).

To expand upon this, I should like to turn to an observation in a video entitled *The Amazing Talents of the Newborn* (Klaus et al. 2011). It shows a series of stills of Andrew, 40 minutes after his birth. Andrew has been dried but not washed or given various treatments, so that the smells of the amniotic fluid are still with him. He has been placed on his mother's abdomen and slowly starts climbing towards his mother's breast and face. The narrator relates that as he does so, the movement of his feet stimulates her uterus to 'clamp down' so that the bleeding stops, while also producing the 'love hormone', oxytocin, resulting in powerful feelings of love. Then it is noted how Andrew looks from her face to her right nipple and back to her face again, and, in the little pauses in between, he sucks his fingers. The narrator describes how there are similarities between the smell and taste of the amniotic fluid and what Andrew will smell and taste of his mother's milk. He continues to look from face to nipple and back again, and then, lifting his head to look at his mother's face, he is put just in the right position to latch on to the aureole, which he does. This awesome interplay of nature and nurture is a good way to exemplify what is meant by early archetypal phenomena and their relation to deintegration.

Bremner points out that behaviours like Andrew's may be viewed as innate, or 'pre-wired', 'if we take birth as the starting point, [but] the fetus's activities in the womb may have been involved in the "wiring up" process' (Bremner 1994, p. 36). For instance, the stepping movements that Andrew uses to crawl are now known to be foetal movements, which may be important in preventing the organism from becoming attached to the side of the uterus. Bremner adds, 'So instead of there being just one dramatic neural reorganization following birth, it seems more plausible that, starting in the fetal stage, there are a series of discontinuities brought about as successively higher regions of the brain become functional' (Bremner 1994, p. 37). This can be seen to describe Fordham's idea of how a phenomenon-less, 'empty' primary self develops even before birth.

The observation of Andrew shows the meeting point of nature and nurture. Fordham held that the match between them need not be perfect. Although newborns like Andrew may be capable of what is termed the 'breast crawl', it is not the actual experience of many babies, in spite of the fact that they do adapt, survive and thrive. Developmentalists refer to this as the newborn's 'flexibility in the range of his affordances', that is, how he makes use of the environment. Fordham believed that the infant also contributes to the environment, and Andrew's stimulation of oxytocin in his mother's bloodstream is a good example of what he meant. However, Andrew also contributed to his own development even before birth because foetal stepping produces neural activity and organisation in the foetal brain.

If archetypes are the result of deintegration and reintegration, how does Fordham account for the collective in childhood? Firstly, it should be clear by this point that he does not believe that the infant is born with a wealth of collective images which then become projected onto the mother. Nor does he believe that 'The unconscious psyche of the child is truly limitless in extent and of incalculable age' (Jung 1931, para. 95). Instead Fordham turns to Jung's likening of archetypal phenomena to a spectrum covering, at the one end, instinctual life (as with the example of Andrew) and, at the other, spiritual life. For Fordham, expressions of the collective in infancy are best understood in terms of a body mythology, as Klein had understood and described. As for the spiritual pole, the child's predisposition to 'develop archaic ideas, feelings and fantasies . . . are influenced and refined by education which in turn, as in feedback systems, provides suitable imagery through which the unconscious archetypes can find expression in consciousness' (Fordham 1976, p. 6). The growing child discovers images around him that contribute to the imagery expressive of the collective. Images become available via the culture at large, such as children's books, television, films and video games. Miranda Davies has referred to the one-sidedness of most of these popular images and the imbalance of power, speed and violence at the expense of smallness, dependency and loss (Davies 1993).

Fordham adds, 'In contrast to the instinctual drives, which are relatively fixed and few in number, the fantasy (or spiritual) component has wide and flexible application' (Fordham 1976, p. 6).

The primary self, the self and the sense of self

What is the difference between the primary self and the self? Rosemary Gordon noted that the primary self 'is a primitive form of the self' (Gordon 1985, p. 267).

To this I have added that the primary self is also a period of development. This raises such questions as when does the primary self begin, and when is the self no longer primary? In this section, I shall divert in order to clarify certain matters, including Fordham's position in relation to current conflicts amongst Jungians who also take a developmental perspective.

Fordham would not be pinned down in dating the beginning of the primary self, other than to say it occurred before birth. It is important to keep in mind that Fordham postulated a psychosomatic integrate. Carvalho warns against 'the danger particularly when the idea of the "self" is pushed back prior to the formation of a nervous system and its function of apperception, [because] the idea invites theologizing, idealization and inflation' (Carvalho 1985, pp. 237–238). Using 'the formation of a nervous system' as a guide, one might consider the primary self to have beginnings as early as 14 days after conception, with 'the formation of the primitive streak and therefore the beginning of the development of the nervous system' (Piontelli 1992, p. 109). If one includes apperception, that is, the cognition of a perception, this may change the dating to, say, around seven weeks, when external stimuli to the peri-oral area will produce a response, indicating neural connections have begun to become established.[1,2,3,4] Bremner considers that 'in practice it is often hard to draw a clear line between perceptual and cognitive processes' (Bremner 1994, p. 52). The same is likely to be the case with the beginning of the primary self.

Carvalho is reluctant to use the term 'primary self' unless talking about the primary integrate after the stage at which it has developed a mind and the functions of mind (Carvalho 1985, p. 237). He states that ' "self" as a term implies some notion of reflectiveness and therefore of mind and awareness' (ibid., p. 236),[5] a position shared by Louis Zinkin. Within Fordham's model, both Jungians are referring to the sense of self.

Fordham distinguished between the self and the sense of self, and for him the difference was major. In 1986 Zinkin published a paper in the *Journal of Analytical Psychology*, in which he criticised Fordham's notion of the primary self:

> Because Fordham is deeply concerned with babies and how they come to have a sense of self, a sense of an inside and outside, he posits an original self . . . which seems to be quite undifferentiated which he sees as deintegrating through an act of spontaneous division.
>
> It is here that I have the greatest difficulty with his theory . . . the baby is at no time undifferentiated even when it is a foetus [*sic zygote*] consisting of only one cell. As a model or a hypothesis of what takes place in infancy I cannot accept that there is an original self. . . . I can agree with it only as a postulate like 'initial conditions' in systems theory language but would regard such a state as preceding the birth of the individual.
>
> (Zinkin 1986, p. 302)

The article was controversial. James Astor, who is and was at the time an authority on Fordham's work, wrote a letter to the *Journal*, stating, 'The Winnicottian idea that the original self is undifferentiated is not one that Michael Fordham subscribes to' (Astor 1987, p. 57).

Zinkin's misunderstanding of Fordham extended to other elements of Fordham's position. Fordham had not postulated a primary self simply in order to account for the sense of self. It was to account for the fundamental unity of the infant before an ego is formed, including the capacity of the infant to relate to and make use of the environment, particularly its human components, as we saw with Jake. Secondly, Fordham had explained that the sense of self arose as self representations became part of the ego, so only indirectly did it come from the primary self. Thirdly, whether the self is differentiated or not depends on what is meant by differentiation. The sleeping infant, Jake, could differentiate between his mother and me, but it is unlikely that he had formed stable internal differentiation in terms of self, good, not-self and bad.

Following this paper, Fordham initiated a personal correspondence with Zinkin that lasted from January to June of 1987. In his initial letter Fordham wrote:

> you [Zinkin] cannot conceive of a self without a sense of 'I' or 'myself', but Jung persistently denies that his 'self' is that and he regularly distinguishes the ego from the self. . . . I was quite horrified at the symposium on the self in the *Journal* [Vol. 30, 3, in which Carvalho's paper had appeared] to see how far our members had departed from Jung in this respect.
>
> (Zinkin 1998, p. 136)[6]

Zinkin responded and Fordham wrote back, enclosing some notes he had made about foetal deintegration and reintegration. They include the following:

> Considering the accumulation of data it would seem wrong to assert, as has been widely done and still is in many quarters, that a foetus has no mental life and so no ego even in the later part of gestation, say after five months when his brain is fully formed. Even before this it would be daring to assert that there are no physical elements from which mental life will emerge.
>
> (ibid., p. 139)

Here however Fordham seems to be regarding the primary self as a concept beyond time and space and therefore existence, at the same time as making efforts to date it (in his notes).

An extension to Fordham's resolution
to Jung's incompatible definition

I shall now return to Fordham's attempt at a resolution of the contradictory meanings Jung attributed to the self. In so doing, I shall address the question of when the primary self is no longer primary.

Fordham concludes his study in the first chapter of *Explorations* with an overly condensed section entitled 'The nature of the self'. I shall expand on this section, which is a reworking of a previous paper (1963, republished in 1973). The chapter was being revised when Fordham was still recovering from a serious illness, when his wife and colleague, Frieda, had become quite infirm and dependent, and while he was under pressure to complete what was undone in his life's work. His purpose in this section of the chapter is to answer the question, 'Can a hypothesis [about what is meant by the self] be formulated closer to the experiences accumulated and capable of being tested by or used to organize them?' (Fordham 1985, p. 31). Fordham's purpose here would be clearer if he had retained the original section heading: 'Attempt at a solution of the theoretical quandary'.

Essentially Fordham's resolution lies in a development approach. Development begins with the primary self, that is, the potential for an individual being with psychosomatic continuity and the capacity to adapt. Deintegration and reintegration lead to the development of stable structures, both somatic and psychic, including an embodied mind and conscious sense of self. This involves the emergence of archetypal structures and forms, and one of particular importance to Fordham's model is the central archetype of order. The term identifying this archetype seemed to be Fordham's way of dealing with the 'problem of nomenclature', that is, the term 'self' had been used to refer to both the archetype and the totality of the self. If a distinction was needed in the conceptualisation, one was also needed in the terminology. Fordham had clearly intended the term to be an alternative to what Jung had meant by the archetype of the self. In the original version of what became Chapter 1 in *Explorations* he wrote, 'The central ego has a special relation to what, with some hesitation, may be called the central archetype of order (archetype of the self, in Jung's terminology)' (Fordham 1963, p. 20).

The 'central archetype of order' had been used by Jung and Perry. To my awareness, Fordham had first used the term in a 1962 paper, 'Ego, self and mental health'. It is republished in *Explorations* as Chapter 7, 'Mental Health', where he states, 'Turning to the possible ways the archetypes may be related to each other, we at once think of the possibility of a hierarchy subservient to a central organizing system, as Jung suggested when he referred to the self as the central archetype of order' (Fordham 1985, p. 117). Fordham again used the concept in his 1963 research study on Jung's meanings of self, in which he pointed out that Perry had used the term to account for images of wholeness in schizophrenia. Fordham expanded on this, drawing out the integrative function of the central archetype, which is evident in the individuation process as well as apart from it (in psychosis) and in early development. Fordham also used the term in a 1964 paper, 'The relation of the ego to the self', revised as Chapter 6 in *Explorations*. In the revision he writes, 'If the "Ich Gefuhl" be considered from the dimension of the ego, then the self appears as part of the ego. But looked at from that of the self, then it would be conceived as manifesting the central archetype of which the ego is a part' (Fordham 1985, p. 108).

It seems that Fordham used the concept of a 'central archetype of order' during the early 1960s, at a time when he was consolidating his model of development. He then dropped the term. It does not appear in either *Children as Individuals* (1969) or *The Self and Autism* (1976), yet it reappears in *Explorations* in the chapters that are revisions of the 1960s papers. Why had Fordham revived the term in *Explorations* and why, once revived, did he not develop it? I suggest that after Fordham started to use 'central archetype of order', he became more involved in, amongst other activities, his clinical research into autism. In his research, Fordham used the concept of self objects to describe the lack of self/other differentiation that was so evident in his clinical studies. He did not need the concept of an archetype distinguished by its function of integration because he was thinking of autism as a problem primarily of deintegration. Why was the idea of the central archetype revived but then not developed? I consider this may be because he realised that the central archetype enabled him to resolve Jung's contradiction via his developmental model and needed to remain. Fordham may not have had the energy to develop it as he progressed into old age, when he needed to prioritise his efforts around the two volumes and numerous reviews, papers and chapters he wrote during the last ten years of his life. He may also not have considered he had the data to develop the concept of a central archetype of order.

I should like to extend the concept as he presented it. To begin, Fordham clearly meant for the central archetype of order to distinguish a particular archetype that has special integrative functions in relation to the archetypes and to the ego. He describes the archetype as follows:

> Integration is the main function of the self [that is, the archetype of order]. . . . That central archetype can be thought of an [sic: as] an organizer of the unconscious: it contributes significantly to the formation of the central ego in which it finds expression especially in conscious experiences of selfhood. . . . In this formulation, the central archetype, being a part system in the total self, can be introjected, projected, can assimilate other unconscious elements, identify with the ego, be the source of religious experience, the source of the central ego, and function mostly in the unconscious in a compensatory manner until it gets realized, i.e., largely integrated into the ego in individuation. . . . At the same time, room is left for the personal life of the individual and his relation to the external world as a whole, within the self conceived of as the superordinate totality.
>
> (Fordham 1985, pp. 31–33)

How might the notion of the central archetype be viewed developmentally? By the end of the first year, most infant researchers agree there is a surge of significant developments. These changes include the beginning of attachment proper, when there is an enhanced awareness of the singularity and significance of the attachment figure, accompanied by the infant's new consciousness of his own individuality and value. Also there are the dawning awareness of a theory of mind, mentioned earlier, and the capacity for empathy (Schore 2002). This period correlates with Stern's domain of subjectivity (that is, of the subjective sense of self) and might be seen as the point at which there is a shift from what Edelman calls primary consciousness, which is shared by most mammals, to secondary consciousness, which includes a basic awareness of one's subjectivity as well as that of another (Edelman 1992). Thus this archetype could be seen to be that of subjectivity, as Young-Eisendrath concludes (Young-Eisendrath and Hall 1987 in Colman 2000). In his study of the self, Colman notes, 'it is possible to think of archetypal processes directed towards wholeness and of a "central archetype" whose centering functions involve the organisation and integration of the psyche as a whole' (Colman 2000, p. 8). Following on from this, I am putting forward that the central archetype of order organises and integrates psychic deintegrates.

In summary, there is towards the end of the first year a vast array of evidence indicating a predominance of integrative processes within the infant's emerging mind, leading, amongst other developments, to a new awareness of the sense of self as an individual. This evidence indicates activities of what Fordham conceived as the central archetype of order, which has a special role in shaping and consolidating the ego. By the end of the first year the emerging archetype becomes shaped via deintegration and reintegration into a more coherent processing structure, resulting in numerous new capacities in relation to subjectivity and mindedness. These include a nascent unified sense of self, such as was seen with the two babies and the doll. In this light, what Fordham termed 'representations of the self' might more accurately be considered representations and pre-symbolic expressions of the central archetype of order. As I conceive it, the archetype arises from early actions of the self, perhaps beginning in utero and being amongst the earliest to deintegrate, and perhaps based in the physiology of the brain and the way it wires together (integrates) circuits that fire together.

This conception of the archetype means that it is intimately linked to the primary self. Yet they differ in two important respects. The central archetype is a part of the whole and, as such, it can be projected, introjected and so forth as Fordham described (Fordham 1985, p. 33). Its primary function is to integrate. In contrast, the primary self and its successor, the self, refer to the whole and function as an integrator and deintegrator.

When is the primary self no longer primary? I view the primary self to refer to a period of early development that is predominated by deintegrates, that is, primitive part objects. Through deintegration and reintegration, contents become both differentiated and consolidated into a more stable ego and internal objects. As the infant begins to have a sense of his own mind and his mother's, internal objects take on a three-dimensional quality and become whole objects in the Kleinian sense. As the changes that begin at the end of the first year develop through the second, one may begin to refer to the self and to its contents and structures by their specific terms within the theoretical model, such as 'ego' or the 'central archetype of order' and so forth. Hence as more clearly defined archetypal structuring occurs, the self moves beyond being primary, although its processes continue throughout life as new deintegrates appear.

Conclusion

This chapter began with some of the difficulties inherent in a study of the self. Jung referred to his circumambulations of the self, and Fordham had his own experiences of the elusiveness of his subject. In their correspondence, Zinkin had written to Fordham, 'when you avoid dating the original self it is not simply that we don't know the date and one day we might find out, but that it has no date. In this sense I entirely take your point that it is an abstraction' (Zinkin 1998, p. 142). Fordham answered:

> I certainly think that dating the original self is not important and am struck and attracted to your idea that 'it has no date'. That seems the obvious conclusion now you have suggested it. If that is so, and I am persuaded that it is, then can we speak of the self as existing? Against that we put Jung's idea, and that of others, which covers cosmic experiences extending to the limits of space and time. That is what I am talking about, following Jung.
>
> (ibid., p. 143)

Here Fordham seems to find himself caught in the rapid and endless shifts that accompany thinking about the self. He has made it clear to Zinkin that the primary self is an abstraction or a concept. He then slides into wondering if the self is a 'thing' that exists, before shifting rapidly back to it being a mystical concept accounting, as Jung intended, for cosmic and mystical experiences.

Overall Fordham was able to keep his conceptual bearings because of the value he placed on theoretical constructs to further understanding. He wrote during the long period in the 20th century when psychoanalysis was defining itself through theory. Fordham appreciated the need to steer a course through the muddles that came from the proliferation of theory that was occurring and had the clarity of thought to do so. Hence he developed his model in a way that led him to sharpen one aspect, theory, while leaving another, phenomenology, 'more unsharp'. This has begun to change, and analytic thinkers are working to balance theory with human experience, so that they are reaching to literature to expand upon their conceptualisations (Britton 1998; Canham and Satyamurti 2003; Williams and Waddell 1991).

Recently Jean Knox has made a plea to re-establish this 'heart of our theory and practice', and James Astor has presented a paper to the Society of Analytical Psychology Analytic Group, in which he argued that literary descriptions of fictional characters may offer something more authentic about what happens subjectively within and between analyst and patient than do clinical accounts (Knox 2004, p. 1; Astor 2004).

The enormous changes in developmental psychology and neuroscience that challenge our theories and offer hope of leading forward can also be seen as part of an endless shift. (6)

> . . . On a huge hill,
> Cragged, and steep, Truth stands, and he that will
> Reach her, about must, and about must go.
>
> (Donne 1633, p. 163)[7]

Notes

1 I am grateful to John Adkins of Jesus College for this concise statement.
2 The term 'deintegration' has proved difficult for those unfamiliar with Fordham. In part this is because it seems to connote an undoing of a negative nature. Fordham intended it to be seen as the unfolding of an integrate that does not undo development but instead is an essential part of it.
3 'The peri-oral area is the first part of the body to come "on-line". The onset of the response marks the point the embryonic period ends and the foetal period begins' (Bremner 1994, pp. 2–5).
4 The word 'self' is of Anglo-Saxon, Old Saxon and Old Norse origins, and Damasio notes that the term does not occur in romance languages except in the reflexive, such as 'self-reflective' and 'self-centred' (Damasio 1999). Nor, I am told, does 'self' occur in the Eastern languages of Hindi and Gugerati.
5 Daniel Stern and Antonio Damasio have in their respective ways also studied the self. Stern and Damasio are careful to use phrases such as 'sense of' or 'feeling' of self, while not getting into the thorny issue of what the self is. Each holds their respective ideas, whether explicit or implied, about an 'emergent' and 'core self' (Stern 1985) or 'proto-self' (Damasio 1999). These are not equivalents to the primary self, but they refer to the same dynamic entity that Fordham postulated.
6 Fordham's attempts to date the beginning of the primary self imply that the concept also refers to the period of development. Here however Fordham seems to be regarding the primary self as a concept beyond time and space and therefore existence, at the same time as making efforts to date it (in his notes).
7 I should like to express my appreciation to David Crosher for pointing out these lines.

References

Astor, J. (1987). 'Correspondence'. *Journal of Analytical Psychology*, 32(1).
————. (1995). *Michael Fordham: Innovations in Analytical Psychology*. London: Routledge.
————. (2004). 'The self-invented personality? Reflections on authenticity and writing analytic papers'. *Journal of Analytical Psychology*, 50(4).
Blackman, S. (1996). *The Oxford Dictionary of Philosophy*. Oxford: Oxford University Press.
Bremner, J. (1994). *Infancy*. Oxford: Blackwell.
Britton, R. (1998). *Belief and Imagination: Explorations in Psychoanalysis*. London: Routledge.
Bullock, A. and Trombley, S. (2000). *The New Fontana Dictionary of Modern Thought*. London: Harper Collins.
Canham, H. and Satyamurti, C. (2003). *Acquainted with the Night: Psychoanalysis and the Poetic Imagination*. London: Karnac.
Carvalho, R. (1985). 'The self as primary integrate: Some observations'. *Journal of Analytical Psychology*, 30(3).
Colman, W. (1999). Personal communication with the author.
————. (2000). 'Models of the self'. In E. Christopher and H. Solomon (eds.), *Jungian Thought in the Modern World*. London: Free Association Books.
Damasio, A. (1994). *Descartes' Error*. New York: Grosett/Putnam.
————. (1999). *The Feeling of What Happens*. London: Harcourt Brace & Company.

Davies, M. (1993). 'Heroic deeds, manic defense and intrusive identification: Some reflections on psychotherapy with a 16-year-old boy'. *Journal of Child Psychotherapy*, 19(1).

Day, R. and Wong, S. (1996). 'Anomalous perceptual asymmetries for negative emotional stimuli in the psychopath'. *Journal of Abnormal Psychology*, 105: 648–652.

Donne, J. (1633). 'Satire 3'. In A. J. Smith (ed.), *John Donne, The Complete English Poems*. London: Penguin, 1982.

Edelman, G. (1992). *Bright Air, Brilliant Fire*. London: Penguin Books.

Fonagy, P., Gergely, G., Jurist, E. and Target, M. (2002). *Affect Regulation, Mentalization, and the Development of the Self*. New York: Other Press.

Fordham, M. (1947). 'Integration, disintegration and early ego development'. *The Nervous Child*, 6(3).

———. (1957). *New Developments in Analytical Psychology*. London: Routledge & Kegan Paul.

———. (1963). 'The empirical foundations and theories of the self in Jung's works'. *Journal of Analytical Psychology*, 8(1).

———. (1964). 'The relation of the ego to the self'. *British Journal of Medical Psychology*, 37.

———. (1969). *Children as Individuals*. London: Hodder & Stoughton.

———. (1976). *The Self and Autism*. London: Academic Press.

———. (1985). *Explorations into the Self*. London: Academic Press.

———. (1988). 'In discussion with Karl Figlio'. *Free Associations*, 12.

Fordham, M., Gordon, R., Hubback, J., Lambert, K. and Williams, M. (1973). *Analytical Psychology: A Modern Science*. London: Heinemann Medical Books.

Frayn, M. (1998). *Copenhagen*. London: Methuen.

Gordon, R. (1985). 'Big self and little self: Some reflections'. *Journal of Analytical Psychology*, 30(3): 261–271.

Hobson, R. (1961). 'Critical notice'. *Journal of Analytical Psychology*, 6(2).

Jacoby, M. (2003). Personal communication.

Jung, C. G. (1926). 'Spirit and life'. *CW 8*.

———. (1931). 'The development of personality'. *CW 17*.

———. (1935a). 'The Tavistock lectures'. *CW 18*.

———. (1935b). 'Psychological commentary on the Tibetan book of the dead'. *CW 11*.

———. (1954). *Answer to Job*. London: Routledge & Kegan Paul.

———. (1963). *Memories, Dreams, Reflections*. London: Collins/Routledge & Kegan Paul.

———. (1971). 'Psychological types'. *CW 6*.

Klaus, M., Klaus, P., Keefe, R. and Fox, N. (2011). *The Amazing Talents of the Newborn*. Clifton, NJ: Johnson & Johnson Pediatric Institute. (A video).

Knox, J. (2004). 'From archetypes to reflective function'. *Journal of Analytical Psychology*, 49(1).

Piontelli, A. (1992). *From Fetus to Child: An Observational and Psychoanalytic Study*. London: Tavistock/Routledge.

Schore, A. (2002). 'Clinical implications of a psychoneurobiological model of projective identification'. In S. Alhananti (ed.), *Primitive Mental States*, Vol. 2. London: Karnac.

Stern, D. (1985). *The Interpersonal World of the Infant*. New York: Basic Books.

Urban, F. (1992). 'The primary self and related concepts in Jung, Klein, and Isaacs'. *Journal of Analytical Psychology*, 37(4): 411–432.

Williams, M. and Waddell, M. (1991). *The Chamber of Maiden Thought: Literary Origins of the Psychoanalytic Model of the Mind.* London: Routledge.

Young-Eisendrath, P. and Hall, J. (1987). *The Book of the Self.* London: New York University Press.

Zinkin, L. (1986). 'Some thoughts on deintegration'. *Journal of Analytical Psychology*, 31(3).

———. (1998). *Dialogue in the Analytic Setting,* eds. H. Zinkin, R. Gordon, and J. Haynes. London: Jessica Kingsley.

Chapter 7

The 'self' in analytical psychology

The function of the 'central archetype' within Fordham's model

Fordham once commented that the term 'self' would not have been used when he was studying medicine at Cambridge during the late 1920s, implying that it was not 'scientific enough'. He gave credit to Jung, who earlier the same decade introduced his formulations on the self (Jung 1921) and was, in Fordham's estimation, 'the first to evolve a method whereby the self could be systematically observed and experienced' (Fordham 1985, p. 102). Fordham noted that it was not until the mid-20th century that psychoanalysts, such as Federn, Winnicott, Hartmann, Kohut, Scott, Klein and Bion, began to become interested in the self, often describing 'the psychology of the self whether or not they have used the term' (Fordham 1987, p. 345). Not long after, scientists too were using the 'self', as developments in brain science drew neurology to philosophy over the mind-brain question, producing such volumes as that cited by Fordham (1987), *The Self and its Brain* by Popper, a philosopher, and Eccles, a neurologist (1977). Thus in the course of the 20th century, it was as if there was a converging sense of need to find a term that captured the unity of the individual, while at the same time suggesting human subjectivity. Even 20 years ago it was with some understatement that Fordham wrote, 'So now there is a complex and often confusing literature to digest' (Fordham 1987, p. 345).

This chapter sets out to examine how Fordham addressed the complexity and confusion surrounding the 'self' within Jungian psychology. This entails exploring an idea that Fordham suggested with such tentativeness that it has been all but lost, yet is, I maintain, useful. I shall be looking at his idea of a 'central archetype' from within the conceptual framework of his model, covering development from infancy to adulthood.

The 'self' in analytical psychology

Within analytical psychology, Fordham disputed whether the 'self' could apply both to the global unity of the human being as well as to subjectivity. He considered that the self was one thing, and the sense – or awareness or experience – of the self was another. The basis of Fordham's thinking rested upon Jung's uniquely extensive and elaborate studies of the self, which drew upon data from adulthood.

DOI: 10.4324/9781003215639-11

Fordham realised very early on that 'if archetypes are universal they must be demonstrable in childhood' (Fordham 1944, p. 5). His earliest published work identified archetypal phenomena and imagery in childhood but said virtually nothing about the self, presumably because he did not expect to find it there, as Jung had maintained that the self became manifest only in mid-life. As Fordham's interest began to focus on ego development, he came, via clinical observations of two children under age two, to the conclusion that early ego development was related to the self in childhood (Fordham 1947). Between 1947 and 1957 he wrote three seminal papers (1947, 1951, 1955). These became the core of *New Developments in Analytical Psychology* (1957), which contains the basic model that has remained: the postulate of the primary self that deintegrates and reintegrates and accounts for development from foetal life to old age (Fordham 1957).

Because his new model was based on the 'self', Fordham not long after began to research the ways that Jung used the term 'self', which included the data upon which Jung's ideas were based. Fordham published his study in the *Journal of Analytical Psychology* entitled 'The empirical foundations and theories of the self in Jung's work' (1963). This study enabled Fordham to recognise a contradiction in Jung's thinking: Jung used 'self' to mean both the totality of the personality and an archetype. Fordham suggested this arose from Jung's 'concept of two kinds of thinking (directed and undirected) to mean that theory and myth are analogues' (Fordham 1963, p. 3). Drawing upon directed thinking, Jung arrived at a definition of the self as a totality: 'the self is "my totality" . . . and hence it (also) includes the unconscious. It "embraces and includes the ego" as well' (Fordham 1963, p. 11, citing from Jung 1921, in Baynes 1923, p. 540). However, Jung was also concerned to capture the nature of the experience of wholeness linked to the term, derived from undirected thinking. Here Jung was referring to the self considered as an archetype or, rather, archetypal expressions in symbolic imagery and metaphor referring to the totality of the individual. Jung's thinking thus interlaced myth and model, which Fordham disputed: 'The advantages of theories over myths in scientific studies cannot be contested . . .'' (Fordham 1963, p. 3). Moreover, Fordham argued, the two main ways Jung used 'self' were 'mutually incompatible' concepts because archetypal phenomena referring to the self's totality are, within the theoretical system, only a part of the 'whole' self. For example, in *Psychology and Alchemy*, Jung writes:

> I call this centre the 'self', which should be understood as the totality of the psyche. The self is not only the centre, but also the whole circumference which embraces both conscious and unconscious; it is the centre of this totality, just as the ego is the centre of the conscious mind.
>
> (Jung 1944, para. 44)

Logically this does not work: How can the self be the totality and also the centre (only a part) of the totality? This does however work as a metaphorical statement about subjective experience that Jung associated with an archetype of totality.

Fordham was not arguing about Jung's data but rather looking for logical coherence within the theoretical system. His explanation of Jung's logical inconsistency was that Jung's mind moved back and forth between directed and undirected thinking and the metaphorical and the theoretical.[1]

Fordham proposed a resolution to the contradiction in the theory, by which 'self' would refer to a concept that defined the psychosomatic whole of the personality. Another term would be needed to account for the functioning, imagery and subjective experiences of wholeness that Jung had ascribed to the self when he used the term to refer to an archetype. Because it would confuse matters to call this the 'archetype of the self', Fordham suggested the term 'central archetype'.

The term comes from John Perry, who used 'central archetype' to refer to particular integrative psychic processes that were not necessarily part of individuation, like those processes compensatory to ego states evident in schizophrenia (Perry 1957). Perry's understanding was that these images belonged to 'one class (of primordial images) that describes a centre of order and circumference of delimitation which Jung called the self (Jung 1928, para. 274)'. In other words, Perry's use of 'central archetype' was synonymous with 'archetype of the self'.

In his 1963 'Empirical foundations' paper, Fordham wrote that, besides Perry, Jung had also suggested a centralising archetypal organiser closely related to the ego:

> With reference to schizophrenia Perry suggested that another term be given to the archetype lying behind the images. He used the term 'central archetype'. Jung seems to have considered it also for he refers (1958a, p. 137) to '. . . a central archetype . . . which I have called the archetype of the self'.
>
> (Fordham 1963, pp. 14–15)

It is clear from this that Fordham believed that Jung used the term because he cited what he considered to be the source. 'Central archetype' does not appear in the index of the *Collected Works*, which does not mean that Jung did not use the term, just that its occurrence did not merit indexing. However, further investigation shows that the term is not in the source cited, in the bibliography of 'The transcendent function' (1958a). Instead, Fordhan's writings (1957) are closer to the Perry paper than to anything found in Jung. Perry wrote:

> Since I use the term self-image regularly . . ., I wish to avoid confusion of terms and call the former the *personal self image* and the latter the *central archetype;* this archetype is here conceived as making its appearance at all phases of life and in all kinds of states of integration and disintegration [that is, schizophrenia), and thus is not always associated with the conscious experience of selfhood, in the sense of being an active element requiring long and arduous work of spiritual or psychological development specifically designated by Jung the individuation process.
>
> (Perry 1957, p. 137)

Fordham may have wished to find the term in Jung in order to lend it authority when applied to his own objectives. However, Fordham would certainly not have suggested 'central archetype' if it did not connote what he understood to be Jung's meaning of 'archetype of the self' which, as a central organising and integrating principle, could also be considered the 'archetype of order' (Jung 1944, 1950, 1951, 1954). Although in all likelihood 'central archetype' did not come from Jung but from Perry, Perry's ideas about it served Fordham's purposes. It was important to Fordham to have intellectual clarity and consistency in the theoretical system, and this required distinguishing the definition of the self as the totality from usage referring to an archetype; Fordham's model rested on the totality definition. Added to this, at the time Fordham was working on this matter, he had not yet regarded individuation as beginning in childhood.[2] Hence it would have been useful for him to have a concept of an archetype intimately related to selfhood and the ego, and not part of individuation but applicable to ego development in childhood.

In the last edition of his study,[3] Fordham gave a thumbnail sketch of the distinguishing properties of the central archetype:

- Its primary function is integrative; 'the central archetype . . . transcends and unites opposites' (Fordham 1985, p. 33). This primary function discriminates the central archetype from the self as, according to Fordham, the self integrates *and* deintegrates.
- The central archetype has a special connection with the ego and its development. 'The main body of the ego, sometimes called the central ego, has a special relation to the archetype of the self. That central archetype can then be thought of [sic: as] an organizer of the unconscious: it contributes significantly to the formation of the central ego. . . . (It is) the source of the central ego' (Fordham 1985, p. 32). That is, the operations of the central archetype pertain to psychic functioning and organisation.
- In regard to subjective experience, the central archetype 'finds expression especially in conscious experiences of selfhood' (Fordham 1985, pp. 31–33), whether these expressions are 'spiritual ecstasies or being down to earth and quite ordinary' (Fordham 1986).
- The 'central archetype' does not appear in any of Fordham's writing after 1985, which included several papers about his model, some of which refer to the contradiction in Jung's usage of 'self' as well as modifying certain details to his earlier thinking. Hence Fordham did not eliminate the term, nor did he develop it.

I am proposing that Fordham's idea of a central archetype is useful within his developmental model. I shall argue that it is helpful conceptually, not only because it helps to refine terminology, which was Fordham's original intention in using it. It can also describe in Jungian terminology the deintegration of psyche out of the psychosomatic unity of the early infant self, a process implied in Fordham's statement, 'In treating these twin concepts, psyche and soma, as deintegrates, their origin in the self is not lost sight of' (Fordham 1985, p. 170).

To follow this through, I shall need to identify what could be conceptualised as early manifestations of the central archetype, which would be the early development of consciousness and 'conscious experiences of selfhood' (Fordham 1985, p. 32). This will require turning to developmental studies. I shall also need to provide support from clinical and observational material, which comes from observations of a 14-month-old boy, whose behaviour in relation to me can illustrate how the central archetype can express itself in the deintegration of psyche.

The deintegration of psyche and developments at the end of the first year

In order to examine the emergence of the central archetype, I shall be looking for the early development of consciousness and evidences of expressions of self-consciousness, self-awareness and early mentalisation relating to the sense of self. I shall begin with a relevant statement from Fordham: 'the self being the whole, subjectively there's nothing with which to describe it. It's only when a certain amount of deintegration occurs that you can get an angle observed, and of course what you've observed isn't the whole self, but you can infer the existence of a whole self' (Fordham 1986). This raises the question as to when infants begin to make inferences.

This capacity comes with other new developments that begin to appear between nine and fifteen months. During this period there are significant developments in infant capacities indicating new intimations of the awareness of awareness and consciousness of consciousness. As Stern puts it,

> (There] is a quantum leap in the sense of self [that] occurs when the infant discovers that he or she has a mind and that other people have minds as well. . . . This discovery amounts to the acquisition of a 'theory' of separate minds. . . . The potential properties of a self and of another have been greatly expanded. Selves and others now include inner or subjective states of experience. . . . At this stage, for the first time one can attribute to the infant the capacity for psychic intimacy.
>
> (Stern 1985, pp. 124–126)

The new organisations within the infant led the psychologist (Bremner 1994) to describe the changes as a shift from knowledge based on direct perceptual and environmental input, to that based on representations, including those of self.

In psychoanalytic and Jungian terms, these changes represent ego development. Although still unstable, the ego by the end of the first year has become more or less consolidated and, within it, representations of the self begin to appear, experienced as the new sense of self to which Stern refers. Although there is a new consciousness of the sense of self, early on in this period it is probably best conceived as 'pre-"I"', and lacks the conscious coherence of a two-year-old, who can refer to himself as 'I'.

This new surge in ego development between nine and fifteen months can be regarded as evidence of the central archetype, which 'contributes significantly to the formation of the central ego'; it is 'the source of the central ego' and is expressed 'in conscious experiences of selfhood' (Fordham 1985, pp. 32–33). Put differently, because Fordham conceived the central archetype to be the source of the ego and expressed in conscious experiences of selfhood, ego development during this period – the new consciousness of consciousness, including that of self – can be regarded as manifestations of the central archetype.

The complexity of the changes that mark this period can be seen in the wide-ranging fields of research from which our understanding now draws. They include studies of language development (Trevarthen 1986, 1988), neural development (Schore 1994; Chugani 1998), affective neuroscience (Schore 1994, 2002; Panksepp 1998), emotional development (Sroufe 1995), social and cognitive development (Stern 1985; Fonagy et al. 2002), affect regulation (Schore 1994), attachment (Fonagy et al. 2002) and autism (Hobson 2002) – to name but a few of the sources.

This period is but one of several that occur during infancy. These are now considered to be manifestations of the serial progression of the wiring up of the brain. Harry Chugani (1998) discovered that the development of synapses in the individual infant brain follows the evolutionary path of the species; that is, development moves from the primitive brain stem to the midbrain (which includes the limbic system) and then to the frontal cortex. His research was based on the link between synaptogenesis, which soars just after birth, and glucose uptake in the brain, which can be measured. He discovered that glucose uptake in the newborn is highest in the reptilian core, which regulates primitive vital functions. At two to three months there are increases in the 'old mammalian brain', which 'mediates social emotions' (Panksepp 1998 p. 43). Then

> between eight and twelve months, the dorsal and medial frontal regions also show increased glucose utilization. . . . By approximately one year of age, the infant's pattern of glucose utilization resembles qualitatively that of the adult.
> (Chugani 1998, p. 7)

In other words, the wiring up of fundamental functional parts of the brain has been accomplished by the time the infant is about a year old. This marks the point at which there is mind-to-mind communication, at the heart of which are joint cooperation and shared play (Trevarthen and Hubley 1978). Toward the end of the first year, shared play is possible because of neural developments, and neural developments occur because of shared play during this time. As Trevarthen entitled one of his papers, 'Sharing makes sense' (Trevarthen 1988).

The research team including Peter Fonagy have investigated the development of mentalisation, or reflective capacity (Fonagy et al. 2002), which is the capacity to reflect upon oneself. An early step towards this is the 'social-cognitive revolution' that occurs in relation to attachment at about nine months. This revolution is marked by the acquisition of what they term the 'teleological stance', when the infant develops a new awareness of the relationship between means and ends. This is accompanied by a 'naïve' rationality, whereby infants assume that 'agents pursue their goals in the most rational or efficient manner available to them given the constraints of physical reality' (. . . 1st yr . . . involving joint attention to objects or situations' (Fonagy et al. 2002, p. 225).

Earlier Trevarthen, in his research into the foundations of language development, had observed the infant's new capacity for joint cooperation. He described significant developments at the end of the first year in the infant's ability to perceive his own and others' intentions and to bring together previously separate ways of relating to people and to objects. 'Before this, objects are perceived and used, and persons are communicated with – but these two kinds of intention are expressed separately' (Trevarthen and Hubley 1978, p. 184). But toward the end of the first year, during the period of 'secondary subjectivity', 'a deliberately sought sharing of experiences about events and things is achieved for the first time' (Trevarthen and Hubley 1978, p. 184). Trevarthen emphasises the importance of shared play because it is the means by which the broader culture becomes passed on in various ways, such as conveying information (what a telephone is for), cognitive skills, social mores, language and all that language brings with it.

Shared experiences depend upon shared intentions, and shared intentions rest upon a capacity for making inferences, because intentions lie in the mind and cannot be directly perceived. At this time and not before, if a mother points to an object the infant will follow the direction of the point. Stern notes how infants 'not only visually follow the direction of the point but, after reaching the target, look back at the mother and appear to use the feedback from her face to confirm chat they have arrived at the intended target' (Stern 1985, p. 129). Trevarthen concludes, 'Before the change, the infant has no interest, no comprehension of what is wanted', but at the end of the first year, he is able 'to take a gesture and a spoken message as an instruction' (Trevarthen 1988, p. 193).

Being able to infer is inextricably linked to being aware of another's awareness. Peter Hobson researches autism, which he considers to be a failure in the development of mind.[4] Following Trevarthen's work into secondary subjectivity, Hobson's studies have led him to explore the origins of thinking and mindedness. He notes how at the end of the first year

> [The infant] is becoming aware of the other person's awareness of things, conscious of the other's consciousness. [The baby] is interested in and responsive to what the other person does with things and feels toward things.
> (Hobson 2002, p. 63)

As this occurs, the infant enters into triangulations. As Hobson points out, these are comprised of infant, other (e.g., mother), and object (e.g., toy) or event (e.g., a strange sound) or another person (e.g., Daddy), along with the infant's sense of the relationships between them. Each triangulation, to be tripartite, requires psychological space between the self and the other components of the triangle. Time and again through play the infant will, step by step, encounter new perspectives in the ever-changing relationships between the elements making up the triangulation. With each shift of perspective, there is a slightly new awareness. Judith Woodhead, when describing triangulations involving 'the father', has referred to this dynamic as 'trialectic' (Woodhead 2004). Here, I am expanding the notion of 'trialectic' process to include objects and events as well as others.

To summarise, developments begin to manifest at nine to twelve months, which include the emergence of the capacity to infer along with the dawning of a new awareness of one's own and another's attention and attitudes. This does not mean that these new awarenesses involve conscious thinking. Only later can the baby reflect upon himself to another ('Mummy, I'm hurt') or to himself ('I'm naughty'). When this occurs toward the end of the second year, 'This represents something new, which doesn't happen until the other aspects of the relatedness triangle have been in place for some time' (Hobson 2002, p. 108). It is at this point when the trialectic includes self-reflective function-thinking about understanding and interpreting one's own feeling states and those of others. But before that time, towards the end of the first year, one can see the emergence of the components of this highly important capacity, which provide the foundations for the links that Ron Britton has made between the Oedipal triangle and three-dimensional thinking (Britton 1989).

In summary, around the end of the first year there is a new consciousness of consciousness and capacity for mind-to-mind sharing. These developments lead to varying triangulations and new perspectives, which provide the foundations for symbolisation, language, thinking and theory of mind. It is this which leads Trevarthen to say,

> The mysterious, forward-looking, innate determination of psychic growth is here manifest in a most elaborate form. Indeed, psychological functions that remain central to the highest intellectual and moral achievements of adults in society are expressed in a one-year-old on the threshold of spoken language.
>
> (Trevarthen and Hubley 1978, p. 184)

Within Fordham's model and my expansion of his idea of a central archetype, this can be regarded as the emergence of manifestations of the central archetype, the deintegration of psyche and the beginning of having a mind.

A clinical observation: Vejayan

This section aims to provide support from clinical and observational experience for evidence of manifestations of the central archetype, detailed in the previous section.

The boy I shall call Vejayan was 14 months old when I observed him playing with his mother in a mother-baby in-patient unit where some of my NHS work is based. His mother had suffered a severe depression after Vejayan's birth, and he had spent much of his young life in the unit. They both attended a mother-baby group I ran, where, earlier in his babyhood, his mother seemed crushed by the weight of her depression. This was evident from the overall sense of deadness she bore and wore upon her face. There was little physical or emotional contact between them; during baby massage, her hands stilled or were withdrawn to her lap, and making eye contact required prompting and encouragement. For his part, Vejayan too was still and avoidant. When he was old enough to sit up, he would squirm on her lap, leaning and reaching away from her, wriggling towards others in the group, persistently trying to distance himself from her and her depression. Gradually her depression diminished, and she emerged as a pleasant, rather passive woman, who showed courage in addressing serious domestic problems. Throughout the time Vejayan and his mother were in the unit, various nurses cared for and played with Vejayan when his mother was too withdrawn to do so. By the end of his first year, Vejayan had become attached to her and, as he entered toddlerhood, he became a lively and popular baby in the unit. I often came across him stomping hurriedly and unsteadily along a corridor, grinning and wildly waving his arms, with a good-natured nurse in pursuit.

The videos I took of Vejayan arose from a regular staff group discussion of infant observations and studies. When possible, we use videoed observations, given that the mother is well enough and willingly gives consent.[5] When staff and I watched the video with Vejayan and his mother, I became concerned about two things. The first was that there was virtually no truly shared play between them, which I knew to be essential to development. As one person in the group commented, 'The play doesn't go anywhere'.

> Vejayan plays with a ball, kicking it about aimlessly, chirpily chattering and sometimes stumbling as he moves alongside a shelf of toys, occasionally holding onto it. If the ball came her way, the mother would kick it back in his direction, but not being aimed especially for him to catch, and his attention not being aimed at receiving the ball, it bounced off elsewhere. He seemed quite happy playing essentially on his own. Only once did he look at his mother, glancing up at her briefly with a serious, rather worried expression on his face.
>
> After a while, Vejayan goes to her and she pulls him up on her lap, where he stands up facing outward, holding a plastic skittle, looking chuffed and crowing as he knocks the skittle against his other hand and then his head. His mother smiles up at him and he knocks the skittle against her temple. Smiling and affectionate, she says, 'Naw, naw'. He imitates her, emphasizing the end of each word with a slight uplift: 'Nawuh, naw-uh', and pressing his face against hers, cheek to cheek, with each utterance. Playfully, but a bit roughly, he sways back and forth as they alternate their singsong 'naws', first away from her then back against her face, pushing his mouth against it. He starts to roar – excited! – and stands tall and swings the skittle up and down in the

air until it's thrown onto the floor. He returns to swaying back and forth, smearing her face with gooey 'kisses', the 'naw-uh' becoming an aggressive 'ooo-UH', when his face comes up against hers. She objects when the 'kisses' are replaced with pinching fingers. He turns away and gives an excited call, whereupon his voice changes and becomes whiny, increasingly becoming more complaining and grating. Eventually she softly intervenes, 'Vejayan . . . Vejayan . . . naughty boy' as he swings back and forth against her. She clearly had had enough of the persecutory tone of his whingeing.

It is evident that Vejayan and his mother are affectionate with one another, although their interchanges do not get beneath the surface. As if pursuing a 'deliberately sought sharing of experiences' (Trevarthen and Hubley 1978, p. 184), he tries to touch upon both their minds with the skittle, banging it first against his head and then hers, as if he knows there are thoughts inside to which he wants access. He smears her face with gooey, sticky 'kisses', a kind of relating that Esther Bick and Donald Meltzer called 'adhesive' and 'two-dimensional' (Bick 1986; Meltzer 1975). Their exchange, despite its warmth, remains face-to-face rather than mind-to-mind, before dissolving into his persecutory whingeing and her soft admonition.

Left with a sense that there was a mind behind his mother's face that was not available to him, Vejayan was not only frustrated but also without something to engage the focus of his attention. So he flitted from one thing to another, the brevity of his concentration being noticeable and worrying. Overall, I was concerned that Vejayan functioned primarily in a two-dimensional way, and it was unclear whether he had the capacity for shared play, three-dimensionality and mind-to-mind relationships. If he did not, there was cause possibly for serious concern, indicating autistic tendencies and/or the beginning of behaviour and relationship problems. I was also concerned that most of the nurses watching the video considered that, given his liveliness and the warmth of their interaction, Vejayan and his mother were playing normally. I wondered if the nurses might become more aware of play that 'went somewhere', and the group agreed to ask Vejayan's mother if I could do a second video, when I would play with Vejayan.

My aim was to see if I could engage Vejayan by following his interest and then invite shared play. To begin, he engaged with me, and he engaged with toys, but these did not come together into a triangulation of conjoint activity that could 'go somewhere'. His concentration shifted quickly from one thing to another, and he became excited and aggressive.

> Vejayan bangs a bucket around noisily and aggressively. His mother tries to quieten him but he bangs on it until he throws a small ball my way. I catch it up and ask him if he would like to play ball. He throws the bucket in my direction and his mother protests. I carefully roll the ball back to him. When the ball reaches him, he brings the ball my way. I catch it up and ask him if he

would like to play ball. He throws the bucket in my direction and his mother protests. I carefully roll the ball back to him. When the ball reaches him, he brings it back to me rather than rolling it. I reach for the bucket and invite him to put the ball into the bucket. Thereupon Vejayan forcefully throws it inside. He squeals in over-excitement and throws the ball willy-nilly. His concentration bounces around as much as the ball, and his excitement and aggression escalate. When he throws the ball toward his mother – clearly intentionally – she firmly tells him 'No'.

This persisted for what seemed a long time, and I became discouraged and began to sense that my plan might fail. Vejayan, now playing on his own, drifted off behind a small Wendy house, perhaps in his retreat just as dejected as I was. His mother and I conversed as much as we could, given the limitations of language. Eventually Vejayan seemed interested, and we encouraged him to come and play again. He came to us, on his way picking up the lid to a small plastic carry-out cup.

Near us was a large, mushroom-shaped, toy house, into which various shapes fit through corresponding slots in the hemisphere of the roof, with a door at the bottom of the 'stem' from which they could be removed. On the surface of the roof were objects that spun, turned or could be pushed, which he and his mother had previously banged against in a two-dimensional way.

> His mother tries to support my efforts to play with him by drawing his attention to the mushroom house, banging on its surface apparatus. He slips down and follows her in this two-dimensional play, becoming excited and throwing the plastic lid at the house, and then grasping the knob on the house top and leaning over it, as if trying to grasp and conquer something about it.

From what followed I now think that what he was trying to grasp was its interior quality. Rather than get frustrated he began to string together something like a series of thoughts.

> Vejayan is clearly getting frustrated and his mother hands him the skittle. He tries to put the skittle into one of the holes on the roof but can't get it to go inside. He turns and with intention looks around for something, then finds the plastic lid and inserts it into his mouth. Almost instantaneously he inserts first his hand, and then the narrow end of the skittle, into the hole.

For just a brief moment he explored perspectives on 'container-contained'. There was the direct experience of 'container', when his mouth encapsulated the lid, and the direct experience of 'contained', when his arm went inside the toy. Lastly there was the projection of a part of himself into a container when he inserted the skittle inside the toy.

Finally Vejayan dropped the plastic cap into the house, where it disappeared and became a 'no-breast'. He tried unsuccessfully to retrieve it through the slot where he dropped it:

> Speaking to him, I offer to help him find it, and look at and point to the door at the base of the toy, from which he can retrieve the lid. I feel hopeful that here we have a chance for shared play, but Vejayan seems unable to follow the line of my gaze or my pointing. Curiously, rather than following my gaze and point, he retraces them back to my face, behind which lies my intention. He stoops in order to look up and into my face, poking at it. I smile and say, 'That's my face, Vejayan!' But he seems frustrated that he can't make out what's going on. He tries to put the bucket over my head, and, when I prevent this, he puts it over his own head, when his mother intervenes. He seems to be blocking out mind-to-mind communication, as he can't infer what I'm trying to convey. I encourage him time and again to look down at the door, and his mother tries to help, but he just doesn't 'get it' so I retrieve it for him. His frustration throws him off balance, and he tumbles over and cries in emotional hurt and frustration. His mother distracts him by pounding on the top surface of the roof. He does try again with the lid, but soon gives up and goes to his mother.
>
> Feeling discouraged, I find myself examining the toy and discovering that the roof has an outer shell that turns and must be in place for particular objects to fit through their corresponding slots. When I 'get' how the toy works, my left hand, which turned the knob on the top, automatically lifts with a flick in a brief unconscious flourish of satisfaction. Vejayan meanwhile stands next to his mother with one hand on her knee, watching what I am doing, When I notice this, I repeatedly show how the lid can go into the top and then come out the bottom, telling him so as I demonstrate. He studies the situation for several moments, then leans forward just a bit, looks at me and makes a little sound.

It was a musical, not a speech, vocalisation, purely expressive and hence rather like the unconscious flourish of my hand when I had 'got' how the toy worked.

> He takes a step toward me and the toy, I hold out the lid to him and ask, 'Do you want to do it?' He takes the lid and inserts it into a hole in the roof and then stoops down and opens the door. The lid's fallen to the back of the base of the toy, out of sight, so I tip the toy so that it falls out and he picks it up. 'Well, brilliant!', I say and he immediately inserts the lid through the top again and retrieves it without help from behind the closed door at the bottom. He repeats this several times.

The play at last had gone somewhere. Vejayan had eventually been able to see what I had in mind, which, despite being as invisible to him as the lid was inside the house, was, like the lid, reachable. What was curious was the little song-note he emitted just when he clearly 'got it'. I conferred with Miranda Davies, who is a singer and now a retired child analyst, who identified the pitch of Vejayan's song-note as the C above middle C. She noted that when I told him, 'Well, brilliant', my 'Well' was also the C above middle C. Hence Vejayan and I were metaphorically singing from the same song sheet.

Self representations and the emergence of the central archetype

I should now like to turn to the two barely noticeable 'eureka!' moments in the observation, which would not have been evident if they had not been caught on videotape. The first was the flourish of my hand, dance-like rather than gestural, when I discovered how the toy 'worked'. The second was Vejayan's song-note, song-like rather than a communicative vocalisation, when he inferred what I was implying. The words 'eureka' and 'heuristic' are related and refer to finding out or discovering something for oneself. This is not the same as imitation, projective identification or a state of identity.

Vejayan's frustration toppled him externally and internally, and he reverted to two-dimensional functioning, banging on the surface of the toy. But when he recovered and stood at his mother's knee, he turned his attention back to the toy and me. From that perspective he entered two triangulations: of himself, his mother and the situation; and of himself, the toy and me being interested in the toy. We can assume from what followed that he integrated his perceptions into a new thought, but this was not simply a cognitive phenomenon. It was heralded by a 'song-note', which I see as an expression of what Fordham called a 'self representation': 'A self representation is that which gives rise to a preconscious sense of self and other' (Astor 1995, p. 59). It is a 'sense of being oneself' (Fordham 1985, p. 120), which is an early, pre-symbolic representation of the self in the ego; 'self representations . . . [require] some degree of ego development . . . and are obviously partial . . . though something of the primary self clings to them' (Fordham 1976, p. 13). 'Some of them refer . . . to the total self as Jung maintained' (Fordham 1976, p. 56).

Thus the song-note, like the movement of my hand, can be seen as an expression of a sense of self of which there is some consciousness. In our respective eureka moments, each of us felt, 'I found it!', and the 'I' to which we referred is a pre-conscious inference of a taken-for-granted unity of our respective beings. This was accompanied by spontaneous, irreducible phenomena that were purely expressive – merely an announcement of a new reintegration of the self. When a new thought (but not thinking) emanated out of this, Vejayan grasped it *as his own*. He could successfully act on this new thought because he now possessed it. Despite my gestures and efforts to share my idea, when Vejayan inferred what was in my mind, he felt it to be his thought, not mine.

These eureka moments represented a fleeting, momentary awareness of the unity in our respective senses of self, which referred to the wholeness of the self, defined by Fordham[6] It is true that very young infants are no strangers to musicality and rhythmic movement. I have heard a newborn less than a day old vocalise distinctly musical notes as her family talked about her and seen babies only a few weeks old 'dance' as they watch the movement of a mobile above them. But these are direct responses to the world and are different from Vejayan's song-note and the flourish of my hand. Our eureka moments, with their accompanying self representations, required the achievement of an awareness of our respective selves, an awareness not yet available to young infants.

Yet self representations viewed as representations of the self are not entirely logically consistent within Fordham's model. Conceptually, 'the primal self cannot be represented but its *deintegrates can*, and from these inferences can be made about the self' (Fordham 1994, p. 76; my italics).[7] Rather self-feeling ('Ich Gefuhl'), with its representations and symbols, 'would be conceived as manifesting the central archetype of which the ego is a part' (Fordham 1985, p. 108). Hence I am modifying Fordham's idea of self representations as representations of the self in the ego, to state that self representations and self are more aptly considered as representations and symbols of the central archetype.

In furtherance of this, Fordham noted that the primary function of the central archetype is integrative; 'it transcends and unites opposites' (Fordham 1985, p. 33). Vejayan's song-note can be seen as an expression of an integration of his sense of other, of object and of self, emerging from the space provided by a triangulation of the constituents. Vejayan's new thought, fused as it is with self feeling, can be seen as ego development resulting from the same integrative activities that Fordham, from Jung, ascribed to the central archetype.

Archetypes, as Fordham summarised them, are 'typical and universal, . . . at once mental and physical' (Fordham 1986). Brain developments occurring at the end of the first year are typical and universal, and hence they can be conceived to be archetypal. Furthermore they are physical, the result of brain activity in which circuits and systems firing together become wired together; and they are mental, as is Vejayan's having a new thought, even if it cannot yet be considered mentalisation.

Just how brain becomes mind remains unknown; however various eminent researchers inquiring into this mystery have forged possible new links between body and mind. One of these is Roger Sperry, a neurophysiologist, who spelled out a hypothesis involving the principle of emergence[8] a concept which rose up in science and philosophy during the mid-20th century (Sperry 1977; Tresan 1996). Sperry suggested that consciousness was an emergent property and was separate from, although dependent upon, brain activity. Basically, emergence holds that the whole is irreducibly more than the sum of its parts. An example of the principle of emergence is water, which is irreducibly more than its constituent two hydrogen and one oxygen atoms.

Sperry was awarded a Nobel Prize in 1981 for his work on the bilaterality of the cerebral cortex, two different systems of consciousness. He pointed out that these become, in normal circumstances, 'single and unified' (Sperry 1977, p. 376).

Sperry was cautious when he introduced the conclusions from his work in a lecture in the mid-1960s, when he put forward a view that consciousness is

> a dynamic emergent of brain activity neither identical with, nor reducible to, the neural events of which it is mainly composed. . . . [It is] not conceived as an epiphenomenon, inner aspect, or other passive correlate of brain process- ing, but rather to be an active integral part of the cerebral process itself, exert- ing potent causal effects in the interplay of cerebral operations. In a position of top command at the highest levels in the hierarchy of brain organization, the subjective properties . . . exert control over the biophysical and chemical activities at subordinate levels.
>
> (Sperry 1977, p. 382)

Sperry points out the evolutionary advantage to humans of having 'two mutually conflicting modes of cerebral processing, holistic-spatial and analytic-sequen- tial' (Sperry 1977, p. 376). 'Consider', he asks, 'the tactical difference between responding to the world directly and responding to inner conscious representations of the outside world' (Sperry 1977, p. 385). This is the advantage that Vejayan was acquiring through shared play, when he integrated new perceptions, observed from new perspectives, and abstracted them into a new thought. He grasped this new thought to be his own, whereby he could internalise it by successfully testing it out on the toy on his own.

Here the 'central archetype', 'emergence' and developments at the end of the first year converge to form an understanding towards the early deintegration of psyche. According to Fordham, the central archetype contributes to the formation of the central ego and its primary function is integrative (Fordham 1947). This links with Sperry's 'single and unified' consciousness and Vejayan's coming to possess a new thought. The central archetype 'transcends and unites opposites' and therefore has a transcendent function, just as does Sperry's concept of emer- gence, which unites mutually conflicting modes of consciousness. The central archetype finds expression especially in conscious experiences of selfhood, as Vejayan expressed in his song-note.

Deintegration of the central archetype from infancy to adulthood

The emergence of capacities at the end of the first year can be seen as a devel- opmental prelude to symbolisation, story-making, morality and the variety of subjective experiences of the self that Jung had reserved for later life. What is left to be done is to link early self representations to symbols of the self in later development.

Developmentally the earliest manifestations of the central archetype are pre- symbolic, such as Vejayan's song-note and the scribbles drawn by a little boy, who was one of the two children from whose activities Fordham hypothesised the self in childhood. The boy, who was around Vejayan's age, drew repeated circles until he could say 'I', whereupon the circles stopped.

The capacity for (but not necessarily the acquisition of) symbolisation, as Jung regarded symbols, develops at around four years (Fonagy et al. 2002). At this point there are evidences of reflective function and theory of mind, indicating the child's capacity to represent representations. This could be expected to apply to self symbols referring to the child's wholeness of being. In fact Fordham described this kind of self-image from his own childhood, when he was around four. In his *Memoirs*, he recalled an experience that occurred as his family were moving from Surrey to Hampshire.

> A lot of packing was going on and it continued until we left the first house in my life when I was three or four years old. I do not remember arriving at Clapham Junction. (I am convinced that I was told and remembered the title of that station at the time.) My mother and I were together; I was sitting on her knee in a railway carriage looking out of the window. I thought we were at the centre of the world and all trains came to Clapham Junction where our train had stopped. I felt important and secure.
>
> (Fordham 1993, p. 27)

Fordham's reflection conveys his sense of wholeness, of being 'at the centre of the world'. Simultaneously it is of self-integrative processes of the central archetype, expressed as a self image, or symbol, of a junction where 'all trains came to' and 'where our train had stopped'. (The memory disregards the fact that trains also departed from Clapham Junction.)

The emergent processes of self-image creation are now recognised to be evanescent and fleeting, less comparable to the fixed properties of H_2O, and more to schools of certain fish or flocks of certain birds. These burst into an overall form and move as a unit until dissolving into entities behaving as individuals. The sight of a flock of starlings preoccupied Samuel Coleridge, who made the following entry in his journal as he was leaving the Lake District to start a new career as a journalist.

> Starlings in vast flights drove along like smoke, mist, or any thing misty without volition – now a circular area inclined in an arc – now a Globe – now from complete Orb into an Ellipse & Oblong – now a balloon with the car suspended, now a concave Semicircle – & still it expands & condenses, some moments glimmering and shimmering, dim & shadowy, now thickening, deepening, blackening!
>
> (Holmes 1989, p. 253)

Richard Holmes, Coleridge's biographer, wrote,

> This image haunted him for years after. . . . It is an image of shifting energy and imagination, a protean form or a force field, lacking fixed structure or

outline, a powerful personality without a solid identity, or unified will – 'without volition'. Clearly this was some sort of self-image for Coleridge, both stimulating in its freedom of 'vast flights' and menacing in its sense of threatening chaos or implosion, 'thickening, deepening, blackening'.

(Holmes 1989, p. 254)

This captures the ceaseless movement of both consciousness and unconsciousness, one state blending into or clashing against another in what appears to be the way emergence functions to create mind and enable mind to create and recreate itself. The terms 'representation' and 'image' seem inappropriate because they convey an impression of something static. These symbolic expressions are ephemeral and elusive, rising up, emerging into consciousness seemingly from nowhere and then disappearing again. Jung famously experienced this kind of self-image of mind reflecting on mind, evidenced in the changing mandalas in his series of drawings during 1918–19. He referred to them as the 'ultimate'; 'Formation, Transformation, Eternal Mind's eternal recreation' (Jung 1963, p. 221).

This then is a very brief sketch of the deintegration of the central archetype, from infancy to adult life.

Summary comment

The subject of this chapter is the self in Jungian theory as Fordham came to view it, having made it the conceptual centre and basis of his model. Working out his model required it to be logically coherent and consistent, so when Fordham discovered a contradiction in the ways Jung used the 'self', a resolution was required. Fordham separated the 'self' defined as a psychosomatic totality from expressions of its wholeness in human psychic experience. For this he suggested the term 'central archetype'. This resolved the contradiction via his developmental model; the self is primary, and the central archetype is a deintegrate. What I have here pressed to clarify is that the logical consequence of this is that phenomena associated with the self should be regarded as manifestations of the central archetype.

Curiously Fordham, having suggested the term, neither developed nor dropped it, although he preserved it in the culmination of his work, *Explorations into the Self* (1985). I am arguing for the value of this concept, based on my own studies into infancy and Fordham's model. 'Central archetype' serves as a conceptual tool providing logical consistency to Jung's theory of the self. It offers a more precise way of describing the deintegration of mind because it accommodates the wealth of data from infant research not available to Fordham, while demonstrating how readily his model comprehends it.

As a deintegrate out of which the ego develops, the central archetype provides a link between early ego development and the primary self. Locating the emergence of its early phenomena at the end of the first year marks the closing of what I have elsewhere considered to be the period of the primary self, and the early beginnings of psychic phenomena, including symbolisation, which were the data of Jung's work (Urban 2005). This link preserves Fordham's view, following Jung, that the individual self is woven into the whole fabric of one's life. In Fordham's model, the self is not emergent or a construct derived from others or a process alone, but inherently, bodily and essentially one's own.

Notes

1 In his biography of Jung, Vincent Brome noted that Jung 'imagined himself to belong to the type called Logos – or thinking-dominated man, but in fact the intuitive-sensation functions came first and the Logos last' (Brome 1980, p. 125). In contrast Fordham was a very fine conceptual thinker, who greatly admired Jung's intuitive powers, so evident in the way he gleaned ideas of the transference from the *Mysterium Cunjunctionis*.

   The term 'deintegration' has proved difficult for those unfamiliar with Fordham. In part this is because it seems to connote an undoing of a negative nature. Fordham intended it to be seen as the unfolding of an integrate that does not undo development but instead is an essential part of it.

   'The peri-oral area is the first part of the body to come "on-line". The onset of the response marks the point the embryonic period ends and the foetal period begins' (Bremner 1994, pp. 2–5).

   The word 'self' is of Anglo-Saxon, Old Saxon and Old Norse origins, and Damasio notes that the term does not occur in romance languages except in the reflexive, such as 'self-reflective' and 'self-centred' (Damasio 1999). Nor, I am told, does 'self' occur in the Eastern languages of Hindi and Gugerati.

   Daniel Stern and Antonio Damasio have in their respective ways also studied the self. Stern and Damasio are careful to use phrases such as 'sense of' or 'feeling' of self, while not getting into the thorny issue of what the self is. Each holds their respective ideas, whether explicit or implied, about an 'emergent' and 'core self' (Stern 1985) or 'proto-self' (Damasio 1999). These are not equivalents to the primary self, but they refer to the same dynamic entity that Fordham postulated.

   Fordham's attempts to date the beginning of the primary self imply that the concept also refers to the period of development. Here however Fordham seems to be regarding the primary self as a concept beyond time and space and therefore existence, at the same time as making efforts to date it (in his notes).

2 I examine the 1960 and 1928 versions of 'The transcendent function' as well as searched other possible sources in the Collected Works. It was not until 1965 at Fordham came to be convinced that the individuation applied to childhood. Up until that time, 'I argued that because of the differences between the relation of the ego to the self in childhood and in later life, individuation did not take place in childhood . . .' (Fordham 1985, p. 44). His conclusion first emerged in a paper entitled 'Individuation in childhood'. which Fordham presented to the Third IAAP International Congress (1965). It was published in J.B. Wheelwright's compilation of the proceedings (Wheelwright 1968). It appeared with minor alterations as chapter 4 in *The Self and Autism*, where Fordham wrote 'By the age of two, therefore, an infant can achieve every essential element of individuation in the sense that Jung could have accepted (Fordham 1976, p. 40).

3 The 1963 paper was reprinted in *Analytical Psychology: A Modern Science* (1973) and then revised to be the first chapter of Explorations into the Self (1985).

4 This is consistent with the conclusion that for Andrew from his studies into autism, namely, that autism is a failure of deintegration and reintegration.

5 The video was this intended for observational purposes, which Vijayan's mother understood, and does not represent an interaction primarily intended as parent infant psychotherapy as it is usually carried out. Each video recording requires informed consent,

obtained within procedures established by Health Trusts, which Vijayan's mother understood and granted.
6 Here I am understanding 'that we are dealing not only with successes phases but also with simultaneous domains of self experience beyond childhood' (Stern 1985, p. 19).
7 Here Fordham is not viewing inference as conscious, but as a function of an integrated state.
8 Jean Knox has written a fine paper in the *Journal of Analytical Psychology* on emergence, which parallels my own but coming from a different vertex. Knox's overall aim is to integrate archetypal theory with attachment theory. Mine is an examination of Fordham's developmental model, both historically and in the light of developmental and related research.
   The aim of Knox's 2004 paper is to put forward, 'that mind and meaning emerge out of developmental processes and the experience of interpersonal relationships rather than existing a priori' (Knox 2004, p. 161). This statement is an apt description of Fordham's model using different terminology. Fordham (who wrote about parent infant-interaction in the 1930s) (Fordham 1937) thought in terms of deintegration, 'unpacking' (of the original integrate) and unfolding rather than 'emergence'.
   Knox uses the term in its common sense meaning, whereas I am thinking here of 'emergence' in a more specific way, drawing upon Sperry's description of this principle. My doing so has a certain economy, as Sperry notes the way the brain functions integratively to produce consciousness, whereby subjective experience can act 'top-down' and effect change in lower parts of the brain. These functions are covered by Knox via an exposition of relevant research.
   Lastly, where is Knox applies 'emergence' to archetypes in general, I focus here on the development of an archetype linked to, and muddled with, the concept of 'self', which Fordham argued should be defined as the totality of the personality.

References

Astor, J. (1995). *Michael Fordham: Innovations in Analytical Psychology*. London: Routledge.
Bick, E. (1986). 'Further considerations of the function of the skin in early object relations'. *British Journal of Psychotherapy*, 2.
Bremner, J. (1994). *Infancy*. Oxford: Blackwell.
Britton, R. (1989). 'The missing link: Parental sexuality in the Oedipus complex'. In J. Steiner (ed.), *The Oedipus Complex Today*. London: Karnac Books.
Brome, V. (1980). *Jung*. London: Granada.
Chugani, H. (1998). 'The biological basis of emotions'. In J. Warhol and S. Shelov (eds.), *New Perspectives in Early Emotional Development*. USA: Johnson & Johnson Paediatric Institute.
Fonagy, P., Gergely, G., Jurist, E. and Target, M. (2002). *Affect Regulation, Mentalization, and the Development of the Self*. New York: Other Press.
Fordham, M. (1937). 'How children learn to grow up'. *The Psychologist*, September.
———. (1944). *The Life of Childhood*. London: Kegan Paul, Trench, Trubner.
———. (1947). 'Integration and disintegration and early ego development'. *The Nervous Child*, 6(3).
———. (1951). 'Some observations on the self in childhood'. *British Journal of Medical Psychology*, 24(2).
———. (1955). 'The origins of the ego in childhood'. In C. G. Jung (ed.), *Studien zur analytischen Psychologie*. Zurich: Rascher. Trans. by Bader and Hastern as 'Uber die Entwicklung des Ichs in der Kindkeit'. *Zeitschrift fur Analytische Psychologie*, 2(4).

————. (1957). *New Developments in Analytical Psychology*. London: Routledge & Kegan Paul.

————. (1963). 'The empirical foundations and theories of the self in Jung's works'. *Journal of Analytical Psychology*, 8(1).

————. (1964). 'The relation of the ego to the self'. *British Journal of Medical Psychology*, 37.

————. (1968). 'Individuation in childhood'. In Wheelwright (ed.), *The Reality of the Psyche*. New York: Putnam.

————. (1976). *The Self and Autism*. London: William Heinemann Medical Books.

————. (1984). *Fordham at Ghost Ranch*. Videotaped Interview with Murray Stein and Nathan Schwarcz-Salant.

————. (1985). *Explorations into the Self*. London: Academic Press.

————. (1986). *Portrait of Analyst*. Filmed interview with Roger Hobdell.

————. (1987). 'Actions of self'. Chapter 16 in P. Young-Eisendrach and J. Hall (eds.), *The Book of the Self: Person, Pretext and Process*. New York: New York University Press.

————. (1993). *The Making of an Analyst*. London: Free Association Books.

————. (1994). *Children as Individuals*. London: Free Association Books.

Fordham, M., Gordon. R., Hubback, J., Lambert, K. and Williams, M. (eds.) (1973). *Analytical Psychology: A Modern Science*. London: Heinemann Medical Books.

Hobson, P. (2002). *The Cradle of Thought*. London: Macmillan.

Holmes, R. (1989). *Coleridge: Early Visions*. London: Penguin Books.

Jung, C. (1921). *Psychologische Types*. Ziiriich: Rascher. Trans. *Psychological Types* by H. G. Baynes, 1923. *CW 6*.

————. (1928). *Contributions to Analytical Psychology*, H. G. Baynes and C. F. Baynes. London: Routledge & Kegan Paul.

————. (1944). 'Psychology and alchemy'. *CW 12*.

————. (1950). 'Concerning mandala symbolism'. *CW 9*.

————. (1951). 'Aion: Researches into the phenomenology of the self'. *CW 9ii*.

————. (1954). 'Transformation symbols and the mass'. *CW 11*.

————. (1958a). *Die Transcendente Funktion*. Zurich: Rhein-Verlag. Trans. 'The transcendent function'. *CW 8*.

————. (1958b). 'Flying saucers: A modern myth of things seen in the sky'. *CW 10*.

————. (1963). *Memories, Dreams and Reflections*. London: Collins and Routledge & Kegan Paul.

————. (1971). 'Psychological types'. *CW 6*.

Knox, J. (2004). 'From archetypes to reflective function'. *Journal of Analytical Psychology*, 49(1).

Meltzer, D. (1975). 'Adhesive identification'. Contemporary Psychoanalysis, 11.

Panksepp, J. (1998). *Affective Neuroscience: The Foundations of Human and Animal Emotions*. Oxford: Oxford University Press.

Perry, J. (1957). 'Acute catatonic schizophrenia'. *Journal of Analytical Psychology*, 2(2).

Popper, K. and Eccles, J. (1977). *The Self and Its Brain: An Argument for Interactionism*. London: Springer International

Schore, A. (1994). *Affect Regulation and the Origin of the Self: The Neurology of Emotional Development*. Hove, UK: Lawrence Erlbaum Associates.

————. (2002). 'Clinical implications of a psychoneurobiological model of projective identification'. In S. Alhanati (eds.), *Primitive Mental States, Volume 2*. London: Karnac.

Sperry, R. (1977). 'Forebrain commissurotomy and conscious awareness'. *The Journal of Medicine and Philosophy*, 2(2). Reprinted in *Brain Circuits and Functions of the Mind: Essays in Honour of Roger W. Sperry*, ed. C. Trevarthen. Cambridge, UK: Cambridge University Press.

Sroufe, A. (1995). *Emotional Development: The Organization of Emotional Life in the Early Years*. Cambridge, UK: Cambridge University Press.

Stern, D. (1985). *The Interpersonal World of the Infant*. New York: Basic Books.

Tresan, D. (1996). 'Jungian metapsychology and neurobiological theory'. *Journal of Analytical Psychology*, 41: 3.

Trevarthen, C. (1988). 'Sharing makes sense: Intersubjectivity and the making of an infant's meaning'. In R. Steele and T. Treadgold (eds.), *Language Topics*. Amsterdam: John Benjamins.

Trevarthen, C. and Hubley, P. (1978). 'Secondary intersubjectivity'. In A. Lock (ed.), *Action, Gesture and Symbol: The Emergence of Language*. London: Academic Press.

Trevarthen, C. and Marwick, H. (1986). 'Signs of motivation for speech in infants, and the nature of a mother's support for development of language'. In B. Lindblom & R. Zetterstrom (eds.), *Precursors of Early Speech*. Basingstoke, Hants: Macmillan.

Urban, E. (2005). 'Fordham, Jung and the self: A re-examination of Fordham's contribution to Jung's conceptualization of the self'. *Journal of Analytical Psychology*, 50(5).

Woodhead, J. (2004). '"Dialectical process" and "constructive method": Micro-analysis of relational process in an example from parent-infant therapy'. *Journal of Analytical Psychology*, 49(2).

Reflections on research and learning from the patient

The art and science of what we do

Jung's final statement, 'We need a different language for every patient' (Jung 1963, p. 153), should be taken not as a denial of the value of theoretical guidelines for psychotherapy, but rather as a suggestion that the treatment of the patient is an art.

Over three decades ago, John Bowlby argued for psychoanalysis to seek empirics beyond its own parameters if it was to maintain its claim to be a science (Bowlby 1979). Since then the picture has changed, and research, particularly that into infancy, neurobiology and attachment, has been given a place within the controversies and literature in psychoanalysis and analytical psychology. A good example is the recent *Journal of Analytic Psychology* Conference in Boston USA[1] which directed attention to the potential enrichment that contemporary research can bring to Jungian understanding and practice; indeed, various elements of this research have been instrumental in the development of my own studies and clinical work. However, what follows will not elaborate on that contribution, which, like theory, is peripheral to my purposes here. Rather, I shall focus on learning from the patient. I shall begin with a premise: Interpretative analytic work is based on a three-dimensional configuration comprising two people with minds or, rather, minds-in-the-making, sharing interest in objects of thought and feelings (or lack of them). Put simply, the object of interest, whether a toy or a memory the patient recalls, serves as a kind of 'constant' in relation to which there are two different positions made up of a complexity of attitude, affect and meaning. These differences allow both parties to separate their minds from one another while becoming more deeply engaged with one another's selves. This triangulation lays the foundation and provides the ongoing means for realising our human capacities for abstraction, language, imagination, symbolisation and reflection.[2] Although interpretative work may be ingrained in our professional identity, this triangulation may or may not be held in the minds of our patients to any workable degree. What follows concerns just this and might be seen as an account of 'Formation, transformation; actions of the self in the mind's creation'.[3]

Firstly I offer a condensed outline of the developmental shifts in the infant's field of interest that provide the experiential components of three-dimensionality: self, other and object. Secondly, I show how the infant and child are active in the creation of their minds, presuming the participation of a mindful other. Implied in

DOI: 10.4324/9781003215639-12

these are considerations for working with patients for whom interpretations do not work. Herein lies the art of what we do.

Formation: observations of Baby Harry

In the same year Bowlby delivered his case for the recognition of attachment research, Edinburgh Professor Colwyn Trevarthen concluded that 'psychological functions that remain central to the highest intellectual and moral achievements of adults in society are expressed in a one-year-old on the threshold of spoken language' (Trevarthen and Hubley 1978, p. 184). Trevarthen researched the precursors of language, drawing upon observations of 'normal' mothers' responses to their babies during the first year. His research therefore included behaviours other than social interaction. Extracts from Lynn Barnett's filmed observation[4] of the infant I shall call Harry at four different points over his first year illustrate the shifts in the infant's interest noted by Trevarthen. These incremental changes move from self with other to self with object, and then, at the end of the first year, these are integrated into a triangulation of self, other and object.

These shifts of attention are typical and universal, that is, archetypal, and are manifestations of post-natal neurological developments dependent upon parental interaction. At birth and during the neonate period (birth to two months) the infant's behaviour is regulated by the basal ganglia, which is associated with instinctual action and survival (fight, flight, freeze). (Pictures 1 and 2: Harry at three and a half weeks 'Self') Notice Harry's engagement in his feed (*Picture 1*) and, afterwards, his post-feed, freeze-like trance (*Picture 2*).

At this point there is a new quality and intensity of attention to the mother's face, which is highly evocative and elicits expressive responses (*Picture 3*). Previously the infant looked at his mother's face; now he looks into it.

Around six weeks to two months the mid-brain and limbic system come 'on-line'. The most obvious features of this change are face-to-face interactions marked by emotionally rich exchanges of smiles and vocalisations ('proto-conversations').

At around four to five months, there is a shift in the baby's interest from his mother's face to objects that she animates, which then become an interest in themselves (*Picture 4*). Towards the end of the first year highly important developments occur in the neocortex. The baby's focus of interest shifts back and forth between the toy (*Picture 5*) and the other's face and gestures (*Picture 6*). Up until now the baby has taken the lead in social interaction, but at this point the baby turns to another for guidance. Now the baby looks behind the face and searches into the other's mind. At this point, self, other and object come together in shared play to create an 'idea' in the infant's emergent mind of what the game is about.

Transformation: observations of a toddler

As described in see Chapter 7, Vejayan's mother had suffered an acute post-natal depression just after his birth, not long after which she was admitted, with

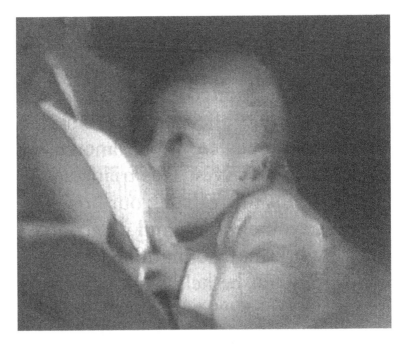

Picture 1 Harry at three and a half weeks: Self – attentive

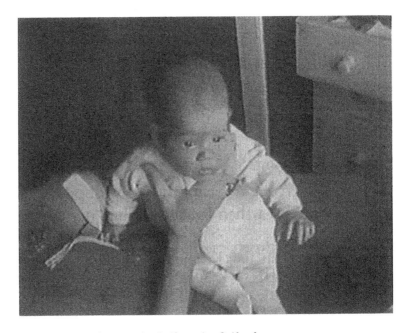

Picture 2 Harry at three and a half weeks: Self – freeze

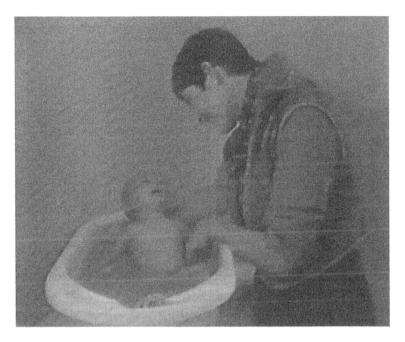

Picture 3 Harry at five weeks: Self and other

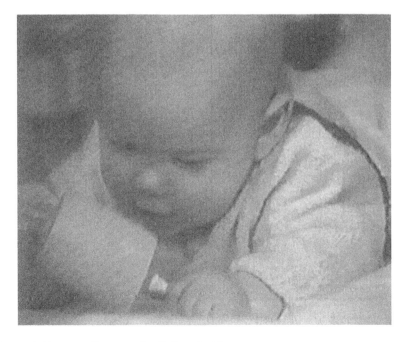

Picture 4 Harry at five months: Self and object

Picture 5 Harry at five months: Self, object and other

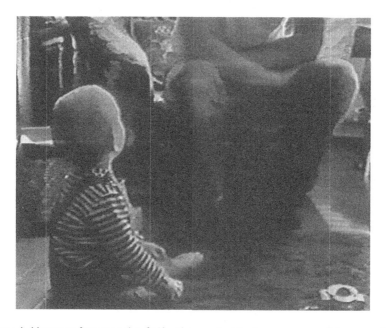

Picture 6 Harry at five months: Self, other and object – one second later on from Picture 5

Vejayan, to the perinatal in-patient mental health unit where I work. They regularly came to my mother-baby group, where I frequently observed Vejayan, only a few months old, twist his whole body away from his mother in order to avert what he registered of her lifelessness. There were times when she was too withdrawn to look after her baby, and nurses cared for Vejayan. Over the months Vejayan's mother improved and took pride in her son and authority for his care. Not long before she was discharged, when Vejayan was 14 months old, I videoed them playing together.[5] What I saw aroused my concern because there was no shared play; Vejayan seldom looked at his mother' s face and moved quickly from one activity to another until becoming excited and boisterous. At one point Vejayan approached his mother and stood on her lap, held by her. He playfully tapped a skittle against his own head and then his mother's, then swayed back and forth, touching, then more aggressively knocking, his head against hers. Their interactions were sensation-based and two-dimensional; Vejayan and his mother were head-to-head rather than mind-to-mind. I then videoed Vejayan and myself, while I tried to engage him in shared play. I started by inviting him to put an object he was holding into a bucket, which he did, but soon he became distracted and messed about. Twenty-five minutes into the session, I returned to the bucket play, intentionally trying to engage him in the three-dimensional property of the bucket: It could contain something else within it. Although Vejayan could not make sense of what I was doing, from what followed very soon afterward he had gleaned something from my behaviour.[6]

Frustrated by not understanding my intentions, he smacked his hands against a large toy. He sauntered off and picked up a small plastic lid he had earlier thrown away and put it into his mouth. At the time I regarded his behaviour as distracted and disorganised, but when I studied the video, Vejayan was clearly looking intentionally for the plastic cap. When he found it and put it into his mouth, he almost simultaneously put his hand into an opening on the top of the toy (*Picture 7*). He was thus actively experimenting in a coherent way, deliberately trying to comprehend 'insiderness' and 'container' (his mouth) and 'contained' (his hand) by using direct sensation (see Bower 1977).

I initiated a game of putting the cap into the top of the toy and then retrieving it from a door at the bottom. Too physically close to be able to see the toy and me together, Vejayan was unable to infer what I had in mind to do with the toy. Tired and uncontained, he stumbled over, got upset and went to his mother's knee. In so doing Vejayan positioned himself within a physical triangulation of himself, me and the game (*Picture 8*). From that advantage he watched me as I demonstrated the game. He then leaned forward, emitted a little joyful note of recognition and discovery, came close and repeated what I had shown him. His song-like note (the C above Middle C) marked the instant when what he saw through direct, sensate perception was transformed into something mental: He 'got it'. This marked the emergence of a triangulation of self, other and mental object.

Picture 7 Vejayan's experiment with three-dimensionality

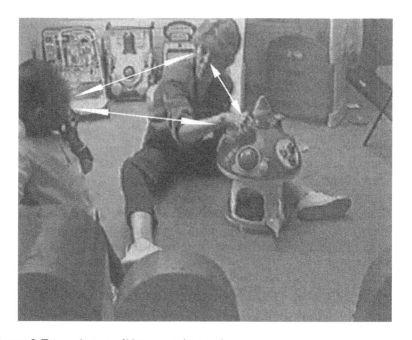

Picture 8 Triangulation of Vejayan, other and toy

Formation, transformation: clinical work with a young boy

The boy I shall call Bryan had been grossly neglected during his first two years when developmental capacities are particularly sensitive to and dependent upon parental care. His behaviour and responses revealed deprivations in each of the domains of self, self and object, and self together with other and object. The degree of Bryan's neglect was evident in his lack of the most elemental human social norms, including face-to-face intimacy, mutuality, turn-taking and seeking protection from another. Social Services removed Bryan from his mother's care not long after his birth and placed him with his father. That arrangement broke down when Bryan was around two years old. At the same time his younger sister was taken into care at birth and the siblings, who had never met, were fostered with separate families. A year and a half later, Mr. and Mrs. B. adopted both children. By the end of their first year together as a family, Bryan's behaviour had become unmanageable.

I've distilled the following clinical material to show how Bryan, despite gross deprivation during his first two years, was active in re-forming delusional assumptions and revising early relational memories. By the end of treatment, Bryan was transforming mindless dread into benign three-dimensional space. Bryan was five and a half years old when he began his once weekly treatment over a fixed-term two-year period in my NHS clinic. His adoptive mother, wanting to avoid the negative connotation of the treatment, had explained to Bryan that he would be seeing a 'nice person who was interested in getting to know him'. When I first met Bryan with his adoptive parents, he appeared impressively confident until Mr. and Mrs. B. left the room.

Once alone with me, Bryan carefully explored a few of the toys in his toy box, then went to the window and saw his father open the car door, presumably to get something. Bryan said, as if to himself, 'They're going and leaving me'. He found a toy cheetah in his toy box and told me that the cheetah – 'the fastest animal in the world' – was his favourite in the zoo.

By his third and final assessment interview, Bryan's anxieties dissipated into physical activity. Running in place beside me, he showed me how he could run faster than a horse. He then became the horse, racing furiously till he suddenly dropped over and 'died'. He repeated this several times. I said he seemed troubled that his parents left him alone with me. Although I was sure his parents would be in the waiting room when we finished, he seemed to believe that they would go away without him, and he worried whether he would be fast enough to catch up with them.

Once treatment had started, Bryan seemed to anticipate every session as a prelude to abandonment. He had, after all, experienced other 'nice people', that is, social workers, who 'were interested to get to know him' before he was removed from one carer to be given over to another. Bryan's response to being left was not as organised as securely attached behaviour, which might have resulted in asking for his adoptive parents. Rather, separation for Bryan was a threat to his sense of survival, expressed in fight/flight/freeze behaviours. Much later I heard that Bowlby had said that most animals run away from danger, while humans run towards safety. Bryan just ran – and did cartwheels and somersaults, and climbed on furniture and the window sill – then suddenly dropped onto the floor in feigned sleep. Marginally more collected, he then insisted on escaping to the lavatory. I did little more than absorb this in baffled impotence.

The following is an example of his over-activity at three months into treatment. I had accompanied him to the lavatory and waited outside. I heard him call me, distress in his voice. When I went in, he asked anxiously, 'Is it going to flood?' I then noticed the toilet bowl, full to the brim with excreta, soiled water and dissolving shreds of toilet paper. I told him it was only blocked and sorted this out. Returning to the room, I felt protective of him and wondered if I had proved myself to be a safe person. But Bryan became quite manic and turned two cartwheels. He wadded two balls of paper, labelled one his poo and the other mine, blew his nose into them and threw them at me. He violently kicked the wall and then a metal cabinet, denting it. I physically restrained him, holding him from behind, while he kicked the wall again and shouted, 'Stand off!' I said I would stand off; first I'd count to five and then both of us would take three steps away from each another. This we did.

From time to time I initiated what I hoped would become shared play. Occasionally I introduced Winnicott's squiggle game, which is based on the imaginative powers of recognising familiar shapes, say, of animals, from simple scribbles. On reflection, I was acting out my wish to help Bryan and his omnipotence. This got nowhere. Bryan had no imagination; moreover, he had no notion of how to relate to me. And nor did I to him.

When, further into treatment, Bryan started climbing up the safety grill over the window, Bryan's bodily activity became communicative because I could identify my projective identifications six months into treatment:

> Bryan climbed onto a chair and from there to the windowsill, then clambered nimbly as a monkey up the safety grill over the window to the top of it, eleven feet up. From there he crowed down to me contemptuously, 'Look! Look!', as he touched the ceiling. I felt humiliated. I was tremendously anxious that he would fall. There was no point in trying to coax him down as it only drew attention to his position of power and my helplessness. If I left the room to get his mother, it might make him anxious and possibly lose his grip. I knew perfectly well that the anxiety, helplessness and humiliation had their sources in Bryan, and, equally, that making an interpretation on this basis would make me look only more ridiculous. I stood and waited until he decided to come down.

Soon after he started his episodes of climbing the grill, I said that we both knew that climbing up that high was dangerous. He looked at me with genuine mystification; 'Danger?' he queried. I saw that my sense of safety was for him to be on the ground, whereas his sense of safety was based on primate instinct, that is, climbing like a monkey up a tree. Worried about Bryan's risky behaviour, I consulted my supervisor. I realised that Bryan's climbing had a secondary aim of eliciting me to exert control, which would only heighten anxiety rather than contain it. When he next climbed the grill, I told Bryan I would not look at him or speak to him while he was at the top of the window, but I would when he came down. I then looked down at the floor, much like a foraging mother monkey, while keeping him in my peripheral vision. This brought him down and his climbing soon stopped altogether.

Besides Bryan's fight/flight actions, there were his feigned freeze responses. Initially there was the 'dead' horse in the assessment interview and the post-hyper-activity 'collapses' into sleep. These brief, still periods evolved, almost impercep-tibly, into quiet moments that could become overtures to relating. There were several occasions when he appeared from seemingly nowhere to be beside me, almost touching, his eyes fixed on mine. Face-to-face, from barely a hand-span away, he gazed intently into my eyes with an expression of wonderment and awe. These were moments when we shared the most remarkable, unspoken intimacy.

Thus it was a sharp surprise when, with explosive impulsiveness, he kicked me hard or punched my nose and left a lasting sting. It was as if he were terri-fied of the closeness that Harry, looking up at his mother from his bath, found so pleasurably engaging. Fordham was in his seventies when he treated his last child patient, a boy not dissimilar to Bryan, who climbed to the roof of Fordham's consulting room. Fordham admitted that he 'loved him like anything' (1975). I felt the same toward Bryan. Despite this, I considered finishing at the end of the first year because there had been little change outside his sessions or seemingly within them.

It was only when I countenanced giving up that I began to notice that Bryan was changing and was more amenable to being distracted from his aggressive-ness. Toward the end of the first year, we briefly played together. Bryan seemed cheerful, telling me about a picnic when some friends came along. He wadded up his shirt and initiated a friendly game of catch. We tossed the shirt back and forth cooperatively and after several exchanges Bryan said brightly, 'Let's do this the whole time'. No sooner had he said this than he insisted he needed to go to the lavatory.

He returned aggressive and complained of being bored. He kicked at some toys on the floor. Trying to re-engage him, I suggested that we play a picture-story game. When it was his turn he drew a picture of a boy on the grass next to a rocket, with a speech bubble above the boy, inside of which was 'Aaaaagh! Heeeeelp!' I found myself looking for a question I might ask about his picture, but this was superseded by my sense of our mutuality today. I said 'Aaaaagh' with pretended agony. He joined in and pretended to collapse onto the floor. He asked me to say it again and again, which I did. By now cheerful again, he recollected the time when he drove with his adoptive parents to pick up his younger sister.

Transformations: the second year of treatment

Bryan returned after a long summer break having grown and changed into a 'boy's boy'. It was World Cup time as we entered the second year of treatment, and session after session he played solo football with a small foam ball, scoring repeatedly and declaring he was Wayne Rooney. His movements were clumsy and ineffectual, even for a seven-year-old. With no emotional link between us, I found it insufferably boring. Yet we stumbled on, not much aware that our relationship was becoming what Bryan later called 'getting on together'. Bryan's regular flights to the lavatory continued. His adoptive mother told me that what she knew of Bryan's history was sketchy and unreliable. With this caveat, she passed on a disturbing vignette; as a toddler, Bryan was left alone in his crib while his father went out with friends. The mattress of the crib had been removed, presumably so it would not be soiled when Bryan wet and fouled his nappy. This became a vivid and discomforting image in my mind. Even if historically untrue, it had the ring of psychic truth. I speculated that for Bryan the lavatory was a refuge from others and from the pain and shame at feeling such a loser when it came to eliciting care. Equally it was a chamber of self-comfort, imbued with self-sensations and self-odours, that is, a prison of self-dom. What was clearer was that the lavatory was part of Bryan's birth theory; he had told me that babies are born out their mummies' bottoms. The following comes from a session 18 months into treatment, just after he returned from another sortie to the lavatory. It was the first time that a useful interpretation arose out of our interchanges:

> Bryan noticed the calendar on the wall. He turned each page carefully until finding his birthday, and pointed to it. I said, 'Maybe you're thinking about your birthday because you've just done a poo. It seems you feel you were inside your birth mother's tummy until, on your birthday, she did a poo and you came out of her bottom. But you believe that she then just flushed you away'. There was a pause. Still looking at the calendar, he asked in an interested way, 'When's your birthday?' I said, 'I think you're wondering if I was once inside my mummy's tummy, and whether I too was born when my mummy did a poo'. He was on the floor now, leaning into the space beneath a small table. He pointed to an empty phone socket there and asked me what it was. I told him I thought he was wondering what it was like to be in the space inside a mummy's tummy, just like he was wondering about things in the space under the table. That he wanted so much to understand how it was that he had a birth mummy he was inside of, but then had a different mummy he lived with now.

A few weeks later, Bryan was playing quietly on the floor near me. He cautiously slid under the side of my chair and carefully manoeuvred himself, on his back, face upward, into the space underneath. I always wore trousers when seeing him, and I adjusted my legs to accommodate his apparent intention to push himself between them. As this was happening, I realised he was revising his delusional birth phantasy to become a 'natural birth'. When our eyes met, I welcomed him with a soft hello. Not long after Bryan asked if he would be coming 'forever', I explained that we would be finishing in a few months.

Soon he protested against coming to his sessions, and his behaviour deteriorated badly. In our penultimate session, his adoptive father had to carry him into the clinic, with Bryan clinging to him like a baby monkey. As soon as we went into the room, Bryan aggressively heaved a chair around and then, taking another, struggled to fit the two together. Sensing a slight change of mood, I said I thought the chairs were the two of us together. With that, and for the first time, Bryan constructed a three-dimensional space: a 'cottage', with a blanket for the roof. He went in and out of the cottage, and in and out of the room, and to and fro between excitement with his new construction and aggression.

Eventually he walked determinedly out of the room, saying nothing. I followed and found him sitting on a chair in the corridor. He looked at me with hostility, pushed past me and marched to the end of the corridor. I feared he would leave through the door there, but he returned. He stepped up onto the seats of a row of chairs along the hallway and strode toward me. Now at my height and eye-to-eye, Bryan glared at me menacingly, thrusting his face into mine.

I struggled with a sense of failure that our ending was little different from the way we had begun. I didn't want to part humiliated in a contest of wills and therefore had to say something. A useless interpretation came to mind; 'I think you're upset about the ending'. This was as obvious as it was trite and dismissive. I knew from some of my own vulnerable moments in analysis when my analyst would issue forth (for so it felt) with an interpretation. That only made me feel singled out and belittled, that no one else ever felt that way, certainly not the speaker. I 'knew' Bryan would feel the same. Fordham's phrase 'working out of the self' came to mind, which was his idea of what was needed at just such critical moments. It seemed a long time before a sentence began to form. I said, 'Our finishing affects me, too, Bryan'. It was true and, from what followed immediately on, Bryan heard it to be so.

Bryan instantly jumped off the chair, raced past the door to our room and, to my further surprise, to the room adjacent. He opened the door, realised that someone else was inside and dashed into our room. There he energetically constructed more rooms to his 'cottage', excited at how big it was, now calling it not a 'flat' but an 'apartment'. I said he was building an imaginary apartment in his mind for our being together after we finished, just like he and I would be together in my memories of us. He took the soft teddy from his box, hugged it close and said in a baby voice that he loved it. He took the teddy inside his 'apartment' and added more 'rooms' until the session ended.

It was only in reflection that I recognised the meaning of Bryan's actions. He first rushed into the wrong room as if re-enacting an implicit relational memory of a 'no-entry' maternal mind, comparable to the toddler Vejayan knocking his own head against mother's when her mind was inaccessible. As if revising this experience Bryan then dashed into our room, where he had constructed a three-dimensional space. Only now it had the capacity to hold feelings inside, just, as he now knew, my mind held feelings like his. In this Bryan was transforming the dread of abandonment into a tolerable sense of being apart, an 'apart-ment'. Furthermore it was a three-dimensional mental space that could hold loving feelings, and thus – for a moment – Bryan could own what via my projective identifications I had known throughout the treatment of his love. Here was an emergence of a mind different from his assumptions and the creation of an internal good object.

The self and what we do

I have tried to show how Harry, Vejayan and Bryan all possessed capacities for engagements that enabled them to be active participants in the creation of their own mental development. This is what Michael Fordham termed 'actions of the self'. In this Fordham is distinguishing an infant self that is preliminary to ego, awareness of consciousness and self-consciousness. Of course development is equally dependent on early interactions. Herein lie the differences between Harry, Vejayan and Bryan. Both Vejayan and Bryan had in infancy registered painful mis- and mal-attunements. Whereas Vejayan was of an age when he was still open to change, Bryan was far less so. The deprivations imposed on Bryan registered not simply as lacunae but as a desolate domain of affect coupled with innumerable repudiations. As the awareness of the sense of self and others develops during toddlerhood, so can counter-developmental protective mechanisms, which serve to protect a fragile sense of self-worth and of life being worthwhile. Fordham termed these defences of the self, which operate dynamically via the primitive mechanisms identified by Klein, in particular, projective identification. (6) This is different from transference and counter-transference, which Fordham had restricted to its original use as transferring parental representations onto the analyst (Fordham 1979). Defences of the self refer to primary, non-conscious experiences, what I have referred to as 'primary self functioning' in order to indicate functioning prior to the emergence of the awareness of consciousness (Urban 2005, p. 589–590). As Fordham describes this, 'there is no unconsciousness but rather more or less violent attempts to do away with the bad object' (1985, p. 153), what I have here termed flight/flight/freeze responses. Subjectively, there is 'impoverishment of self-feeling' and 'feelings of emptiness, formless terror and dread' (Fordham 1985, p. 159). Once, early in his treatment, Bryan climbed over furniture until he sat triumphantly on the top of a tall filing cabinet. Then he suddenly slumped over and spoke slowly, with feeling, 'I'm just bad'. Being 'just bad' was Bryan's fundamental assumption underlying his delusional transference. Fordham maintained that delusional transferences can contain reparative elements that refer to 'archetypal forms aiming to re-establish relatedness although seemingly in a malignant form' (Fordham 1985, p. 159). I have described this in terms of acting out that relates through projective identification. It can also be seen in other archetypal expressions of instinctual behaviour that aim toward relatedness, which are linked along a spectrum to symbolic expressions. For instance, I observed Bryan's climb up the grill to be 'like a baby monkey', that is, an instinctual flight response toward safety, whereas there is also a spiritual aspect to the safety of heights; for instance, 'I will lift up mine eyes unto the hills, from whence cometh my help' (Psalm 121:1).

Fordham's aim was to establish a physiological basis for archetypal theory, and this is currently acknowledged in what might now be called 'top-down/down-up' neurological interconnectivity. Drawing directly from Jung, Fordham linked the opposite ends of the archetypal spectrum by citing similar behaviours in parallel situations at each pole (Fordham 1957). At the spiritual pole he instanced the mystical experiences of Mechthild of Magdeburg, who was tortured by the devil until she submitted to him, saying, 'Do whatsoever God allows thee to do!' At that point the devil held back, saying, 'Because thou givest thy soul meekly to torment, I lose all my power' (ibid, p. 25). At the corresponding instinctual pole Fordham cites Konrad Lorenz's description of two wolves. The larger one had pressed its younger competitor into submission until the latter exposed its jugular. At this point, Lorenz observed: 'the victor will definitely not close on his less fortunate rival. You can see he would like to, but he just cannot' (Fordham 1957, p. 26).

Although Fordham emphasised the protective purposes of defences of the self, he also implied their link with developmental deficits because these primitive defences interfere with deintegration and reintegration. In a 1979 paper Fordham wrote of his clinical discovery of an effective intervention that penetrated defences of the self. Here he wrote of how he came to identify with his patient's affective projections, felt empathy and respect for her, and started to speak without knowing what to say. His patient responded to his affect, and her transference changed. Numerous analysts were working at the time to adapt their responses to similar, difficult-to-reach patients. For example, in 1993 the child psychotherapist Anne Alvarez explicitly put forward from her experience that these patients' deficits needed to be distinguished from defences and made an argument for modifications to traditional technique (Alvarez 1993). In the same year, Fordham restated his 1979 clinical discovery of 'an interpretation which is not based on theory but came out of the self':

> That involves trusting one's unconscious, in which projective identifications are active. . . . You must look and listen to your patient as though you have never seen him before so you will not have any knowledge of him. In that way you will be open to him and be in the best position to experience his state of mind today. As you listen you will begin to experience [the patient's] mood and then have some thoughts or feelings, etc. about him. It is out of this that an intervention will arise.
>
> (Fordham 1993, pp. 637–638)

I see 'working out of the self' as a spontaneous, internal temporary state of integration within the analyst, simultaneous with identification with the patient's affective state. The integration is neurologically 'top-down and bottom-up'. When I exposed to Bryan that I too had humbling feelings about our finishing, I revealed not only that I had feelings but also, in the way I said it, who I was at that moment. Bryan's lightning reaction was like a flash of neurological top-down/ down-up connection – very like Mechthild and the wolves – that seems to have triggered relatedness and developments in his own mind. Would this have been working out of the self if it had 'not worked'? 'What works' is part of a dynamic between and within our selves and our patients' selves. When I worked out of my self, Bryan responded out of his.[7] Does working out of the self mean abandoning interpreta-tive work? Not at all; it means being clearer when interpretative work is failing because the patient needs a more direct and immediate emotional contact (in con-trast to physical).

Does working out of the self mean abandoning interpretive work? Not at all; it means being clear when interpretive work is failing because the patient needs a more direct and immediate *emotional* contact (in contrast to physical touch). This contrasts with when the patient is ready – even seeks – to know more about himself, for instance, when Bryan pointed out his birthday and asked about mine. At this point he seemed to be open to questioning his basic assumption that he was 'just bad' and to regard the other, that is, wondering something about mothers and birth. When I spoke out of my self and Bryan reacted out of his, what happened was the equivalent of the fulfilment of those outstretched fingertips of God and Adam on the ceiling of the Sistine Chapel. Michelangelo certainly knew of that igniting touch, the conjunction of creation and discovery, which the Boston Change Process Study Group calls a 'moment of meeting'.[8]

> These occur from the personal engagement between analyst and patient that has been constructed over time and [has] acquire[d] its own history. It involves basic issues . . . and includes more or less accurate sensings of the therapist's and patient's person. When we speak of an 'authentic' meeting we mean communications that reveal a personal aspect of the self that has been evoked in an affective response to another. In turn, it reveals to the other a personal signature, so as to create a new dyadic state specific to the two participants.
>
> (Boston Change Process Study Group 2000, p. 26)

What the Boston Change Process Study Group learned from research is very close indeed to what Fordham learned from his patients: that is, the transformative con-nections of emotional depth that occur out of a compelling motivation for relat-edness. This links what we do with art. Peter Schjeldahl notes in his review of a recent exhibition at New York's Museum of Modern Art, 'The proof of any art's lasting value is a comprehensive emotional intensity: it's something that a person needed to do and which awakens and satisfies corresponding needs in us' (Schje-dahl 2013).

'Formation, transformation; eternal mind's eternal recreation': the art of what we do

Taking the bus home one afternoon not long ago, I overheard a teenage girl announce to her school friend, 'Some of my ideas are my own'. None of the ideas here are mine or new. I've intentionally not expanded on the sources I have drawn upon in order to emphasise observing and learning from my patient. But I'm not demeaning research from whatever reliable source or theory and technique confirmed through practice. Neil MacGregor, the Director of the British Museum, wrote about the challenge of identifying ancient objects held by the museum. This can equally apply to the objects held in others' minds:

> We acknowledge the limits of what we can know with certainty, and must then try to find a different kind of knowing, aware that objects must have been made by people essentially like us – so we should be able to puzzle out why they might have made them and what they were for. . . . Can we really ever understand others? Perhaps, but only through feats of poetic imagination, combined with knowledge rigorously acquired and ordered.
>
> (MacGregor 2010, p. xviii)

What is mine and new, as with Vejayan and Bryan, is what I have discovered and simultaneously created from my own inner resources and how that has become for me more than the sum of its parts. I have not tried to define what it is that we do because my point is the holistic and emergent nature of what we do with our patients, with our instruments of theory, research, technique, experience and imagination. Jeremy Eichler, classical music critic for the *Boston Globe*, published a profile of the German violinist Christian Tetzlaff. He writes, 'Since the time of Paganini violin virtuosos have tried to overwhelm audiences with feats of agility. Tetzlaff is after something different' (Eichler 2012, p. 34). Tetzlaff tries to understand the mind of the composer: 'Interpretation, Tetzlaff believes, should ultimately be an act of compassion' (p. 38) and 'whether you can allow yourself to be touched by things, to be receptive to other people, to be in the pain of the composer' (ibid., p. 39). The Finnish composer and conductor Esa-Pekka Salonen, who has worked with Tetzlaff for over two decades, states:

> What always strikes me when I hear him playing, and when I work with him myself, is that it's not about the violin. It's about music being realized, and abstraction becoming reality, through the violin. He happens to play it extremely well, but that's not the point.
>
> (ibid., 34–35)

Acknowledgement

I should like to express my appreciation to Lynn Barnett for her permission to use stills from her video series 'Sunday's Child'.

Notes

1 'Attachment and Intersubjectivity in the Therapeutic Relationship', JAP XIth International conference, with sponsorship from the New England Society of Jungian Analysts, the C.G. Jung Institute (Boston), and the Child Analytic Project Fund (Society of Analytical Psychology, London) April 4–7, 2013, Boston, MA.
2 For more about the triangulation see Chapters 3 and 4 in Hobson, P. (2002) The Cradle of Thought. London: Macmillan.
3 This is a variation of Jung's quote from Goethe regarding 'the ultimate': 'Formation, Transformation; Eternal Minds' eternal recreation'. (Jung 1963, p. 211). It is pertinent that inGoethe's play Faust must touch a key given to him by Mephistopheles to a tripod in order to enter the mysterious realm of pure ideas (archetypes, Platonic forms) (Goethe 1954).
4 Lynn Barnett is a British child psychotherapist who filmed a longitudinal observation of a boy, entitled 'Sunday's child'. I have changed the babies name at the request of Miss Barnett (1988).
5 For a more detailed account of these eobservations of Vijayan see Chapter 7.
6 For a more detailed account of these observations of Vijayan see Chapter 7.
7 It is a patient's spontaneous response that consequently quickly changes the relationship that, in my view, is the hallmark of working out of the self.
8 The five points characterizing moments of meeting listed by the BSPSG (pp. 26–27) comprehensively describe my 'moment of meeting' with Bryan in our penultimate session.

References

Alvarez, A. (1993). *Live Company*. London: Routledge.
Barnett, L. (1988). *Sunday's Child*. Ipswich, UK: Concord Video.
Bowlby, J. (1979). 'Psychoanalysis as art and science'. Paper delivered to the annual Canadian Psychoanalytic Society, Quebec City, 1978. Published in the *International Review of Psychoanalysis*, 6: 3–14.
Bower, T. (1977). *The Perceptual World of the Child*. Glasgow: William Collins.
Eichler, J. (2012). 'String theorist'. *The New Yorker Magazine*, 27 August.
Fordham, M. (1957). 'Biological theory and the concept of the archetypes'. In *New Developments in Analytical Psychology*. London: Routledge and Kegan Paul.
———. (1975). Personal communication with author.
———. (1979). 'Analytical psychology and countertransference'. In *Contemporary Psychoanalysis*, 15, 4. Also in *Counter-Transference: The Therapist's Contribution to Treatment*, eds. L. Epstein and A. H. Feiner. New York: Jason Aronson.
———. (1985). *Explorations into the Self*. London: Academic Press.
———. (1993). 'The Jung-Klein hybrid'. *Free Associations*, 3(4): 28, 631–641.
Goethe, J. (1954). *Faust, Part II: Theodore Martin*. Translated, introduced, revised, and Annotated by W. H. Bruford. London: J. M. Dent.
Jung, C. (1963). *Memories, Dreams, Reflections*. London: Collins.
MacGregor, N. (2010). *A History of the World in 100 Objects*. London: Allen Lane.
Schjedahl, P. (2013). 'Shapes of things: The birth of the abstract'. *The New Yorker Magazine*, 7 January.

The Boston Change Process Study Group. (2000). *Change in Psychotherapy: A Unifying Paradigm.* London: W. W. Norton.

Trevarthen, C. and Hubley, P. (1978). 'Secondary intersubjectivity'. In A. Lock (ed.), *Action, Gesture and Symbol: The Emergence of Language.* London: Academic Press.

Urban, E. (2005). 'Fordham, Jung and the self: A re-examination of Fordham's contribution to Jung's conceptualization of the self'. *Journal of Analytical Psychology,* 50(5).

Elizabeth Urban – list of publications

Papers

1989 'Childhood deafness: Compensatory deintegrations of the self', *Journal of Analytical Psychology,* 34:143–157.

1990 'Childhood and the child within: views of an analytical psychologist', *Journal of the British Association of Psychotherapists,* 21:3–19.

1990 'The eye of the beholder: work with a ten-year-old deaf girl', *Journal of Child Psychotherapy,* 16:63–81.

1992 'The primary self and related concepts in Jung, Klein and Isaacs', *Journal of Analytical Psychology,* 37:411–432.

1993 'Out of the mouths of babes: an enquiry into the sources of language development', *Journal of Analytical Psychology,* 38:237–256.

1996a '"With healing in her wings . . .": integration and repair in a self-destructive adolescent', *Journal of Child Psychotherapy,* 22:64–81.

1996b With Miranda Davies, 'Fordham and the SAP infant observations: an interview with Gianna Williams', *Journal of Child Psychotherapy,* 22:49–63.

1998 'States of identity: a perspective drawing upon Fordham's model and infant studies', *Journal of Analytical Psychology,* 43:261–275.

1999 With Meira Likierman, 'The Roots of Child and Adolescent Psychotherapy in Psychoanalysis', Chapter 2 in *The Handbook of Child and Adolescent Psychotherapy: Psychoanalytic Approaches.* London: Routledge.

2000 'Infant observation, experimental infant research and psychodynamic theory', *International Journal of Infant Observation,* 3:64–79.

2003a 'Supervising Work with Children'. Chapter 4 in *Supervising and Being Supervised,* J. Wiener, R. Mizen, and J. Duckham (eds.). London: Palgrave.

2003b 'Developmental aspects of trauma and traumatic aspects of development'. *Journal of Analytical Psychology,* 48:171–190.

2004 'Working psychotherapeutically with infants and young children: the contribution of experimental studies', *International Journal of Infant Observation,* 7:61–75.

2005 'Fordham, Jung and the self: a re-examination of Fordham's contribution to Jung's conceptualisation', *Journal of Analytical Psychology,* 50:571–594).

2006 'Unintegration, disintegration and deintegration', *Journal of Child Psychotherapy*, 32:181–192.

2008 'The "self" in analytical psychology: the function of the "central archetype" within Fordham's model', *Journal of Analytical Psychology*, 53:329–350.

2009 'Conjugating the self', *Journal of Analytical Psychology*, 54:399–403.

2013 'Reflections on research and learning from the patient: the art and science of what we do', *Journal of Analytical Psychology*, 58:510–529.

2013 'End Notes: Commentary for two unpublished papers by Michael Fordham', *Journal of Analytical Psychology*, 58:454–469.

2014 'Introduction to three clinical papers', *Journal of Analytical Psychology*, 58: 309–313.

2015 'Michael Fordham and the *Journal of Analytical Psychology*: The View from Hangman's Hill', *Journal of Analytical Psychology*, 60: 497–506.

2018 'On matters of mind and body: regarding Descartes', *Journal of Analytical Psychology*, 63:228–240.

Reviews and commentaries

1990 Journal Review of 'The therapeutic utilisation of countertransference' by W. Steinberg', *Journal of Analytical Psychology*, 35:355–356.

1992 Book Review of *Diary of a Baby* by D.N. Stern, *Journal of Analytical Psychology*, 37: 243–244.

1993 Book Review of *From Fetus to Child: An Observational and Psychoanalytic Study* by A. Piontelli, *Journal of Analytical Psychology*, 38:493–494 (4).

1994 Book Review of *Live Company: Psychoanalytic Psychotherapy with Autistic, Borderline, Deprived and Abused Children* by A. Alvarez. *Journal of Analytical Psychology*, 39:265–267.

1996 Book Review of *Children as Individuals* by M. Fordham, *Journal of Child Psychotherapy* 22: 153–156.

2003 Book Review of *Primitive Mental States, Vol 2: Psychobiological and Psychoanalytic Perspectives on Early Trauma and Personality Development* by S. Alhanati, *International Journal of Infant Observation*, 6:117–122.

2004 Obituary: Dorothy Davidson, *Journal of Analytical Psychology*, 49:125–127.

2012 Commentary on 'Transcendent function or group dysfunction? Comments on 'Transcendence, transmission and transformation: the transcendent function in infant observation' by Virginia Humphrey and Beth Barmac. *Journal of Analytical Psychology*, 57:247–253.

2018 Response to Roger Brooke's critique of 'On matters of mind and body: regarding Descartes'. *Journal of Analytical Psychology*, 63:573–700.

Index

Page numbers followed by 'n' indicate a note on the corresponding page.

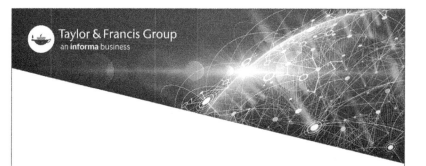

Made in the USA
Las Vegas, NV
28 August 2022